PRAISE FOR *Thrumpton Hall*

Winner of the PEN/Ackerley Prize for Memoir of the Year

One of the Best Books of the Year
(*The Times Literary Supplement* [London])

"The masterpiece for which her previous novels and biographies have prepared the way. . . . It is the convincing portrayal of a number of complex personalities altering in intense and precarious relation to one another that makes her memoir so moving."
—Tim Parks, *New York Review of Books*

"This enthralling book is not just another tale of restoring—and living in the decaying magnificence of—an English country estate. The story that Miranda Seymour unfolds against the background of Thrumpton Hall has enough drama—and psychodrama—to give playwright Harold Pinter a run for his money. There is comedy in her father's house, but festering emotional wounds, slights, and injuries invest it with the stuff of tragedy. . . . Miranda Seymour's unsparing account of life with her father is a chilling portrait of obsession and selfishness, a fascinating picture of a singular family dynamic."
—*Los Angeles Times*

"Beautifully written. . . . A story of house-love that borders on madness. It's also the story of her father, and not the least of its accomplishments is that it instantly catapults him into the front rank of impossible and eccentric English parents. . . . Both comic . . . and immensely touching. . . . She brings a historian's scrutiny to her family's story, and walks a careful line between sentimentalizing her father on the one hand and turning him into a monster on the other."
—*New York Times Book Review* (cover review)

"Miranda Seymour's wonderful memoir is a kind of posthumous conversation with her father. The ending is particularly powerful. What a gripping, poignant, dramatic, emotionally searing book she has written." —Joyce Carol Oates

"A memoir that reads like a mystery. *Thrumpton Hall* is a daughter's eloquent attempt to parse her damaged father and the insular world that he loved." —*People*

"A story of heartfelt love and loathing, told with wit, delicacy, and a considerable amount of understated indelicacy as well; it is also a delightful period piece, an evocation of a very recent time that is long gone. . . . [A] heavyhearted but light-handed reflection on love, memory, and truth." —*The Sunday Times* (London)

"A brave and revealing book that helps us to reconsider the price of privilege, and the lives of people 'bred to sound bored.' . . . Above all, this book shows that nothing can meet the want of love—or match the gift of it." —*The Times* (London)

"A memoir that reads like a fairy tale gone wrong." —*The Times Literary Supplement* (London)

"Undeniably graceful and often brilliant writing." —*Washington Times*

"Utterly riveting and weirdly unusual, this moving memoir is a touching and deeply personal insight into a private family, and a true upper-crust English eccentric." —*Daily Mail* (London)

"An extremely well-told tale of an unexceptional man. . . . Writing this deeply personal account of her family must have been a cathartic experience for Seymour. For the reader, it is a treat to catch an author at the height of her descriptive powers, exposing the agony of parental disappointment with honesty, sensitivity, and touches of brilliance." —*The Guardian* (London)

"This is an extraordinary book. Miranda Seymour has written a family memoir whose honesty appalls even as it compels, but its secondary achievement is to draw, almost from the corner of its eye, a portrait of Englishness in the last century that encompasses class, ownership, landscape, money, manners, and clothes. It is consistently fascinating and occasionally horrifying and will make a good deal of modern autobiography look feeble and colorless in comparison. . . . This story of a family colluding in its own unhappiness strives for the truth and something more: an elegance and wit to make it memorable." —*The Observer* (London)

"A brilliantly crafted true story, *Thrumpton Hall* gains depth and complexity from its willingness to explore the ethical dilemma of revealing painful family secrets. There is more to learn about human nature in this short memoir than in many novels two or three times its length." —Pat Barker, Booker Prize–winning author of the Regeneration Trilogy

"[A] gem. . . . Bizarre and fascinating. . . . *Thrumpton Hall* is disarming in its honesty, endlessly surprising and oddly touching." —*The Spectator* (London)

"The story is fascinating and Miranda's honest, frank, and in-depth account of her father's life proves a captivating read." —*Evening Chronicle* (Newcastle, United Kingdom)

"The tale Seymour tells is so strange and sad, so sordid yet touching, that you find yourself caught between wonder that she waited more than a decade to write it—and wonder that she was able to put pen to paper at all." —*The Evening Standard* (London)

"A moving and almost uncomfortable book. . . . She brought off this extraordinary account of her father triumphantly." —*Derby Evening Telegraph* (United Kingdom)

"A mesmerizing, quintessentially English story." —*Mail on Sunday* (London)

Suzanna Allen

About the Author

MIRANDA SEYMOUR is the author of many acclaimed works, including biographies of Mary Shelley, Henry James, and French racing driver Hellé Nice. She has also written four children's books and a collection of stories set at her former home on Corfu. She lives in England.

Also by Miranda Seymour

Fiction
The Stones of Maggiare
Daughter of Darkness
Count Manfred
The Goddess
Medea
Madonna of the Island: Tales from Corfu
Carrying On
The Reluctant Devil: A Cautionary Tale
The Telling

Non-fiction
A Ring of Conspirators: Henry James and his Literary Circle
Ottoline Morrell: Life on the Grand Scale
Robert Graves: Life on the Edge
Mary Shelley
The Bugatti Queen: In Search of a Motor-Racing Legend

Children's Books
Mumtaz the Magical Cat
The Vampire of Verdonia
Caspar and the Secret Kingdom
Pierre and the Pamplemousse

Miscellaneous
A Brief History of Thyme

THRUMPTON HALL

A Memoir of Life
in My Father's House

MIRANDA SEYMOUR

HARPER  PERENNIAL

NEW YORK • LONDON • TORONTO • SYDNEY • NEW DELHI • AUCKLAND

HARPER ● PERENNIAL

First published in Great Britain as *In My Father's House* in 2007
by Simon & Schuster UK Ltd.

First U.S. hardcover edition published in 2008 by HarperCollins Publishers.

HarperCollins books may be purchased for educational, business, or sales pro-
motional use. For information please write: Special Markets Department,
HarperCollins Publishers, 10 East 53rd Street, New York, NY 10022.

FIRST HARPER PERENNIAL EDITION PUBLISHED 2009.

Library of Congress Cataloging-in-Publication Data
is available upon request.

ISBN 978-0-06-146658-8

09 10 11 12 13   RRD   10 9 8 7 6 5 4 3 2 1

To my beloved husband, Ted Lynch

CONTENTS

PART TWO
THE HOUSE: POSSESSION

ACKNOWLEDGEMENTS

I would like, for his perseverance and faith in this book, to express warm gratitude to Anthony Goff, my agent and friend. I could not have wished for a wiser editor than Andrew Gordon, whose judgement proved invaluable. In the U.S., endless thanks to their counterparts, George Lucas and Rakesh Satyal. This book owes much to all of these gentlemen.

My gratitude also goes to Alan Hollinghurst for his unfailing support and wise counsel. Thanks also to Edwina Barstow, Hannah Corbett and to my excellent copy-editor, Robyn Karney. My warm appreciation also goes to Reginald Piggott for sorting out two complicated family trees.

I owe a debt of a different kind to my mother, whose support has meant everything to me during the course of preparing and writing what proved to be a difficult book for us both.

I thank my brother for having allowed me to feel that I could write as I wished, and as I felt. This was generous, and made a great difference to my approach.

I have been continuously grateful for the friendship and excellent company of my son and daughter-in-law, and for the restorative and understanding love of my husband – and first reader.

AUTHOR'S NOTE

The subject of this book is often referred to as 'my father'. He was, in fact, 'our father'. As the son of the house, my brother knew him from a different perspective.

This is the story of my father in relation to myself. It is, in that sense, only a partial truth. It does not attempt to reflect my brother's views, although I believe that he shares some of mine.

Some names have been changed.

'It seems, perhaps, a strange and unnecessary thing to go prowling back into the recesses of the past and to lift the decent curtain which has covered the weary ugly follies . . .'

– Lord Howard de Walden, my mother's father, in a letter to his five-year-old son; Gallipoli, 1915

'What do you know about your own family anyway? They're such secretive organisms, I can't be doing with them.'

– James Brooke to William Beckwith: Alan Hollinghurst, The Swimming-Pool Library (1988)

THRUMPTON
HALL

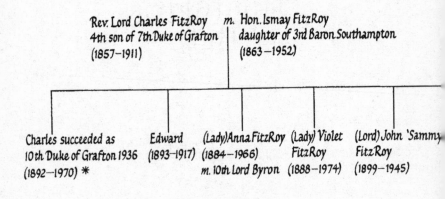

Rev. Lord Charles FitzRoy
4th son of 7th Duke of Grafton
(1857–1911)

m. Hon. Ismay FitzRoy
daughter of 3rd Baron Southampton
(1863–1952)

Charles succeeded as
10th Duke of Grafton 1936
(1892–1970) ✳

Edward
(1893–1917)

(Lady) Anna FitzRoy
(1884–1966)
m. 10th Lord Byron

(Lady) Violet
FitzRoy
(1888–1974)

(Lord) John 'Sammy
FitzRoy
(1899–1945)

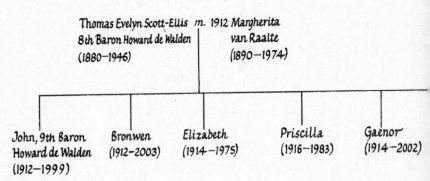

Thomas Evelyn Scott-Ellis
8th Baron Howard de Walden
(1880–1946)

m. 1912 Margherita
van Raalte
(1890–1974)

John, 9th Baron
Howard de Walden
(1912–1999)

Bronwen
(1912–2003)

Elizabeth
(1914–1975)

Priscilla
(1916–1983)

Gaenor
(1914–2002)

(Lord), (Lady) = raised to title on succession
of 10th Duke of Grafton in 1936.

✳ Father of Hugh, 11th Duke of Grafton (1919–)
and favoured cousin Oliver (1923–1944).

These family trees show links between the main characters
in the book and are not intended to be comprehensive.

Family connections

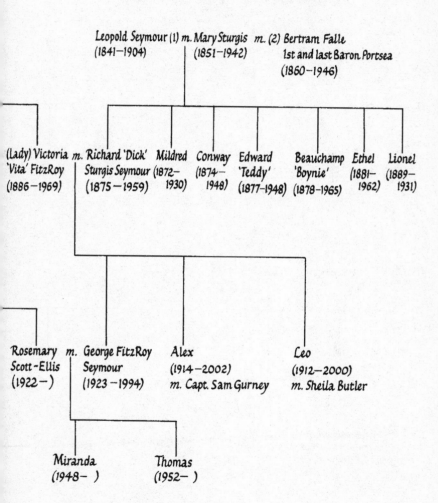

Leopold Seymour (1) m. Mary Sturgis m. (2) Bertram Falle
(1841–1904)   (1851–1942)   1st and last Baron Portsea
                                      (1860–1946)

(Lady) Victoria m. Richard 'Dick'   Mildred   Conway   Edward   Beauchamp   Ethel   Lionel
'Vita' FitzRoy   Sturgis Seymour   (1872–   (1874–   'Teddy'   'Boynie'   (1881–   (1889–
(1886–1969)   (1875–1959)   1930)   1948)   (1877–1948)   (1878–1965)   1962)   1931)

Rosemary m. George FitzRoy   Alex   Leo
Scott-Ellis   Seymour   (1914–2002)   (1912–2000)
(1922–)   (1923–1994)   m. Capt. Sam Gurney   m. Sheila Butler

Miranda   Thomas
(1948–)   (1952–)

PROLOGUE:
IN MY FATHER'S HOUSE

'Three obituaries!' a fierce old relation wrote after my father died. 'What on earth for! What did he ever *do*?'

The point was fair. Her own late husband, a handsomely moustached man with an outstanding war record, was of the type who earn such tributes. But George FitzRoy Seymour – he was concerned that the FitzRoy, recording some royal bed-hopping in the seventeenth century, should never be overlooked – had done no such service to his country. He had no war record. Long and dutiful service as a magistrate had earned him commendations and praise, but no official honour. The fat red handbooks in which he listed his London clubs – Pratt's and Brooks' in the issue of 1982 – offered no history of worthy activities, while revealing (father 'great great great grandson of Marquess of Hertford'; mother 'sister of 10th Duke of Grafton'; wife 'daughter of 8th Baron Howard de Walden') that here was a man who took exceptional pride in his connections. It saddened him that he had no title. His links to those who did were a solace.

Eccentricity has not always been encouraged by the prim editors of *Debrett*. Invited to list his recreations, my father omitted motorbikes and wrote instead: shooting, deerstalking and tennis. Identifying himself as Lord of the Manor of Thrumpton provided a greater source of satisfaction.

His address provides the clue to George FitzRoy Seymour's most substantial achievement. Deposited with its childless owners as a baby, he fell in love with the House that always seemed to be his natural home. His vocation was announced in one of the first roundhanded essays he wrote as a schoolboy. When he grew up, he wrote, he wished to become the squ'arson of Thrumpton Hall, combining the role of landowner and parson as his uncle, Lord Byron, the poet's descendant, had done before him. He would look after the tenants. He would be kind to his servants, especially when they grew old. He would cherish and protect the home he loved. The master who marked the essay, repelled by such priggishness, scribbled a terse comment in red crayon, advising young Seymour to find a style and topic more suited to his years. The following week, my father handed in eight pages on the importance of preserving the family monuments in Thrumpton's village church. He was eleven years old. No suggestion had been made that he would ever inherit the House to which he had vowed his love. Uncertainty was not one of his failings.

My father died in May 1994. A gust of wind blew in through a newly opened window, rippling the yellow hangings of the bed on which he lay. My brother went along the landing to find our mother and consult her about hymns for the funeral. I walked out into the garden. Reaching up into the swaying branches of the lilacs, I snapped them off until I stood knee-deep in the heavy swags of blossom I had never, until that moment, been licensed to cut. Returning to the House, I pushed at the wooden shutters of the rooms on the ground floor, parting them to let in a flood of lime-green light. Standing, hands on hips, at the far end of the garden, I hurled shouts at the red-brick walls and arching gables until they echoed back their reassurance: *Free! Free!*

In the little village church later that week, the vicar spoke of my father as 'a man with a wound in his heart'. The description, which startled nobody, could have been a reference to the anguish he had recently experienced. It seemed more likely that the vicar, a man who had known my father for thirty years, was thinking of his aching need for a love greater than any one person had been able to provide.

We buried his ashes privately, in the garden of the House to which he gave his heart. The wording on the tablet that marked the spot was borrowed from Christopher Wren's epitaph. *Si monumentum requiris, circumspice.* The pride of it, loosely translated here, felt right: *If you wish to know me, look around you. Here I am.*

We chose the words and here, still, he is. On troubled nights, he comes to me in dreams, stalking back through the front door to survey his home and take charge of it once more. He complains that unknown people are sleeping in his room; that his cupboards are filled with the sordid clothes of strangers. Speaking in a flat voice, thinned by resentment, he explains that he intends to put the House, his home, not ours, to rights. We buried a phantom, a creature of our own wishes. We wanted him dead. Our mistake. He never died. He just went travelling.

A white hand reaches out to pull down a parchment-coloured blind at one of the library windows. Wearily, he reminds me of the need to protect precious leather-bound books and rosewood tables from the glare of daylight. Helpless, I watch him take his familiar place at the head of the long dining table. Awaiting instructions, I find myself dismissed to a side seat, far away. He observes, looking pained, that the silver is tarnished, that the wine has been insufficiently aired, and that the soup plates are cold. Standards have slipped, but all will be well again. Everything, once again, is under his control.

I watch his body harden into the familiar lines of authority. I long for him to leave. I know he never will.

It takes days for the sense of dread to wear off, not only of his reproachful spirit, but of having failed the House, of having been unworthy of his expectations.

His taste was not always for objects of beauty. This morning, I came across a battered white plastic chair in the courtyard at the back of the House, turned east to face the morning sun. The seat is soiled, the shape is ugly. I want to throw it away. Sam Walker disagrees. Sam and I read our first books together at the village dame school where Sam's aunt kept order with a ruler and a whistle. Sam has grown up to be a true Nottinghamshire man, plain-spoken and reserved. He's worked at the House for forty years.

'You can't get rid of that,' he says. 'It's your father's chair.'

'The seat's broken. I'm sure he didn't mean us to keep it.'

Sam Walker's belief in preservation is legendary. Old lamp fittings, massive radiograms, towel racks, broken deckchairs; they never disappear. They go to rest in one of the stables to which only Sam holds the key. Their return may be a matter of years, not months, but their time will come.

Resolute, I fold my arms. 'There's no reason to keep it now.'

Sam looks at the wall behind me. 'Your father always sat on that chair when . . . he carried it down to the lakeside every afternoon he was here after . . .' Hesitating, he stares harder at the wall. 'You know. After it happened.'

Long-jawed and high-cheeked, Sam's eloquent face could have been carved by a medieval mason. At this moment, it conveys no expression. The message is clear. The chair may look empty, but it still has an occupant.

The chair stays.

I can never hope to banish my father's presence from the House that possessed his heart. I can make my peace by trying to understand what made him the man he was. Sifting through the drawers of diaries and ancient letters – like Sam Walker, George FitzRoy Seymour was a man who threw nothing away – I can assemble the fragments and see plainly what I always knew: that a single passion governed his life, a love so great and so certain that he was willing to sacrifice everything and everybody for it. 'Dear Thrumpton, how I miss you tonight,' he wrote in 1944, when he was twenty-one and had just paid a summer visit to his uncle's home. 'As I grow older the House exerts an ever greater hold on me – I love every tree and stone on the place, and every hold and corner of the place. God send I never have to leave for ever.'

The House, constructed from rosy bricks and crowned with curved stone gables, stands among the meadows flanking the River Trent, in the middle of England, a hundred miles to the north of London. Starting life as a modest Nottinghamshire manor house built in the time of Shakespeare, it was enlarged twice. An ambitious owner redesigned it in the seventeenth century, to incorporate a large carved staircase and a grand reception room on an upper floor. In the 1820s, the House gained a courtyard, a library and a lake. The estate, easily encompassed by an hour's brisk walk, is surprisingly varied in its landscape, incorporating traces of an Iron Age fort and a Roman trading post. An eighteenth-century stone weir breaks the level of the river that runs alongside the park's expansive fields; pretty copses and airy beechwoods climb a long line of hillside that blocks out all evidence of the twenty-first century. (Until, that is, you walk the ridge along the hilltop and look the other way, out to where a distant line of motorway traffic snakes across a green plain and cooling towers puff steam clouds at the wingtips of low-flying aircraft. This landscape has a different kind of beauty, a kind my father did not acknowledge.)

'God send I never have to leave for ever.' There's no doubting Thrumpton's charm, but what was it that could lead a boy of twenty-one to make such a declaration? How could bricks and mortar exert such power? What was 'the wound in his heart', so painful to see, so difficult to comprehend?

To find the answer, time has to be turned back and confronted.

'I'm sorry, but I simply don't see the point.'

My mother and I have been discussing my wish to write this book for ten years. Anger and self-pity have kept me on hold.

Listening to myself as I talk to friends, telling them the stories, polishing the details, I hear sourness in the tone, feel rage twist a knife in my throat, and know the time hasn't yet come. I've wondered if my mother's way, the path of silence, is the wiser option. There are things it's easier to disclose in private than expose to public view. There are things I've never understood, that I'm not sure I want to examine.

'It's not as if you'd be writing one of your biographies,' she goes on. 'He's your father.'

'Was,' I say fiercely. '*Was*.'

We're sitting late over supper in the kitchen of the House, our faces lit, like uneasy conspirators, by a couple of candles.

'I don't know,' she says after a long pause. 'What do you want me to do?'

'Be my conscience. Tell me when I go wrong.'

She gives me a sharp sideways look. 'I can *tell* you. It doesn't mean you'll *do* anything.'

'I'll listen.'

'It doesn't strike you,' she says after a pause, 'that you're too like him to be objective?'

'Like him!' I can feel the heat of blood rushing to my cheeks. '*Like* him?'

She winces. 'Is that so dreadful? Did you hate him so much? He did love you, you know.'

'After his fashion.' *Don't do this to me*, I think. *You know what he was like. You know what we went through. Don't make me soft, not now.*

'Well,' she says, standing up and brushing crumbs off her skirt, 'you're set on it and I can't stop you. But you've gone wrong already.'

'I have?'

'I'm afraid so.' Solemnly, she nods. 'Cutting down lilacs? Darling, do you still not know the difference between lilacs and a buddleia, a butterfly tree? In our own garden? Good grief, George must be turning in his grave.'

Even a phrase like that can summon him back. Later, brushing my hair before the dim glass in my bedroom, I catch the flicker of a shadow behind me, hear the sudden squeak of a pressed floorboard.

'Goodnight!' I call. I wait for my mother's voice to answer me, but the House is asleep inside the tall closed shutters. Not a sound is to be heard now in the muffled quiet but the deep steady thud of my own heart and the busy rattle of a distant train.

PART ONE

The House: Obsession

1

DICK AND VITA

'I expect you'll be talking about Barbara Castle,' my mother remarks. We're having breakfast on a winter morning. When I glance up, it's to see her feet stretched out towards the fire as she admires a new treasure, a pair of slippers fluffed out to resemble startled baby owls.

'I will?' Am I about to hear revelations of something too improbable for fiction, news that my true-blue father had a secret affair with an aristocrat-averse old politician who wouldn't – or *would* she? I want to sound casual, but I'm dismayed. This won't fit the story I want to tell. It's out of character.

'Sounds interesting,' I say carefully. 'Something I've missed?'

The owls withdraw under the table. My mother raps the dome of her egg with a spoon and rallies herself from a moment of slipped moorings.

'Castle-maine! Who did you think I meant? You know, Charles II's mistress, the one he made Duchess of Cleveland. I can't imagine anybody writing a book about George and leaving her out. Dreadful money-grubber. Nothing to boast about that I could ever see.'

I'm relieved – and she's right. It's inconceivable that I should omit to mention the connection my father most treasured. Snobbery is, after all, a significant aspect of the man. I can't, in describing a passion for houses and great estates, undervalue the Euston link, the precious ducal kinship.

Extract from Frederic Shoberl's *The Beauties of England and Wales*, 1813:

EUSTON, a village, pleasantly situated on the Lesser Ouse, was formerly the lordship of a family of that name. It afterwards descended to the family of Pattishall, and from them to Sir Henry Bennet, who . . . built Euston Hall; and left an only daughter, Isabella, married to Henry Fitzroy, one of the natural children of King Charles II, by the Duchess of Cleveland, who was created by his father Earl of Euston and Duke of Grafton, and was the ancestor of the present noble proprietor of Euston.

'I love your Euston,' my father wrote to his mother in 1942. He was nineteen, and enjoying a rare overnight stay with his favourite FitzRoy cousin at the Hall. It was the Hall, the Duke of Grafton's country seat, on which my father always dwelt when he spoke to us of Euston. I imagined that this was where his mother, the Duke's granddaughter, had grown up.

This was a misconception. Vita FitzRoy had not lived at the Hall. Her home, never alluded to by my father, was at the rectory across the road.

Vita kept a diary from the age of eight. Her daily entries conjure up a cheerful picture of life at the turn of the century in East Anglia, a part of England that had not altered much since Frederic Shoberl made his entry on Euston in 1813. Water was heated on the rectory's kitchen range; oil lamps and candles lit the rooms;

Vita and her two sisters shared a bedroom, and a schoolroom governess, until their mid-teens. On summer days, they knotted up their long serge skirts and bicycled into Bury St Edmunds where, on one occasion, they saw a blue man, a giant and a midget, who were visiting the market town with Buffalo Bill's travelling circus; in the evenings, they clustered round their mother, Ismay, while she read to them from the novels of Walter Scott. Sometimes, when their boisterous brothers came home from boarding school, the girls played silly family games: Puff Poilliard, Rumble Puppy, Teapot and Up Jenkins.

Vita was a lively, hot-tempered child. 'I fought with Fraulein at my music lesson,' she noted during the summer she turned fourteen. 'This morning [I had] another fearful row with Fraulein. Afternoon. Row continued with fearful heat.' A day later, feeling penitent, she noted that Fraulein had kissed her and did not seem cross.

'I love your Euston,' my father had written. He never comprehended how little affection Vita felt for the large, handsome Hall and its owner, a grandfather who was rarely there. She responded with excitement, not dismay, in 1902, when a large portion of the Hall went up in a blaze. Five horsedrawn fire-engines lumbered up the village street, too late to save the grand staircase and the finest staterooms. Vita, thrilled and awed, watched the spectacle with her father, the rector, from the top of the church tower.

A year later, Charles FitzRoy was diagnosed with tuberculosis. Less work, and plenty of rest in a warm climate: this was the doctor's prescription. A handout from the rector's father would have helped him to follow it. But the Duke of Grafton, glumly contemplating the devastation of Euston Hall, decided restoration and enlargement of the family house came first. Charles FitzRoy was forced to settle for taking holidays at Eastbourne; at home, the dust of bricks, mortar and stone chippings blew across the road, whitening the rectory windows and caking his throat. Euston Hall, when the expensive work of renovation had been completed, was larger than ever. The Duke, who preferred Wakefield Place, his home in Northamptonshire, stayed away.

George FitzRoy Seymour's maternal grandfather, the Reverend Lord Charles FitzRoy. He died of tuberculosis in 1911, the year in which George's parents married.

The sense of straitened circumstances at the rectory comes through the diaries more poignantly because it is mentioned so seldom. Vita wore an old dress freshened up with new buttons and a frill of lace for her first grown-up dance. When rich friends invited her to stay, she was ordered to decline. The servants of rich families expected lavish tips; the rector's family couldn't afford them. 'Mother says it would be too extravagant,' Vita told her diary; instead, she was sent on a cost-free visit to her grandfather's house, in Northamptonshire.

Her stay began agreeably. Two days after her arrival, Vita cautiously noted that the Duke had been quite good-tempered – 'so far.' On the third morning, a female guest sneezed at breakfast; pressed to explain herself, she admitted to a cold. Typhoid fever could not have caused more alarm. Rising from his chair at the head of the table, the host waved away a whimpered apology and stalked out of the dining room. He was not seen again. An order was despatched, via the butler, that the house must be vacated by nightfall; Vita was offered the consolation of a parting gift. Unwrapping it at the rectory that night, she found only a signed and plainly framed photograph of her grandfather.

At the beginning of 1908, Charles FitzRoy and his family faced a domestic crisis. His youngest daughter, Violet, had fallen in love with a military man; aristocratic genes did not console Nigel Maitland-Wilson's parents for Miss FitzRoy's shortage of cash. They wanted evidence that her family could support her; when Violet shed tears, the rector decided to help raise money by selling his favourite horse, and set about it without consultation. When he returned from Bury market with a beaming smile on his face and thirteen pounds in his pocket, even Vita knew he had been duped: 'Dad could never be a good horse-dealer or a bargainer in *anything*,' she noted. Still, brightening, she thought that he was looking 'awfully well – for him'. She was being optimistic. Tuberculosis had begun to strip the fat from Charles FitzRoy's athletic frame. He had three years left to live.

Dancing offered Vita a release from worry as her father's illness became increasingly hard to ignore. At the age of eighteen, her favourite treat was to stay over for a dance at one of the local big houses. In the past, the three sisters had always gone together, often sharing a bed in some freezing room up in an attic. Anna, the oldest, announced that she was bored by dances; Violet (the Maitland-Wilsons had reluctantly consented to their son's engagement), was a married woman. Vita, in the late spring of 1908, was obliged to look for a new companion.

She found one in her cousin. Linda Nelson was smartly turned-out and boldly spoken. She smoked, drank cocktails, expressed doubt about the existence of God, and drove her own car. Linda shared Vita's love of dancing, but she was not eager to go about with a girl who wore home-made dresses. When Vita admitted that she couldn't afford to buy new ones, Linda urged her to write to the Duke. Surely, however stingy he was, the old wretch could afford to buy his granddaughter a dress?

Fuelled by Linda's untipped cigarettes ('we smoked until we felt quite ill'), Vita concocted and despatched an elaborately affectionate letter. The response, to her amazement, was prompt: for her next dance, Vita wore silver kid slippers and a brand-new blue voile dress with a shimmering glacé lining, paid for by a cheque from the Duke.

'Hereward Wake and I had great fun dancing together,' she reported to the diary the following day. 'He is most awfully jolly and nice.' She had taken a tumble on the floor, but Hereward had helped her to her feet, 'and I wasn't a bit hurt'. She wondered if Sir Hereward's unusual name meant that he was descended from the Saxon hero, a thought she found most romantic. (She had just read Scott's novel, *Ivanhoe*.) A week later, Hereward and she were in each other's arms once more. A dinner service of pure gold had been laid out in the Marble Hall at Stowe, an architectural wonder-house in Buckinghamshire, soon to change use and become a boys' school. Two bands had played in relays until the sun came up. 'Danced in the ball room, the drawing room, the dining room and the Hall!' Vita reported with glee. 'We danced all night!' Later, they walked beside a stream towards William Kent's Temple of the Worthies, where she admired busts of Milton and Shakespeare. She doesn't mention whether Hereward kissed her.

Perhaps Sir Hereward failed to live up to his heroic name; perhaps Vita's zest for dancing wore him out; all I know is that she never mentioned him again. A few months later, she was invited to a houseparty in Scotland. The guests included the raffishly named

Tiger Howard, Lord and Lady Strathmore, Aubrey Herbert, Neva Trefusis, Richard Seymour and a Mr Gore. 'All young,' Vita noted, 'and very jolly.'

'Jolly' is just the word for it. They started by going to a fancy-dress ball, at which Vita showed up as a Romney painting of 'Flora', after having her cheeks rouged by Tiger Howard; on the following night, they stayed home and had 'great sport' after dinner, romping in the drawing room to the music of a pianola. 'Mr Gore dances too beautifully,' Vita noted, and added he was said to be the best dancer in London. 'He is awfully nice, too,' she added, 'most amusing – in fact, I like him far the best.' They collaborated in a game of charades the following night; on the next, Mr Gore and she beat all the rest in a game of billiards.

Hereward had been forgotten or surpassed; more surprisingly, my grandmother had not a word to say about Mr Gore's friend and companion, the man she would later marry. Her only reference to Richard Seymour on this occasion was a brief mention of the date on which he, together with Mr Gore, returned to London.

Am I missing the story of a love affair? Vita abandoned her diary the following year; she did not resume it until well after her marriage. Did Mr Gore – so graceful on the dance floor, so deft at croquet, so swift on the tennis court – capture my grandmother's heart that summer, only to break it? Did my shy grandfather catch her on the rebound? The letters and diaries have nothing to say.

Vita married Richard Sturgis Seymour (he was always known to his friends and family as Dick) in April 1911. Her father, who took the service himself, died that autumn; her mother told Dick that worries about the marriage had shortened the rector's life.

Ismay FitzRoy was a troublemaker who always showed a flair for the dramatic statement; nevertheless, there was cause for concern. Dick Seymour's career was flourishing when he visited Scotland with his friend, Mr Gore. He had served both as First Secretary and as a hard-working head of Chancery in Paris, Vienna and Berlin; now, aged thirty-two, he counted on being summoned to head an embassy, a position for which he was well prepared. Instead, in the summer of 1911, just after his marriage to Vita, he was ordered to prepare for a transfer from Berlin to Copenhagen. This was a disagreeable shock. Copenhagen was a charming city, but for a diplomat of Dick Seymour's age and experience it meant only one thing: demotion. In 1911, a well-educated, hard-working man's career had abruptly been thrown into reverse.

This was baffling to Dick, and distressing to his wife's family. Seeking explanations, they found none. Dick's chief, Sir Edward Goschen, pleaded for him in a private letter to Sir Edward Grey, the Secretary of State. Richard Seymour was a man of complete integrity, he pleaded; he was known for his conscientiousness, his industry and his intelligence. He did not deserve such treatment.

Grey never answered. Dick, bearing his humiliation with grace, thought he knew why. Grey's secretary at the time was William Tyrrell, a man referred to in all Dick's personal notes as 'the black knight'. For reasons that have never been clear, Tyrrell loathed Dick Seymour. The family think that Dick may have disparaged his colleague's olive complexion (he had an Indian grandmother). All that can be said for certain is that Tyrrell treated Dick as an enemy and took steps to block his advancement. It was, my grandfather wrote fifty years later, 'a dirty business'.

Copenhagen marked the beginning of an end to Dick Seymour's career. In 1917, he was offered another disappointing position, at The Hague; in 1920, he and Vita were despatched to the Legation at Bangkok. Although awarded the trappings of success (a fine house, plenty of servants, daily contact with Siam's young ruler), Dick knew that his position carried no weight. He was coming into middle age and his chances of being offered a decent post were vanishing. Worryingly, for a father of two young children, he still had no home of his own.

'Surely we must some day get something if we only stick to it,' Dick wrote to Vita from The Hague in 1917; five years later, back from Bangkok and with a third, most unexpected baby on the way, they at last found a house in Surrey that seemed affordable. Dick's Bostonian mother, born Mary Sturgis and always known as May, had meanwhile sold her vast mansion on Piccadilly. Grumbling of fallen circumstances, she moved to a slightly smaller home, in Eaton Square. May promised to provide her son with some furniture; two weeks later, she packed up and sent off her contributions: two brass-handled penwipers and a set of old-fashioned kitchen scales.

'Well, you know what that was about,' my mother comments. 'Beastly old woman: she was keeping the money to buy that wretched Bertie Falle' – she rhymes it with Hall – 'a title. When you think of the money she had! And the jewels!'

The only remaining evidence of May's wealth – she was co-heiress to a banking fortune – is in a portrait that she gave to my father. (She liked young George for sharing her passionate interest in ancestry.) Stroking the surface of the paint, I can feel the sharp points of light with which the artist has dutifully picked out every one of the two hundred pearls in the spectacular necklace that May sold in 1930 to help buy her second husband a barony.

May was fifty-three when Dick's father died in 1904. Bertie Falle, a broad-shouldered and chestnut-haired young politician from Jersey – he was considerably younger than May – was already her lover. In 1906, she married him. From then on, May's prime object in life was to obtain a barony for her adored Bertie. It took thirty years and the equivalent today of over half a million pounds; in 1936, Sir Bertrand Falle (Bertie had been more respectably honoured in 1916, for his services as MP for Portsmouth) finally became Lord Portsea.

Lack of furniture aside, Dick and Vita were overjoyed to be settled at last in a home of their own. Hill House, a low, creeper-clad house near Godalming in Surrey, was where my father George

May, my father's paternal grandmother,
seen here shortly before her death in 1942.

was born in 1923, when Vita was thirty-seven. The celebrations at his birth were overshadowed by a sudden deterioration in Dick Seymour's health. He felt pains in his side; his appetite waned; he experienced difficulty in breathing. Lady Falle wrote to suggest that her son should try eating less; Vita, remembering her father's slow death, insisted that Dick must see a specialist. The verdict was alarming; Dick had weak lungs, asthma and a bad heart condition. A change of climate was prescribed.

He got it. Dick's career had been on hold since his return from Bangkok. In 1924, he received a new posting. The London specialist, when he heard that his patient was being sent to La Paz, expressed concern. No middle-aged invalid suffering fom breathlessness and a weak heart should be expected to take up a new life fourteen thousand feet above sea level, where gasping babies turned blue and strong men fainted if they walked uphill at normal speed. La Paz was a deathtrap for the weak. The appointment was surely a mistake?

There had been none. Dick, conscious that his old enemy had become a force to reckon with in the Foreign Office, was convinced that William Tyrrell had chosen him for the post.

The appointment was for an indefinite period. Hill House would have to be sold. The two older children, Leo and Alexandra, aged twelve and eleven, would remain at their English schools and spend holidays with relations. But what, Vita wondered, was to be the fate of her precious baby, the child she had lovingly named in memory of her friend George Vyse, a cripple who had died at the age of thirty?

It's possible that her memory of George Vyse's fragility and early death heightened Vita's sense of her baby's need for special care. Her first impulse was to take George with her to Bolivia; advised of the potential risks to his health, she racked her brains for a solution. George was such a delicate little creature: who would be worthy of such a precious charge?

Dick's mother – bright, hard and engrossed in the social round – was out of the question. Violet Wilson, Vita's younger sister, had gone to India with her husband; Anna, married at long last, but possessing no children of her own, seemed an unlikely candidate for baby care. This left only Vita's mother.

Ismay FitzRoy had been living alone for almost ten years when, in 1920, she fixed a widow's eye on the dapper little baron who was courting Anna, her eldest daughter. It was noticed that Ismay had started to wear unsuitably girlish hats. A sharp-tongued cousin commented that rouge must be responsible for such uncommonly flushed cheeks in a woman past her prime.

Her children were outraged, and not just by the rouge. As a mother, Ismay had never shown much affection for her eldest daughter; surely, now that plain, awkward Anna was thirty-five, she could be allowed some happiness? Charlie Byron, a shy bachelor who had recently inherited a handsome country home from his aunt, was an ideal match. True, he was capricious, old-fashioned and nearing sixty; nevertheless, he owned a house in London and two estates, in Essex and Nottinghamshire. Unlike his grandfather's cousin, the poet, of whom he stoutly disapproved, this Lord Byron possessed a character of flawless respectability.

Charlie Byron had never been much troubled by women during his placid residence as the rector of Langford, on his family's Essex estate. Forced now to decide whether flirtatious Ismay or bashful Anna would make the better chatelaine for his new home, he dithered, and declined to commit himself to either. Ismay became imperious; Anna, seeing her last chance of marriage slipping away, grew tearful. Urgent family consultations were held; Anna's oldest brother decided to take the initiative. Escorting his nervous sister to Nottinghamshire, Charles FitzRoy rang the bell at Thrumpton

George FitzRoy Seymour's maternal grandmother, Ismay FitzRoy, in 1918, shortly before she set her cap at Charlie Byron, the bashful rector of Thrumpton.

Hall, greeted his host, ordered him to take Anna into the billiard room – and bolted the door. It was winter. The billiard room was chilly. Lord Byron, growing a little shrill, demanded that he should be released. Charlie FitzRoy sat still, and waited. An hour later, Anna emerged, an engaged woman. Six months later, she became Lady Byron.

Ismay FitzRoy was displeased, but undefeated. If she was not to have a husband, she intended to have fun. Sammy, her youngest son, a raffish lad of twenty-three with a weakness for drink, was ready to help.

From a distance, I can warm to the old lady's spirit when I read her accounts of vagabonding around England with young Sammy in a splendid touring car, known as 'the hooter'. As a mother, however, Ismay did not strike Vita as a suitable guardian for her beloved George. Time was drawing on, and her options were limited. It was true that Anna had no children and no experience of caring for them. Thrumpton was, nevertheless, equipped with servants, a large garden and, should George fall ill, a trustworthy doctor in the next village. Anna sent word that her husband was willing to give little George house room, so long as he caused no disruption.

By the end of September 1924, Vita had made the decision that would prove so momentous in shaping my father's life. As his parents set off for the Liverpool docks in preparation for their journey to South America, George, by then a toddler of almost two, smartly dressed in a white wool knee-length coat, and clinging tightly to the hand of his nursemaid, climbed the staircase to his new quarters, a dimly lit range of rooms on an upper floor known as the Barracks. Thrumpton Hall, a large and isolated house in south Nottingham-shire, was to be his home for the undetermined future. He was, as Charlie Byron impressively informed him, the only child to have lived there for three hundred years.

2

❧

EXILE

Travelling slowly towards La Paz, Vita was torn between longing and dread for the voluminous, close-written letters from her mother that now formed her chief contact with the family. Reports on their destination were discouraging. La Paz was said by everybody to be quite frightful, Ismay FitzRoy wrote. Angry not to have been put in charge of her grandson, she added a grim report of his situation. Poor little George! She had seen him at Thrumpton and noticed how hard he clung to his nurse's hand when he was brought downstairs. The house was enormous and fearfully gloomy; scarcely a lamp in the place and oozing with damp, not at all suitable for a child so prone to coughs and colds. Still, George looked sweeter than ever. Such a pity that Charlie Byron and Anna insisted on keeping him hidden away in those dreary rooms on the top floor. What fun he might have had, living with his grandmother!

Ismay's calculated words had the desired effect. 'Beloved little George,' Vita wrote in anguish. 'I can't bear to feel I'll never see him in frocks and rompers again.' Twisting her knife harder in the next letter, Ismay wrote that she had not at first wanted to mention how eagerly George had run out of the Byrons' house to greet her, or how he burst into tears when he saw no sign of 'mummy'. Shedding tears herself, Vita was tempted to wonder if she could abandon Dick on their arrival, and take the next steamer back to Liverpool.

I have kept a photograph of Dick and Vita Seymour in their old age. Snapped in their daughter's garden on a summer afternoon, they sit beside each other on an iron bench. Dick looks wistfully at the camera; Vita keeps her hands clamped together on her lap. You could cut the photograph in half and never guess that these two had once been a couple.

'I wouldn't have wanted to be on that boat to La Paz with her,' my mother says. 'She could be quite cruel, you know, when she was angry.'

My father's parents as I remember them, an old couple,
seated side by side but not companiably.

I answer that I think either of us would have been equally irate. Vita, after all, had married a man who seemed likely to offer her a pleasant future in Paris or Berlin, not indefinite exile on the other side of the world. My mother, who has been reading a book about diplomatic wives, takes the view that Vita should have accepted her fate with a better grace.

'But it must have been so frustrating for her, feeling they deserved a better posting and not being able to do anything about it.'

'Why did you say that was?' my mother asks. 'Something to do with Dick's temper?'

'His temper?'

'Dreadful!'

I'm astonished. I was ten when my grandfather died. I can remember his wheezing chuckle, the slow blink of pale blue eyes, enlarged by the thick lenses of old-fashioned glasses. Nothing more. There's no image of violence in my childhood memories of him; there's no evidence of it in the wistful memoir he began to write while he was in La Paz, or in the mild letters written earlier, when he was at The Hague during the War and longing to be reunited with his family. He wrote to Vita of his bewilderment at the way he was being cold-shouldered by the Foreign Office, and of his love. 'I miss you and the children dreadfully,' he told her; 'I wish the time until we meet could go a little faster.' Dick Seymour sounds kind and a little sad, just as he always seemed to me.

And yet. I'd forgotten something that may be relevant. Not long before my grandfather's death, my father dropped me off to have tea with the old couple at their London flat. The live-in companion opened the door and told me that Mr Seymour had gone to bed for the day. He was too ill to be seen. I was to go into the front room and take care not to talk too loudly.

Sitting by the window that looked out across a flint-grey Thames, I played a game of snap with my grandmother and sipped the diluted orange squash which always tasted different in London from the country, brinily chemical. I asked if I might go to the bathroom. As I walked towards it, something darkened the end of the passage and rushed at me with a roar.

Confusion and rage reddened the air; my fear could not have been greater if a mountain bear had sprung out of a cupboard and shown its claws. Turning, I fled back into the safety of the front room. My grandmother stood with her back against the window, looking down at me with an anxious stare that warned against making a fuss. I picked up a book and opened it, pretending to read while the words ran together in a jumble of black markings. Behind me, I could hear my grandmother and the companion, whispering urgently. They glanced at me and left the room. Listening at the door, I heard two deep, harsh shouts, heavy movements of something being dragged, and a moan. I sat down quickly and began turning the pages again. It seemed as if my grandfather's place in the flat had been usurped by a frightening stranger, who had to be controlled.

The memory is a striking one and my mother insists that Dick Seymour could be terrifying when enraged. Still, his writings offer no confirming evidence. Even Ismay, who clearly despised her son-in-law, never mentioned his temper in her troublemaking letters to Vita. Call it family loyalty if you like, but I think my grandfather was shabbily treated.

I think, too, that Vita's attitude may have hindered his advancement. My grandmother was not the sort of woman who had stiffened the Empire's backbone. Prepared to loathe La Paz before even setting foot in Bolivia, she kept a record of life there that made Job's trials sound lightweight. The rain never stopped. The house was hideous. The housekeeper had no knowledge of English or French (surely Vita could have tried to learn a few phrases of Spanish?); the high altitude kept them both in a state of constant exhaustion.

Marooned in a country she detested, among people with whom she found no common bond – she despised the Bolivians and made no attempt to hide her boredom from the ladies of La Paz's diplomatic colony – Vita lived for the postbag and for news of her children. Leo and Alex were said to be flourishing, but how could she bear to think of George, so young still that he might – this was her greatest fear – forget her and begin to look on Anna as his mother?

She had lost him; she was convinced of it. She had left him behind because she feared the risk to a delicate child's health of such a journey. Now, regretting her decision, she fumed at the unhappiness her husband's stalled career had inflicted. Everything, she confided to her mother and to Anna, was so unjust. The one treat she had keenly anticipated, a train journey to Lake Titicaca, Cuzco and Machu Picchu, ended disastrously when Dick turned blue from lack of breath and had to be transported back to La Paz and confined to his bed for a month. All requests for proper medical treatment had, as usual, been ignored. Dick's new deputy, meanwhile, put in a plea of ill-health and was granted permission to leave on the spot. Embassy servants carried him to the train on a stretcher; when Vita peered though the window of his compartment, she saw the lively young deputy sitting upright and laughing at her as he waved goodbye.

Surely, Ismay FitzRoy wrote, dear Lady Falle could use her political connections? Was Dick entirely without – she might as well have said 'guts' – influence over his own mother? Timidly, Dick wrote to beg for help and to admit, with characteristic understatement, that life in Bolivia was becoming a little bleak. A word to Lady Falle's friend, Mrs Austen Chamberlain, could do so much for them (Chamberlain was the new Foreign Secretary to Baldwin's government). Any assistance that his mother could offer them to cover the older children's school bills would be gladly received.

The response was worse than either he or Vita could have feared. Lady Falle was afraid that she did not have a penny to spare for school fees, but she had done as they wished. She had spoken to the Chamberlains. The news was excellent: Dick was offered an immediate transfer: to Bogotá. Such a chance would not come again; she urged him to accept.

Dick was a dutiful son; even so, he flinched. 'We never had a moment's thought about refusing,' Vita confided to her diary, 'but the shock of such an offer after Bangkok and La Paz was really *awful*.' Their colleagues agreed; better to stay in La Paz than sink to Bogotá.

The final straw for Vita came in a letter from her mother. It brought the news that dear little George now addressed Anna Byron as 'mummy'. She had suffered enough. Booking a passage home, she left her husband to solace himself with the memories of his schooldays. Arriving at Liverpool after a year's absence, she was greeted by a letter from Anna. George had just returned from a weekend with Ismay. 'And directly he got into the hall,' Anna wrote with tactless pride, 'he said: "I've come home now!"'

How old do you have to be to form a passion that will endure for a lifetime? The answer in my father's case seems clear. Abandoned at the age of two, he had given his heart to Thrumpton. No human love would ever displace it.

3

❧

THE HOUSE

My mother has found a newspaper cutting about Mrs Wescomb's Winter Ball, held at Thrumpton Hall in 1840. The gushing prose ('a scene of profuse hospitality and festivity . . . a most elegant supper . . . the graceful pleasures of the dance . . . a brilliant display of loveliness and beauty') was churned out for every grand event of the time. What startles us is the news that over a hundred people were shepherded up the grand carved staircase to dance in what the newspaper describes as 'the upper drawing room'.

'A hundred people!' My mother and I gaze at each other, open-mouthed. The frail wooden floor of this pretty rose-pink reception room has collapsed twice in the last seventy years. The idea of fitting a hundred dancers, not to mention Mr Quick's quadrille band, into such a delicate structure, is beyond our imagining.

The Wescombs had plenty to celebrate in 1840 and no serious concern for the cost of a collapsed floor. A bachelor uncle had just left Thrumpton Hall to Miss Lucy Wescomb, a girl of seventeen.

At the age of twenty-one, she could claim her estate; until then, Lucy's mother was formally in charge of: one large red-brick Jacobean house, a thousand acres of land, four farms, thirty employees, fifteen cottages, and three lively, strong-willed daughters in their teens. As if that were not enough, Mrs Wescomb was still supervising Langford, another estate of a thousand acres in Essex, east of London, where the girls had all grown up.

Lucy and her favourite sister later married two brothers, descendants of the celebrated Lord Byron. Since Lucy had no children, her nephew became her heir. Charlie Byron – my father's uncle – was born on the Essex estate in 1861; fifty years later, he was still the bachelor rector of Langford, patiently waiting to inherit – but only for the duration of his own life – a house he scarcely knew.

'So cruel, those life tenancies,' my mother sighs. 'When you think of having all the work and care of upkeep, and always knowing that your home isn't your own.'

I glance at her. Thrumpton now belongs to me; does she mind living as a guest in a house to which she gave the best part of her life? Is that what she's thinking? Or is she remembering the Welsh castle in which she grew up, always supposing that her parents owned it, until the day the owners returned, and my mother's family were forced to leave? I can't tell. It's not always easy to read my mother's thoughts; she's had too long to learn how best to hide them.

My father was brought up on tales of Lucy Byron's reign. To me, she sounds a monster; to him, and to the Thrumpton villagers who told him their memories, Lucy was a character. Why should they have minded when she refused to have a pub in the village, when beer was always available from the Hall's own brewhouse? Hemming and repairing Lady Byron's bedsheets didn't strike them as inappropriate work for girl pupils at the village school. Neither could she be blamed for having an eye for a handsome lad (Lucy's seven footmen were strikingly good-looking) or for keeping her title after her husband died and she married her cousin Mr Philip Douglas. Everybody knew her as Lady Byron; her tenants and servants shared her pride in the name. Mrs Douglas didn't convey the same glamour.

'Just like you,' my mother says when I comment that this was rather hard on Lucy's second husband. 'Catch you changing your name.'

'That's different. I'm a writer. It's my professional name.'

'Lucy employed over thirty people,' my mother observes. 'What's unprofessional about that? Anyway, she doted on Philip Douglas. I don't suppose he minded.'

Didn't he? I remember the story my father loved to tell, of Lucy sitting bolt upright each Sunday morning in the front pew of the little village church she'd spent a fortune on making her own. (Her first step had been to order all evidence of the House's previous owners to be removed from the walls and banished to the bell-tower.) A plump lapdog lay between the iron hoops that fanned out her long skirt; above the feathered crest of his wife's black crepe hat, Mr Douglas, the rector, spoke mildly to the parishioners of God's message. Lucy, who needed no advice from God, took out her gold repeater watch and stared at it. At midday precisely, even when her husband was still in mid-sentence, she thumped the tiled floor with her ebony cane. The congregation rose for the last hymn; the rector, putting away his notes, crept back down the pulpit steps.

'Dreadful old woman!' my father said, beaming approval.

It was good of Lucy to build a block of alms buildings for the poor, and to allow the villagers the freedom of the estate for their Sunday afternoon strolls. I've also heard how a sick coachman was dismissed after twenty years of service for allowing Lady Byron to catch a cold from him. I've heard of children being ordered to curtsey and doff their caps whenever she passed by, and of a family being evicted from their cottage because they missed a week's rent.

But time has softened the sharp edges in village memories and these stories have to be coaxed into the light. The old ladies I interview want to bathe the past in gold. They'll only tell me how grateful their parents were for Lady Byron's garden fete and the Christmas party up at the House, with supper for all the children of the village, their presents stacked ready and beautifully wrapped under a candlelit tree. Lucy lived in a handsome home cared for by twenty-two house-servants, while her village workforce shivered in unheated cottages with outside privies: the contrast doesn't appear to bother their descendants at all.

'Of course it doesn't,' my mother says, sounding strangely like my father. 'Village people didn't like to travel in those days. They lived at home, they married locally, and they all worked for the big house. It was a good system. They weren't just servants, you know. They were our friends.' And she tells me about the laundrymaid everybody in the village knew as Aunt Alice. 'She was still wearing Lucy Byron's underwear when I came here,' my mother says. 'Beautiful, lace-edged. You'd never see it outside a museum today. Lucy left every stitch of it to Alice.'

I don't know what to make of this. Did owning Lucy's lace bloomers and being addressed as a relation make up for years of scrubbing linen and for hands chafed raw with bleach and carbolic? Alice seems to have thought so, and so does my mother.

'We were friends,' she says again. 'That's what your generation never understand.'

Lucy Byron had been dead for over a decade when my father arrived at Thrumpton for the first time on a damp autumn evening in 1924. Her presence still governed the House. Lucy's last portrait looked down the Carolean carved staircase which, on her orders, had been coated with treacle-black varnish; her ugliest contribution to the House, a Victorian billiard room, squatted beside it like a crematorium; her laurels and yews filled the garden with clumps of darkness. The household remained buried in the nineteenth century, as it had been when Charlie Byron, Lucy's nephew and heir, first visited it as a boy. This was how he was content for it to remain. This was the rigid form from which my father took his blueprint for the future.

'Fancy if they take electric power through Thrumpton and you have it *and* the telephone!' Vita wrote to her sister from La Paz in 1925. Anna, after four years of marriage, was still struggling to accustom herself to life in a house that had no gas, no telephone

Anna Byron, my father's childless aunt, sitting out on a garden wall at Thrumpton in 1928. George FitzRoy Seymour, already adopted as the child of the house, was five years old.

line, no electricity and no mains water supply. From the pulpit in Thrumpton Church, her old-fashioned husband warned the congregation against the dangers of progress; in Charlie Byron's home, a jangling row of bells, each pealing an identifiable note, called servants to their duties around the House throughout the day. A single oil lamp was carried into the drawing room at dusk; George's nurse, bringing her charge down to wish his aunt and uncle goodnight, was given a small tallow candle to light their way back to the top floor.

And yet this was the House that won my father's heart. I have trouble in understanding how this happened. Some of the details of his first years there are farcical: I can't imagine the feelings of a small boy who is woken each morning by Miss Sarah Death (a housemaid) and who has his small shoes polished by Mr Percy Crush (a footman). Others make me shudder. I know that Anna Byron was under her husband's thumb, but how could she have allowed a frightened child to be left alone, night after night (Nurse Ethel preferred to spend her evenings chatting in the Servants' Hall with Mr Crush, Miss Death and Mr Shotbolt, the butler), in a chilly, carpetless room at the top of the House? The Byrons themselves slept in cosier quarters on the floor below; up at the top, so my father always told me, when the wind rattled the windows, he could hear the sound of a girl crying. Sixty years earlier, in Lucy Byron's day, a housemaid, ordered to leave when she got pregnant, had hanged herself from the skylight outside his bedroom door.

'Rubbish!' my mother exclaims. 'Absolute rubbish!'

My mother has no time for ghosts. I think those desolate and unattended nights may help explain a fear of solitude so acute that my father could not, in later years, even walk to the end of the village without company.

This doesn't help. I'm not looking for an explanation of his terror, but a reason for the passionate attachment he formed to the House. From the time he first spoke of it as home at the age of three, his love of Thrumpton dominated my father's existence. He wedded himself to the place with a passion that knew no reserve.

How did it come about? Letters that he wrote later use 'an oppressively Victorian upbringing' to justify his taste for a less orthodox life. Oddly, it was one of the most Victorian aspects of his life there that had most entranced him.

'Shotbolt was my ally,' he wrote. 'Shotbolt was my friend.'

Mr Shotbolt, the Byrons' butler, was an asthmatic ex-service-man who had been gassed in the trenches. (He died in 1938, aged less than fifty, of a lung-related condition.) It was the butler who, having discovered that music was the best way to check a small boy's tears, took out his tin whistle. Shotbolt taught my father to sing, whistle, and dance a jig: "Pop Goes the Weasel" and "I Ain't Nobody's Darling" were their star turns in the Servants' Hall. ('It is so nice to hear of my little angel being fond of music and dancing to the rhythm,' Vita wrote wistfully when Anna reported on George's improved spirits.)

On his off-duty afternoons, Shotbolt obtained permission to take Master George out in the park. From Shotbolt, my father learned that a badger will share its sett with a fox's earth, and that the hills at Thrumpton hide shards of bright pottery left over from Roman times. On long Sunday afternoons, when Shotbolt went fishing down by the ferry, my father sat beside him on the bank, watching the play of light on water and listening to stories of the butler's own country childhood, out on the Romney Marsh.

'Very poetic,' my mother says suspiciously. 'He didn't tell me all that.' I suspect that she's forgotten, for my father wrote it all out and typed it up, as a loving tribute to the man who first made him look on Thrumpton as his home.

Shotbolt introduced him to the land; a young electrician took him deep into the bowels of the House and, perhaps, gave him the sense that it could be mastered.

Anna used all the persuasive power of which she was capable to make her old-fashioned husband see that life could not be lived by oil-lamps and candles for ever. In 1927, worn down by her insistence, Charlie Byron gave his consent: the House would be wired. (The image of 230 volts of power coursing below wooden floorboards was too dreadful to be supported; sternly, he insisted on the installation of a transformer to cut all power to half-strength. The House might have become electrified; thanks to its owner's decision, it grew no brighter than in the old, oil-lit days.)

Charlie Byron, looking quite dapper at the time of his marriage to Anna FitzRoy.

It was my father's good luck that the electricians who undertook the job brought with them a fourteen-year-old apprentice. Billeted in the village with the family of the girl he later married, Jack Carter was a gamekeeper's son, a square-chinned, thickset boy with untidy reddish hair, wide lively eyes and, when amused, a grin that sliced into his cheeks. Jack Carter enjoyed exploring the estate as much as Shotbolt had done, and was as willing to share his knowledge of lairs, holes, birds' nests and ferrets.

The occasion for which my father still remembered Jack Carter fondly, after forty years, had nothing to do with woodland wanderings. It was the day when the young electrician offered to show him the House's hidden world, on the other side of a small door at the back of a bolted cupboard on the top floor.

This, given later developments, might seem to lay the ground for suggesting that my father was given a stealthy introduction to sex as a furtive pleasure by his new friend. Having known Jack Carter for much of my early life, I'd take a bet of any size against that possibility. This was an innocent escapade, a treat to cheer a lonely child.

The space between the floors is the best-kept secret of old houses, a secret trail that can be followed, on hands and knees, from the rafters down to the cellar. I've crawled through that door myself as a child, hunting for lost treasure. Lying flat and wriggling forward through long low galleries laid with rushes and propped with blackened timbers, you become part of the fabric, dusty with its history. Odd objects lie here, dropped through the floorboards a hundred years earlier: a pencil stub, a necklace's lost clasp, a scrap of carved wood. Listening, you catch from above the muffled sounds of life – heels clacking across a floor, a bucket being set down, a smothered laugh, a door being shut. Hidden away from the light, you smell wood, straw and mystery. I don't think my father ever read *The Borrowers*. Climbing down into darkness and crawling behind Jack Carter's sturdy boots into the heart of the House, he became part of their between-the-floors world.

I'd like to think that it was here, lying alert and quiet while the coils of wire were carefully unreeled towards the next electric point, that my father made a pact with the sinews of the House that possessed him so entirely.

Or was it made two years later, in 1929, the year in which a Thrumpton neighbour's home, one of the loveliest in England, went down in flames?

'Nuthall Temple!' My mother shakes her head. 'Now, you really are romancing. What on earth does Nuthall have to do with your father?'

These events took place almost twenty years before her marriage. But when I remind her that her husband was at Thrumpton when Nuthall burnt down, and of the horror of fire which he picked up from his uncle's own terror, she hesitantly admits that there may be a connection. She might only be humouring an obsessed daughter's whim: I can never tell.

Nuthall Temple was a ravishing house, built in the eighteenth century by the same team who had made Chiswick House an exquisite homage to Palladio. Beautifully situated, overlooking the lake from which the stone for its columned portico had been quarried, the Temple's chief glory was a vast octagonal room, soaring to the full height of the house and decorated with some of the finest rococo plasterwork in the country, a playful riot of swags and garlands.

Visits were exchanged on a weekly basis between the two houses during my father's first years at his uncle's home. Charlie Byron of Thrumpton and Robert Holden of Nuthall were both latecomers to the task of running large estates; Holden's advantage was that he had a son and heir who loved the Temple and longed to live there.

Death duties made this impossible. Set at fifty per cent in 1918, this tax on inheritance had just been raised once more when Robert Holden died in 1926. Advised that he could not afford to pay and stay, Holden's son agreed to an auction. He had hoped to save his home from destruction by selling it as a country club; nobody, unfortunately, wanted to make the commitment. In 1927, less than a year after Robert Holden's death, the Temple's contents were sold piecemeal.

The auctioneers stripped the house of all its glory; at the end of the day, nothing remained but a magnificent shell and the empty octagonal hall, its breathtaking plasterwork still intact. A few enthusiasts urged that a rescue mission should be undertaken before further damage was done; their pleas were ignored. Nuthall Temple, from that moment, was a disaster waiting to happen.

Little help was on hand for the owners of country houses and their estates in the post-war years. Farming had helped to maintain them in the past; the ending of wheat subsidy in 1921 heralded twenty years of agricultural depression. Increased death duties didn't help. The National Trust was concentrating its limited resources on the preservation of landscape, not houses; no system yet existed for the listing and protection of property that was still in private hands. A new Tory government championed the rights of a property-owning democracy; country houses, with their large empty parks, offered opportunities for development in a time of housing crisis. Nuthall Temple stood just beyond the fringes of Nottingham, a city ripe for expansion.

The end came on a warm summer's day in 1929. 'Nuthall Temple Burned,' ran the local paper's headline: 'A Wonderful Sight'.

The newspaper's own reporter helped to start the blaze. Contacted by a developer who had bought the Temple and wanted to build on its site, the journalist agreed to lend a hand in exchange for exclusive rights to the photographs. The two of them doused the Temple walls with paraffin; at midday, the villagers strolled up the drive to see what was going on. The developer threw in the first lighted brand; the reporter followed suit. In an hour, the Temple was on fire. Cameras snapped as the whole of the West Wing collapsed. The Music Room, gracefully decorated with Adam plaques, stood as a roofless wreck for a minute or two before dissolving into a shimmering wall of heat; the cupola of the great

Octagon came down into the flames in a cascade of golden fragments. Swaggering among the smoking ruins, a group of boys from the village posed as conquerors.

Charlie Byron was horrified. Robert Holden had been his closest friend in the neighbourhood. Miserably, Charlie blamed himself for Nuthall's fate, for not having rallied up support; fearfully, he dwelt on the possibility that Thrumpton might meet a similar fate. This, in the late summer of 1929, when my father was six years old, was the main topic of conversation.

Vita and Dick were both back in England by this time. Dick had accepted a part-time desk job in the Foreign Office; Lady Falle reluctantly contributed towards the purchase of a family house in Evelyn Gardens, west of her own grander home in Eaton Square. Formally, this was George's home; informally, he was spending a large part of each year at Thrumpton.

The Byrons had grown too attached to their small nephew to want to relinquish him when Vita returned to England in 1925; an understanding was reached which allowed George to continue paying long visits to Thrumpton. This was an arrangement that suited everybody. Vita, glad to see him growing rosy-cheeked in his spells away from the city, began to hope that Charlie Byron might be looking for a suitable heir; Anna, regretting the absence of a child of her own, liked having a little boy to spoil and hug; George relished the sense of being universally loved.

Charlie Byron was already in the habit of talking aloud at meals to his dog Bingo, a large and shaggy poodle. As George grew old enough to hold conversations, he displayed a ready sympathy and understanding for his uncle's worries that Bingo, even at his best, failed to show. When Nuthall Temple burned down, Charlie lectured his nephew on the importance of protecting the home they loved from faceless villains: the local council; developers; a land-hungry government. George took it all in as earnestly as if he was his uncle's colleague, rather than a child of six. His mannerisms were already copied from his uncle; in the larger family, George was spoken of as being 'quaint'.

George loved his parents; it was simply the case that a tall, featureless house in West London could not compete against the charms of life at Thrumpton, where, indulged and adored, he was now allowed to do as he pleased. Gradually, he was developing a sense of his own small and slightly pompous person as the son of the House, the heir apparent. 'I want to live at Thrumpton and care for the village,' he wrote in his diary for 1934. He was eleven years old. By then, the sense of commitment was absolute.

Was it the shocking destruction of Nuthall Temple that first put the idea of himself as the saviour of Thrumpton into my father's oddly unchildish mind? Was that the moment when he first understood that a House cannot survive the failure of an owner's love?

My mother claims that I'm being imaginative. I remember how haunted my father was by his fear of fire, how he patrolled his home on winter nights, ensuring the extinction of matches, candles and cigarette butts, pulling iron guards forward to protect wooden floors from a lively spark or smouldering log. I remember too, after his death, coming across a folder of cuttings about the Temple. One photograph had been circled with a heavy black pen. It showed a few broken chunks of wall that had escaped the fire. *Sic transit gloria*, my father had written underneath, doubtless congratulating himself that Thrumpton had, thanks to his single-minded endeavours, escaped such a fate.

4

THE BOY

Travelling home from La Paz, Vita agonised about the possibility that she had forfeited her son's love.

There is no doubt that her desertion of him had been deeply felt. Abandoned once, George never allowed her to forget how much she was adored. (How did Dick feel on the day in 1944 when he was invited to admire a handsome oil painting of Vita for which his twenty-one-year-old son, not he, had paid a hundred guineas? 'Daddy didn't say much,' gives the answer in George's diary.) Aged four, George spent a month's pocket money on buying a pair of finches after Vita's pet budgie died; a year later, fiercely resentful of the father who had returned from Bolivia to usurp his place, he wrote imperious letters from his bedroom in Evelyn Gardens, headed 'extreamly urgent' and summoning his mother to come upstairs 'at once' to share his bed, 'because I am so fritened'. Such demands invariably won her consent.

'Honestly!' my mother exclaims. 'Imagine what would have happened if I'd asked my mother that!'

'I can see, though, after she left him at Thrumpton – he must have felt so insecure about her love.'

'He had Anna running after him as well,' my mother says. 'And silly old Dar.' (She's talking in the language of family diminutives: by Dar, she means Ismay, Vita's mother.) 'They all spoiled him. The things he got away with! Do you remember the story about his putting tin-tacks on the nanny's chair? Vita thought it was frightfully amusing.'

'So did he. That's why he was always telling us about it.'

We've been chatting about my father this morning while wrapping and putting away – for good, I hope – six or seven delicate sets of breakfast china. I never understood why we had to keep so many of these ready for use; it is only this morning that I have learned my father wanted his weekend house-guests to be offered morning tea and biscuits with a wake-up call. Their bedroom curtains would be drawn, the fire switched on, a bath drawn: delightful, if you happen to be visiting a hotel that specialises in Edwardian weekends. I ask my mother whom he had expected to provide this elegant service. She grimaces.

'Who do you think?'

'Him?'

'Oh, quite!'

What age did he dream that he was living in? (This was during the 1990s.) And who, by that time, when he had almost cut himself free from aristocratic society, were the guests for whom a woman in her seventies was expected to play parlourmaid?

'It's how it was,' she says, laying a flower-sprigged saucer in its nest of paper, ready for storage.

A photograph taken in 1931, when my father was eight, offers a pointer to the way things were to go. Taking part in a charity matinee to raise money for The Women's League Services for Motherhood (the celebrated ballerina Lydia Lopokova was the main draw of the day), George Seymour strutted on to the stage of the Cambridge Theatre as Lord Charles FitzRoy, a royal page in a tableau of Queen Victoria's drawing-room assembly. His mother, priding herself on the family connections, had chosen George's role with care. She did not stint him on the cost of a costume: a splendidly frogged silk coat, a feathered hat and silver-buckled shoes guaranteed that her son would be noticed and admired. Intoxicated by his transformation into a Lord, George began to take a keen interest in his ancestry. Vita, who kept small prints of Charles II and the Duchess of Cleveland, his mistress, on her dressing table, was happy to indulge him. From the age of eight on, my father proclaimed his *Roy*-al connection on all possible occasions. There were Fitzroys – and there was George FitzRoy Seymour, an altogether superior

This photograph of Lord Charles FitzRoy (his grandfather) was the model for my father's appearance on stage in 1931.

being in the opinion of himself and his doting mamma.

Vita seems to have shed few tears over the older two children she had left at boarding-schools when she travelled to La Paz; she was grief-stricken by the departure of George, aged six, to a prep school in Kent. 'The loss must fall heavily on you,' a sympathetic headmaster wrote in a letter that can't have lightened her heart with the news that her puny son showed little confidence in himself, was useless in all forms of team sports, and had made no friends.

I'm ready to sympathise. 'Cream' and 'Dregs' were the two categories into which newcomers to my own boarding school were divided by their superiors; a list of those to be envied (Cream) or despised (Dregs) was displayed each week on the notice board, and studied by all. Being cast among the dregs was a lesson in humiliation that nobody forgot. I don't suppose my father's school was any kinder to its misfits.

He could have taken a hint from Oliver FitzRoy, his cousin and schoolmate. Oliver was a good-looking child, the beau ideal of boyhood, generous, sporting, open-hearted. My father worshipped him. He glued himself to Oliver like a shadow, hoping for a share of the sunlight through which his fair-haired, sleepy-eyed cousin strolled with an air of untouchable ease. Oliver glows out of my father's prep school letters like a burnished prince, the victor on the cricket field, the hero of his set.

Why was my father so disliked? Was it for his selfishness? (Other boys cheerfully shared out the spoils sent to them from home; my father squirrelled away his stores of sweets and cakes, to be consumed in solitude.) Was it because he was sickly and skinny? (He loved the school san; it was, he told his mother, the only place at school where the food was good, the bed comfortable, and the rules relaxed.)

Or was it, perhaps, because he struck his schoolmates as a prig?

Dick, since his return from La Paz, had begun writing light verses which, from time to time, he circulated around the family. Vita let it be known that she found Dick's hobby irritating, an excuse to close the door on his wife and claim that he was busy. She took more pleasure in her son's talent for poetry. George's verses were also relayed around the family, after being copied out, for clarity's sake, by a loving mother's hand. Dick's poems were playful; George's were pious. One, composed when he was seven, told of his wish to become a horse and pace along God's holy path; in another, he hoped that no naughty deed would deprive him of a coveted seat near the Saviour's throne. His schoolmates, in less of a hurry to meet their Maker, kept George at a distance; the English master, reluctant to discourage such ardent feelings, praised a promising literary style.

Vita, my father's adored and indulgent mother,
as he first remembered her.

Abandoned once again by his family and bullied by his peers, my father used his pen to salvage some form of control over trying circumstances. Correspondence, assiduously maintained and elderly in tone, became his weapon. Making notes for a letter he planned to send to his aunt at Thrumpton, George reminded himself to sympathise with Anna about the coldness of the village church, and to 'enlighten' her about the unsatisfactory nature of heating provided at his school. 'Ask her for butter,' he added to his memo.

Obsessively prompt himself, George expected payment in equal coin. By the time he was ten, he knew just how to make his displeasure felt when a correspondent slackened. Writing to his parents, he observed that Leo, his older brother, must be *very busy indeed* with dances and his new car (a snappy little MG) since he found *no time to write*; every morning, he told Vita, he looked at the school letter shelf in the *vain* (the word was fiercely underlined) hope of receiving a note from his sister, Alex. Running short of new victims in the family, he addressed himself to God, 'as no one ever seems to write to you'. But even God was not to be trusted; George ordered him to write his answer *clearly* (underlined) and *promptly* (underlined): 'Please have it there by *tomorrow*.'

God failed to respond, although Vita lovingly preserved the letter: George's earthly family found it wise to respond at length, and with speed, if they were not to be rebuked.

A form of power had been discovered. A habit had been formed.

Fifty years later, my father was still hard at work. Crouched at his desk in a corner of the hospitable Thrumpton library on a Saturday afternoon, he peppered the desultory conversation of his guests with the angry rattle of a tiny Olivetti typewriter. They could talk and lounge; he, their host, had vital work to do; a pile of letters – to the rural dean, to his stockbroker, to his lawyer, to an unsatisfactory fishing tenant – was underway. By four in the afternoon, determined to catch the last post-collection of the day, he was in top gear, cramming stiff little sheets of double-spaced print into envelopes emblazoned with a phoenix perched upon a crown. ('I was so intrigued by the crest,' one of the grander cousins wrote to him. 'I've been puzzling over its origins.' A message that can be translated into blunt English as: *You bloody little fraud*.)

'Don't be silly,' reproves my mother. 'Edward the Sixth was the phoenix arising from the ashes of his mother Jane, who died in childbirth. Henry VIII gave it to the Seymours for their family crest.' Listening, I can hear my father tutoring her in the sacred connection, another of those comforting bloodlines by which he linked himself to the throne. *He sits on the right hand of God the Father.* And then, remembering an attention-seeking child who used to boast to visitors to the House of her own descent from kings, I cringe. *Oh mon semblable, mon père,* I'm every bit as bad as you.

As a snob, I can sometimes match him; as a correspondent, George Seymour had no equal. Pouring letters out fast as water flowing from a tipped bucket, he expressed disgust at those slackers who failed to answer by return of post. What did these people *do* with their time? Had they no manners at *all*? Only the blessed select, possessing either titles or fast motorbikes, escaped his censure; they, lucky creatures, could answer as slowly as they pleased. The rest of us were less leniently treated: if we hadn't replied within the day, it proved that we were heartless, careless, ungrateful or even, when his spirits were especially low, all three.

You couldn't win. He wrote like a survivor from Edwardian times, when five daily posts allowed letters to fly to and fro as fast, almost, as email. A prompt answer engendered an immediate response; with it came a strong hint of trouble in store if you failed to answer – again – within the day.

And so it went on.

A present from the Byrons almost compensated for the miseries of a dormitory bed, bullying schoolmates, and absence from the country house George loved. Their present was a reward to a nephew so affectionate that he had asked if he might spend the Christmas of 1933 with them, rather than at Evelyn Gardens with his parents. Charlie and Anna were eager to show their appreciation. Vita had tipped them off that George wanted to invite his cousin Oliver to stay at Thrumpton, but that he was embarrassed because Oliver had a bicycle. The Byrons consulted with each other and reached agreement: George must not be outshone. When their nephew came down to breakfast on Christmas Day, Shotbolt wheeled his gift up to the table: a Kildare bicycle, bright blue, with a bell. Oliver also had a Kildare, but this one was finer and larger, the new hot model for 1934. Forbidden to bring it to school, where he had looked forward to showing off his treasure, George made the Kildare the subject of a protest poem ('You aren't aloud (sic) a bicycle, for fear that you might crash'). Privately, he comforted himself with the prospect of showing his treasure off to Oliver during the summer vacation, when he had been promised he might spend five glorious weeks at Thrumpton.

George FitzRoy Seymour in 1933, a slightly priggish prep-school boy.

The Byrons' gift offered their nephew a rare opportunity to boast about something other than his blood. Aged ten, George was growing embarrassed by his parents' modest means. He minded that his mother wore dowdy clothes, not couture; an outing with a schoolmate's mother in – he swaggered to his parents – 'the biggest and newest Chrysler you have ever seen', sharpened his embarrassment about their own, inferior motor. Writing to his mother before sports day, he begged her to buy a new hat and to park their battered Hillman out of sight. ('For goodness *sake* don't bring that sky-blue car into the drive because the oldest car that anyone else has seems to be about three years, and if you brought in our old bus I should think we would be the laugh of the place.')

George's parents, as he was forced to realise, lacked the means to buy a Chrysler; a brand-new bicycle almost made up for that disappointment. The day on which he was given the Kildare, he noted in his schoolboy diary, had been the most exciting of his entire life.

Oliver FitzRoy's summer visit to Thrumpton provides another marker in the stages of my father's attachment to the place. Vita had given her son the 1934 edition of *The Cyclists' Diary*, complete with useful tips about repairing punctures (ignored) and on places to visit (carefully studied). The July pages of the diary are dense with reports of journeys undertaken, and places seen. He already loved the House and its park; cycling proudly alongside his cousin's inferior Kildare, he became familiar with the row of fishermen who crouched on the riverside tow path; with the road leading away from the village to a plump wooded cone where the last of the English witches had allegedly been burned at the stake; with the smoke-grimed churches of Clifton, Ratcliffe, Kingston and Strelley, in which alabaster knights and their ladies lay stiffly asleep, a veil of reddish marble hooding their eyes.

Oliver left behind an addicted cyclist. Week by week, George notched up the miles: seventy-six in one, eighty-two in another. The marriage of his parents was going through a stressful period; glad to escape, Vita became her son's travelling companion. Reading his records of their trips, I'm amazed by the distances they covered: in a single month, mother and son cycled across the Fens, up to the Lake District, down to the Norfolk coast, and west to Cornwall.

Was it the easy freedom of those days that my father rediscovered in his rejuvenated middle age, roaring through the empty blackness of the Fenland night and out to the shores, the headlights of his latest ebony-flanked machine glaring into the dark? Was it?

Growing up in the rooms at the top of the House where my father spent his first years, I formed my reading habits at a nursery bookshelf. Five foot across and climbing up to the low ceiling, the shelves seemed as appetising as a box of well-wrapped sweets, stuffed with fairy tales, myths, poetry, encyclopedias and – I'm not sure where these came from – some sinister little German stories with gothic print and inky woodcuts, of which the most vivid showed two bad children being roasted alive, trussed up on a garden spit. (A warning, I supposed, to my brother and myself of what would become of us if we misbehaved.)

These were my father's books. None of them captured his imagination so completely as *Antony*, a memoir presented to him by Vita in 1936, when he was thirteen years old.

My mother detests *Antony*, despite the fact that my father chose to give her a copy shortly after they met. 'Ghastly drivel,' she says, 'and so snobbish! I can't think what your father saw in it.'

Antony was a tribute, written by Lord Lytton shortly after his eldest son and heir, Antony Knebworth, was killed in a freak flying accident. Spoiled by doting parents, Lord Knebworth appears to have excelled at sports, disliked hard work, and treated women badly. My father thought him perfect. As soon as he finished reading *Antony* for the first time – he returned to the book each year, with undiminished pleasure – he persuaded Vita to accompany him on a twenty-mile cycling trip from Evelyn Gardens out to Knebworth House, where his hero had spent his boyhood. Lord Lytton, the bereaved father, was away; a gardener allowed the visitors a brisk walk around the icebound garden before their long journey home.

My mother wonders if George's obsession with a good-looking sportsman offers us a first glimpse of what he was to become. She may be right; we agree that it's strange for a boy of thirteen to have shown no similar interest in girls. I'm more intrigued by the fact that Vita chose to give her son *Antony*, a book about a glamorous aristocrat, the heir to a title and a splendid house, in 1936. This was a year of seismic changes in the ranking of the FitzRoy clan; was Vita encouraging George to glory in his own connections? Was she so foolish, and so irresponsible?

It's possible. Vita, too, was a snob. One of my relatives still remembers how angrily she refused to yield her seat to Princess Margaret at some charity performance of a play. Vita would not do it, she said, because she was better born and had more right to the seat than that *common* woman. (I don't think you need to wonder, my relative added in an acid postscript to her letter, why Dick Seymour's diplomatic career failed to prosper!)

In 1936, a cousin's premature death resulted in Vita's brother, Charles FitzRoy, becoming the tenth Duke of Grafton and owner of Euston Hall; his sisters were given appropriate upgrades. My father, reading *Antony*, felt newly at home in this lordly throng; in his school address book, he wrote out a list of all the noble ranks and placed an asterisk beside those to which he had the closest links. Schoolfriends were proudly informed that his uncle had become a duke; tongue in cheek, surely, one wrote to congratulate him for such a thrilling piece of information.

All George now lacked was a title of his own. This would cause him pain until the end of his days. His yearning for one is apparent in the Debrett's entries where, year after year, he linked himself to the nobility ('father himself great great grandson of; mother the sister of; wife the daughter of . . .') Links, however tenuous, were better than nothing at all.

'I love your Euston.' My father was nineteen when he wrote that to his mother, after a visit to the Duke of Grafton's new Norfolk home. At thirteen, shortly after Vita gained her title, George launched a mission to see that she looked the part. Evelyn Gardens was not smart enough for a duke's sister; helpfully, George bombarded his parents with ideas for improving their London home. He spent his holidays researching suitable carpenters and decorators to refit and paint it. Instead of a birthday present, he wanted Vita and Dick to do up their shabby bathroom. (George had already picked out a pink-and-white wallpaper which would, he assured them, prove ideal.) Alex, his older sister, was persuaded to split the expense of buying Vita a fur coat, secondhand, in which, he proudly noted: 'Mummy looked très grande dame'. Sending home dutiful accounts of the school sports day, he digressed to mention an elegant set of velvet curtains he had seen for sale, quite cheap, just the thing to give their drab dining room a lift.

A less passive father would have reined in such precocity and told George to act his thirteen years. Dick, predictably, did nothing. Dick's mother, meanwhile, expressed delight at her grandson's enthusiasm for titles and connections. It was only two years since May Falle herself had become, at a price, Lady Portsea, a baroness. May was enchanted to hear about George's interest in the future of Thrumpton, and the FitzRoy lineage. 'We share an interest in the rock from which we are hewn,' she told him approvingly.

George had observed that his grandmother generally got what she wanted. In the summer of 1936, he told her how upset he was at not being allowed to go to Eton that autumn with his cousin,

Oliver. May was outraged. How could her son be so foolish! Of *course*, George and Oliver must attend the same school. Had it not occurred to Dick what damage might be done to a young boy by such insensitive behaviour? To Eton George must go: in fact, she herself would underwrite all the costs of the dear boy's education. Reminded that she had done nothing of the kind for George's older brother, Lady Portsea stood her ground. All the more reason, she argued, that she should help this time.

This is the only occasion I have been able to find on which Dick Seymour took a stand against his formidable mother. Contributions would be welcomed, he told her, but a decision had already been made. He himself had been extremely happy at Eton (he did not quite say that he had been far happier there than at home). He did not, however, feel it right to send George to a school to which (thanks to May's refusal to help) he had been unable to afford to send his elder boy. George had done well enough in the exams to enter Winchester in the autumn of 1936. He was an intelligent boy; Winchester was a fine school.

The decision was made.

May, on whose support her grandson had depended for a reprieve, was silenced.

5

❧

A PUBLIC-SCHOOL BOY

I'm visiting Winchester on a sultry summer afternoon, hoping to find why my father hated his public school. So far, I'm charmed.

Nestling behind the grey bulk of the Cathedral, the College hides its beauties as cunningly as Oxford and Cambridge conceal their lovely quads and cloisters. I'd forgotten that Jane Austen died here, in a modest house staring out at a high, hard, pebbled wall. Hawkins (Chawkers to the Wykehamists) is the house in which my father began life at the College in September 1936. The housemaster's tall, fresh-faced son opens the door. When I explain my quest, he leads me upstairs to peep into the airy dormitories, and down to the Study in which forty boys still carry out their evening work in wooden booths known as Toys. Hawkins House, on a sleepy day in early August, feels unthreatening. The ceilings are clean and high; light pours through large windows. There's no shade of the prisonhouse here, nothing sinister.

'Anything else you'd like to see?' asks the friendly boy. I shake my head, feeling foolish. I'm baffled.

Back to the book of essays, then, to see what can be deduced from a schoolboy's first year of compositions, complete with the Master's comments.

The Master had to struggle not to lose his temper with his new pupil. He asked for an essay on comic writing and was rebuked for liking Wodehouse ('Personally,' George informed him, 'I do not particularly admire his style.') The Master also liked Scott; George expressed scorn. Scott, in his own opinion, was greatly inferior to Harrison Ainsworth: 'I challenge you to find another book written in such beautiful English . . . There is no other but *Windsor Castle*.' This time, the Master showed his annoyance: 'Nonsense!' he wrote. The subject of 'Relations' gave rise to one of my father's most florid pieces, inspired by memories of Charlie Byron's sermons. 'So does death part us all,' he wrote. 'Our relations who love us die and we stay on, and we in our turn have to leave those whom we have helped. So time goes on, and I think a befitting ending for this humble effort at entertaining the reader is the following verse of a favourite hymn of mine: "Time like an ever-rolling stream . . ."'

The Master had begun to lose his temper; angrily, he reminded George Seymour that he was thirteen, not seventy, and ordered him to alter his style. My father didn't change his style one scrap. The next set topic was 'Friends', a tricky one for a boy who had made none. Tellingly, George expressed a preference for artefacts. Pictures, in his opinion, were more faithful than friends. 'They will still give you all the pleasure within their power. They do their best.' For him, there was only one prevailing certainty, one friendship that could never falter, never betray: the House. This is true friendship, he wrote: 'a place of happy memories and a place which seems in itself to welcome one on one's homecoming.'

Perhaps, on this occasion, the Master felt a little sorry for a boy who had no friendships to celebrate. 'Rather ponderous,' he wrote.

The more wretched my father grew at school, the more fiercely he clung to the House. Whatever the subject he was given to write about, he always managed to turn it into a eulogy to the place he thought of as home. (Evelyn Gardens was never mentioned; you would never guess, reading these schoolboy essays, that their author had a London connection.) Trying his hand at story-writing, he remembered Nuthall Temple's fate and wrote of the destruction by fire of a beloved family home. The features of Thrumpton – tall red-brick chimneys, stone gables, a lake, a library overlooking a garden – are easily identifiable.

At fifteen, my father at last began to acquire a few friends. All of them were younger; all were impressed by his tales of a princely mansion in Nottinghamshire. (Again, not a word had been breathed about Evelyn Gardens.) 'You rotten worm, aren't you ever going to ask me to that house of yours?' wrote one.

It might seem obvious why my father didn't want to ask friends to stay. Thrumpton was not his home. He feared exposure and ridicule. Another reason helps to explain why his essays dwelt on the House with such intensity. He had, for no reason he could understand, been banished.

It's possible that Charlie Byron, a capricious old gentleman, was playing cruel games with a nephew who adored his home; it's more likely, since some distant Byron cousins had revealed themselves just at the time George went to Winchester, that he was rethinking the future. Charlie's first duty, as Thrumpton's owner, was to his own family, not his wife's; the Byron cousins had a greater right to his property than Anna's nephew. This, it seems, is why Charlie decided to bring an abrupt end to George's holidays at the House. Other members of Anna's family paid regular visits during this period; only George was excluded. This unexplained act of ostracism, it seems fair to assume, contributed to my father's memory of the Winchester years as a time of extreme unhappiness.

Death provided a solution to Charlie Byron's quandary. The

cousinly claimants both died young; George, who may never have known how seriously his hopes of inheritance had been threatened, was restored to favour in the summer of 1939, shortly before the outbreak of war. A rambling and affectionate invitation was issued; he was welcome again. He could visit Thrumpton for as long as he wished.

When war was declared, my father was sixteen years old, with a year of schooling left to run and no expectation that his secure world was about to be overturned. Oliver FitzRoy was preparing to follow his older brother to Cambridge; my father – his academic record at Winchester was poor – had no such plans. He had only one clear objective: occupation of the House he loved and to which he had been welcomed back. Lulled by the tranquillity of a golden autumn, he made a leisurely round of favourite haunts, cycling around the sleepy little villages, fishing by the lake, wandering through the high grass of ungrazed fields where, for hours on end, he lay gazing up at an empty, unthreatening sky.

Writing a letter of reassurance to his mother (he had taken to addressing Vita as 'Boo' because, he told her, it made her seem nearer to his age), he took care to relate which of the Thrumpton roses were in bloom, and to tell her that the House – his House – had never looked so lovely.

War? What war? By the time he left Winchester in 1940, he was convinced that all would be resolved. (This certainty, although George did not say so, was based on Charlie Byron's politically naïve reading of international events.) All that mattered, here and now, on the summer evening of his letter, was the scent of tobacco plants, the deepening blue of the sky, the rich rosy glow of sunlit brick. He felt so safe here, so at peace. Dearest Boo: she must not worry. All was well.

6

A GOOD WAR

As a child, I used to pray, deep into my pillow, that my father would die. I never had such violent feelings about my mother. The only part she played in my fantasies of paternal obliteration was that I wanted her to marry a more glamorous man.

A portrait of my mother, red-haired and slender in a wedding-dress of oyster satin, with the archaic smile favoured by Botticelli lending a curve to her cheeks, was painted a year after her marriage. It hangs in one of the rooms of the House that is always shown to visitors. Below the painting stands a framed photograph of the artist, Anthony Devas. Strangers, drawing the obvious conclusion, have often asked if the photograph is of my father. I told them, until I reached my teens and acquired a conscience, that it was. I liked to bask in their admiration of the artist's handsome face and to hear them find some faint resemblance to my own. I liked to think it might be so, that my newly married mother had conducted a secret affair, of which I was the unacknowledged product.

'Was he as gorgeous as he looks in the photo?' I ask my mother.

'Anthony? He was wonderful-looking. *Just* like the photograph. He painted that picture of me at his studio in Chelsea. He used to take me to lunch afterwards, somewhere in Sloane Street. Augustus sometimes came along. It was all such fun.'

I stare at her, dazzled by this easy jump into the past. 'Augustus John? You never told me that before. What did you talk about? Did he try anything?'

She smooths the bright cover of her book with a gardener's hands, square and strong. 'Who, Augustus? I'm not sure he would have dared, not after he fell out with Mummy about the picture he did of her, the one she didn't like. I did know him already, of course. He came and drew us all at Chirk, in the war.'

My mother has grown lively. Her book forgotten, she's ready for a chat about life in the Welsh castle where she grew up. 'Are you writing about Chirk yet? I was thinking – there's so much I ought to tell you. Are you going to say anything about when Kipling came to stay with us, and Shaw? And you mustn't forget about Chesterton and Belloc!'

I'll have to remind her that this is not to be a book about her family, but her husband. 'I haven't reached Chirk. He's only just left Winchester.'

'Better hurry up, if you want my memories,' she calls after my retreating back. 'I won't be here for ever.'

I'm suddenly full of the wish that she might be just that. It's taken all of the ten years since my father's death for my mother to blossom back to brightness as she emerges from the emotional bolthole in which she buried herself in order to survive. I used to hope only that her death should be merciful, quick as a blink or a dropped stitch. Now, I can't imagine life without her. I want her never to die.

I chose Anthony Devas for my imaginary father because he looked so attractive. I also chose him because he looked, even with a paintbrush in his hand instead of a sword or a gun, as though he could play a military hero; my father did not. As a grown woman who has fallen in love with the House and its history, I'm ready to admire the tenacity with which George Seymour pursued his grand obsession; as a small girl, observing him with a hard judgmental eye, I saw unmanliness in my father's caprices and fits of petulance. I noted and disliked his readiness to use emotion to score a victory.

The fathers I admired never cried. Not in public. They were bluff, capable men who lived up to their military titles. One girlfriend acquired at boarding school was dear to me less for herself than for her father, a nobly moustached colonel with a crop of thick white hair and long cheeks striped pink by desert suns. I liked his tales of war. I winced when his wife shouted at him for boring the child stiff, my dear. She's heard it already. We all have. So we had, but never often enough. I wanted to take this old warrior for myself, to be the privileged recorder of his valiant deeds. If he could only be *my* father! (Once, while he was teaching me how to tack a sailing-boat across a small river near their family home, I found the courage to whisper my secret wish; the colonel answered by giving me a complicated set of instructions to keep me busy until we moored and went ashore for lunch. At which point, kindly patting me on the shoulder, man to man, he said that he was going to forget anything I might wish I hadn't said. 'But I *do*—' He strode ahead of me, letting the garden gate swing shut behind him.)

My love for the colonel was heightened by the fact that he and his family lived in a cheerily modern house on a town street. The house was in no way conspicuous. It was neither pretty nor ugly. It represented all that I wished for, at an age when nothing about a journey to London appealed to me so much as a drive through the cosily interchangeable streets of Mill Hill and Hendon and Finchley. There was such comfort in conformity when I was a child, in the Fifties, such danger in being perceived as different. I didn't, dear parents, mean to annoy you when I prayed to live in a house just like the one near the local garage, where a dressmaker worked at a sewing machine in the front window, seated in a theatre set of white lace curtains pulled back with red silk cords. Her pocket-sized lawn was bordered by pink and white flowers; her front door was picked out in contrasting tones of cerise and powder pink. I loved her home. I wanted nothing to do with a monster house filled with creaks and ghosts and pictures with censorious eyes. I longed to shrink our singularity to the colours of an entrance door or to the choice of which tree, flowering cherry or weeping ash, should throw a shadow-cloak over the pavement.

I know why I craved a soldierly father, and why I wanted to be part of that world of reassuring sameness. I don't know why or precisely when I began to wish my father dead. The urgency with which I muttered my secret prayer, night after night, still causes me to feel guilt. My mother doesn't find it strange.

'Children do find it easy to wish their parents dead; it's not just you. I often thought like that about my mother, you know. It's not a crime.'

I do know when I lost my respect for him.

The incident was sparked by some private grief of his in which I, a little girl with fine, mouse-brown hair held back by an 'Alice' band, had no share; my memory is only of the shocking spectacle of a grown man crying. He wanted, he said, to kill himself; all reason for wishing to live had gone. Sitting beside him, I looked sideways at his bent head and the tears falling on to his knees. Sobs blocked my throat when he told me that we would all be happy when he was dead. How could he think such a terrible thing? Weeping, I flung my arms around his neck and hugged him, rubbing my cheek against his. Too young to understand that the atmosphere of drama thickening the air was meat and drink to a nature such as his, I agreed to the pact on which, still sobbing, he insisted. If he promised to do himself no injury, I, too, must swear never to make an attempt on my life.

That set me off. I only had to picture my body, stiff and cold as a starched shirt, to feel emotion swelling to hysteria.

Tenderly, he stroked my hair. 'You and I are too alike, my darling. We feel these things so much.'

'I won't. I'll never — I swear it! But don't — please don't.' I couldn't speak the words. Carefully, he mopped my blotched cheeks with a freshly pressed handkerchief smelling of limes; gravely, we shook hands on our agreement. I went to bed tearful but exalted. It's not often a girl of nine gets to save her father's life.

Readers will spot the flaw: if I wished him dead, I should have welcomed this unexpected answer to my prayer. But suicide comes under another heading; the word, even to a child, is heavy with horror. Suicides, in the myths and folktales on which I feasted during raids upon the tall nursery bookcase, were among the damned, buried at crossroads, forbidden to lie in churchyards. I could wish my father dead by accident. I could not wish that he should take his life.

My father was in the best of spirits the following day. When I asked, a little reproachfully, how he was feeling, he looked surprised. The moment at which I lost respect for him was the one in which I saw that he had no idea what I was talking about. It was all words.

In fact, as I came to understand, my father placed a high value on his life. To approach him with a cold or cough was an act of unforgivable selfishness; to feed him with a dish which threatened to play havoc with his capricious stomach was tantamount to threatening him with murder. Far from killing himself, my father would have been happy to provide the reasons why he, of us all, should be spared. How could we get on without him? Who but he was indispensable to the survival of the House?

An old-fashioned phrase slides into my head. *You wouldn't want to be in a trench with—*

'You're being unfair,' my mother says. 'He never had the chance to fight. We don't know how he would have behaved.'

'We don't know. But—'

She shakes her head. I'm not going to win her assent to this. But I wouldn't have cared to be with my father in a situation where one life had to be sacrificed. It wouldn't be his.

Even as a child, I knew that the war was a bad subject. He was happy to play us a crackling record of Churchill's speeches to the nation, but direct questions were never welcome. The closest I came to knowing what part he had played in his country's defence was the clipped information that he had been ill. I heard my mother describe how a bad-tempered sergeant made her scrub canteen floors with a sanitary towel; from my father, I heard not a word. No word of the bombs, of the Blitz, or the dead: nothing.

The same hunger to conform that made me yearn for a small suburban home fuelled my longing for a father with a military record of which I could boast. It mattered, in the Fifties. Memories of war were close; the recent past was as rich with action as a storybook. Heroes had fought at Dunkirk, endured starvation and torture in prison camps, come home with medals and rank that paid tribute to their courage. But if it depressed a myth-fed child to learn that her father had spent his war years working in a provincial bank, how much more humiliation must it have caused to him?

This was the error I made. It was true that my father was not physically courageous. However, since he never was put to the test, why should I assume that he lacked the moral fibre to act with honour? Faith to do your duty was his family motto: given the chance, mightn't he have acted on it?

My mother has unearthed an old photograph that she thinks will interest me. It shows two young men in army uniform. These are my father's first cousins, Lord Euston and his brother, Oliver FitzRoy, and the picture was taken late in 1943. The wistful look in their eyes may have something to do with the fact that they lost their mother when they were children, or with the more recent loss of a much-loved stepmother. Only a month has passed since then, and their lonely father has already chosen her successor. Their future feels threatened.

Hugh, the older of the two brothers, is about to set off for India with the Grenadiers. As the son of a duke, he's due to be given an interesting time, on the staff of the viceroy. Oliver, the boy my father thought of as his soulmate, looks too young to be tested in the skills of leadership. His is a sweet face, soft, but guarded. He, too, has just joined the Grenadiers. In a year's time, he'll be sent out to fight in France.

Hugh Euston (later eleventh Duke of Grafton) and his younger brother, (my father's idol) Oliver FitzRoy, in 1943.

I like these studio photographs. There's another in this folder of Leo, my father's older brother, also serving as a Grenadier. Alex, his sister, is giggling at the camera on the day after her engagement in 1939. She's twenty-five, and glad to be settling down in Norfolk with a tall, agreeable young officer whose poor sight has spared him from being sent abroad on active service.

Caring for Alex through her first pregnancy gave my grandmother a reason to stay out of bomb-blasted London in the first months of the war. Dick Seymour, staying on alone at the tall red house in Evelyn Gardens, took new life from the sense of constant danger. Telling his wife about his daily walk to 'the club' in Carlton House Terrace, he joked about the plane fights overhead, the falling bombs, the roar of defending guns firing up from the backs of lorries along the borders of Hyde Park and Piccadilly. 'You know how I hate agitations before breakfast,' he wrote, with an almost visible twirl of his umbrella at the impertinent Italian pilots he longed to see brought down.

'Blasted Ice-Creamers!'

For the first time in his life, Dick Seymour and his mother were enjoying a state of mutual admiration. Lady Portsea was impressed by her son's jaunty indifference to danger, and grateful for the regularity of his visits to her home in Eaton Square. He, in his turn, took pride in the old lady who, during some of the worst months of bombing raids, still climbed into her black Victoria carriage for a daily afternoon outing. The renaming of her two coach-horses was her only concession to an altered life: Fred and Ginger had become Churchill and Sarah.

On the subject of my father, however, they were at loggerheads.

Lady Portsea had always doted on her grandson. His announcement, in the autumn of 1940, that he intended to take on one of the Thrumpton farms, won instant support. 'I love to think of you at work on the land – Mother Nature rewards those who cultivate and care for her,' she wrote on paper newly topped with a coronet. (I think I know whom to blame for my father's inordinate love of crests and coats-of-arms.)

Dick Seymour was less sanguine. 'I can't understand how George can be so foolish,' he wrote to his wife. He was disappointed already that their son had shown no wish to follow his FitzRoy cousins to Cambridge and take a degree; couldn't the boy at least be persuaded to take a course in land agency and learn how to make a living at a richer man's expense? Perhaps a job could be found for him at Ragley Hall, home to the head of the Seymour clan, or even at Euston, if Vita was willing to raise the idea with her brother, the Duke?

Dick, it is clear, had failed to grasp what was obvious to the women of the family. George, after leaving Winchester in the summer of 1940, had sped like a homing pigeon to the House he loved and which Charlie Byron was encouraging him to look on as his heritage. University had never interested him – few men could use the words 'clever' and 'intellectual' with such complete disdain. He had no wish to be employed at Ragley, Euston, or anywhere else; his plans for the future did not extend beyond the boundaries of his uncle's estate. When it was explained to him that a seventeen-year-old, with no experience of land management, could not be given a farm for free, he simply lowered his sights and proposed to work for one of the Thrumpton village tenants. Harvesting, and planting sugar-beet, the principal victory crop in the Midlands, required no special skills; a boy who was known to be Lord Byron's nephew was unlikely to be overworked or ill-treated.

Nobody who knew my father ever doubted that he had a will of steel. This was his first chance to use it. He got his way.

'No need to sneer,' says my mother. 'The farms were fearfully shorthanded during the war. He was being useful. And, besides, what else could he have done?'

'Taken the course to learn land agency?'

'Your father! Leave Thrumpton to help run somebody else's estate? Can you imagine?'

Slight though the remaining evidence is of my father's year of working on the land, the effect on him was profound. Bombs fell on Derby, Nottingham and neighbouring fields; another hit the local electricity station and blew out all the windows of Clifton Hall, the nearest big house. At Thrumpton, the only evidence of war was the placing of a searchlight on the hill and a request from the local shepherd to bring his flock down to lower pastureland. Every Friday, faces scrubbed, boots polished with spit, the farm tenants walked up to the Hall to pay their rent; every evening, when his work was done, my father walked through the park and back, with the sun dazzling his eyes, towards the House. He knew, by now, the name of every mound, copse and corner of the land on which it stood; the threat of devastation heightened its value as a precious commodity. Writing to his parents, his prose quickened with love whenever he turned to the subject of the House and the landscape:

Dear Thrumpton. The moon was full last night. I went for a walk by the lake and spent an hour down by the willows looking at the House. I pray no harm will come to it.

He could as well have been writing of a lover, or a child.

Action could not be put off for ever. In May 1941, George put his name forward for a commission in the Motor Battalions. The Byrons, dismayed at the prospect of losing the company of such a willing and solicitous nephew, grew fretful. What would they do without George to run their errands, act as their chauffeur, keep them entertained? Old Lady Portsea, picking window-glass off the staircarpet after a bomb flattened the house next door to her own, sent blessings to her grandson and congratulated him on having chosen to join the 60th (the King's Royal Rifle Corps). Did he know, she wondered, that two of his Seymour forebears had joined the 60th and fought in the Transvaal? Prudently, she omitted to add that they had both been killed.

George had left Winchester, with a glad heart, in July 1940. In

August 1941, he learned with dismay that he was to be drafted back there for his first spell of military training. Bushfield Camp lay west of Winchester, on the Hursley road. Tracking it down in the summer of 2003, I found the way to an empty hillside blocked by an iron farm gate. Beyond it, a derelict track climbed towards the square silhouette of a sentry box; on the gate, the warning sign was plain: *Keep Out*. Arrogance is one of the vices I have inherited from my father; such restrictions apply to other people, not to us. Like him, I expect a volley of cheap charm to rescue me if caught in the act. ('It's your land? I'm most dreadfully sorry! But what a wonderful place!' Parroting the lines, I can hear his own suave drawl.) I climbed the gate and sauntered up the hill.

Bushfield Camp, according to local information, is a site ready for development for housing, or a leisure centre, or a car park. At present, it's abandoned. The neat grid of roads that once marked out the camp's boundaries is just visible between steep banks that, in high summer, are smothered with wild flowers. Bees hum; a small plane drones in the distance; otherwise, there isn't a sound. A rusty sink juts up from a clump of mallow and tansy. The bolted metal doors that block my entry to abandoned buildings are scrawled with messages. Nothing sinister: Ellie loves Paul; John wants a blowjob; Marie thinks John should fuck off.

Standing on the windless hilltop, I try to imagine my father here in 1941, an underweight and – I'll guess – sexually inexperienced eighteen-year-old with the mannerisms and attitudes of an elderly country squire. Was he conscious, as I am, of the irony of his topographical situation at Bushfield? I hadn't, until my visit, realised that he was placed exactly between his two lives, the schoolboy, and the snob. On the left, lay Winchester; on the right, lay Hursley, one of the houses to which his grand connections had provided an introduction. In 1935, he boasted to his mother of his lunch out at Sir George Cooper's home. He had been given a splendid meal, allowed to admire a set of Gobelin tapestries made for Madame de

Pompadour, and taken into a magnificent ballroom designed by Sir Joseph Duveen. By 1941, however, Sir George was dead, his widow banished to a farmhouse after Vickers Aircraft took over the estate as their headquarters for Spitfire development. Did my father revisit Hursley from Bushfield Camp, I wonder? Did he see how they had daubed the Chinese silk wall hangings with a thick layer of grey paint, turned the linen store into a lab and the dancing room into a factory? (*Dear Thrumpton . . . I pray no harm will come to it.*) The fate of houses such as Hursley must have pierced his heart.

The record of what my father actually did during his brief spell at camp is minimal. His diary shows that he underwent drill from six in the morning until four in the afternoon, with a break for lunch. He was then at liberty to do as he pleased, to visit relations, wander around Winchester, or spend the evening with John Persse, a former schoolchum who was also at the camp.

Persse, a horse-loving, unbookish young man whose family lived nearby, thrived on his time at Bushfield; my father was wretched. It was, he lamented to his parents after five days at the camp, 'a frightfully hard life'. Paying a visit to sympathetic elderly relatives who knew how strings could be pulled, he told tales of loneliness, bad food and a sadistic insistence on rigorous exercise. The relatives promised to do what they could: two weeks later, George was released, to spend a month of sick leave at Thrumpton. No record survives to tell me how he felt, after a spell of successful grouse-shooting in Scotland, about being tersely ordered to return to military duties at the end of September.

'Pneumonia,' my mother says briskly when I ask what ended my father's brief army career a year later. She frowns, doing her best to remember what she was told. 'Did they give him the wrong pills? Something like that.'

'He never mentioned anything about a driving accident? Before the pneumonia?'

'An accident?' And she looks so blank that I know she's telling the truth. 'Oh no, darling, he never had an accident. You know what a good driver your father was.'

My father was a fast driver but not, until the last months of his life, a reckless one. He prided himself on the speed of his reactions. He was pitiless in his contempt for any guest who failed to stay on his tail during a nerve-testing dash to some social occasion for which punctuality stood high above kindness. ('Where on earth has he got to? We're five minutes late! My God, that friend of yours is so *slow!*')

Given his attitude, it is unlikely that he would admit to having crashed an army vehicle shortly after his return to Bushfield Camp. His family, while sympathetic, were plainly uncertain of the details; George may not have been in a hurry to provide them. His first request was that he might be sent to Thrumpton for his convalescence; instead, he was despatched to the new military hospital at St Hugh's in Oxford, to be treated for concussion and head wounds. On 12 December 1941, he was moved again, to spend two months at Middleton Park, a country house newly built by Edwin Lutyens and handed over by its owner, Lord Jersey, for wartime use by patients with head injuries.

Middleton Park, its claustrophobic teak and marble interior contrasting strangely with the façade of an eighteenth-century chateau, cannot be viewed as one of Lutyens' happiest achievements. My father loathed the house, taking comfort only in the survival of an unrestored family chapel in the park, and of a peaceful library in which to keep up his correspondence.

Two days after his arrival at Middleton Park, my father sent what he considered disturbing information to, of all inappropriate people, Charlie Byron's underpaid deputy butler, a boy of twenty. Bursting with indignation, George revealed that he was being forced to share a bedroom at Middleton Park with *communists* (the deduction was drawn from the fact that two of his fellow patients had been complaining that workmen deserved better rates of pay). The next step would be revolution; Lord Byron had better prepare himself to be hanged from a lamp-post when he next left home. In the meantime, he, George, intended to do what he could to help these *idiots* to appreciate the selfishness of their attitude, and the importance, while the country was at war, of preserving *tradition* and *loyalty*!

My father expected his correspondents to be prompt – he did not expect them to dispute his opinions. A round, laborious hand suggests that James Hopkins was not especially well-educated; the tone of his letter suggests that my father had chosen the wrong man with whom to share his alarm. Perhaps, Mr Hopkins wrote, my father was unaware of how hard life was for those less privileged than himself? Nobody wanted to assassinate the aristocracy or to be paid above their merits; it was simply the case that society needed to change. The war must be hard on men like my father, Hopkins added kindly, but perhaps this convalescence would prove a real blessing, a chance to listen to people who could open his mind and broaden his views. Hopkins ended this candid and surely unwelcome letter with the news that he was leaving Lord Byron's service to sign up.

My father, for once, did not reply. A few months later, James Hopkins was killed in action.

The only other surviving evidence of my father's stay at Middleton Park is a spectacularly hideous rug: lime green was, to his annoy-ance, the only available shade of wool. His diligence in creating this monstrosity was fuelled by zeal: by showing the so-called communists a representation of his beloved Thrumpton, he hoped to soften and humanise these misguided men. His scheme was disclosed in his diary. The results were not recorded.

My father returned to duty at Bushfield in May 1942. Two weeks later, he caught pneumonia and was sent back to St Hugh's, Oxford.

His condition was serious; the fact that he failed to attend the funeral of Lady Portsea confirms it. She had been, with the exception of his mother, his favourite relative.

Family affection always came second to his love of the House. When George was released from St Hugh's, he accepted an invitation from Charlie Byron to complete his convalescence at Thrumpton. The proposal was not without self-interest; gardeners were hard to find in wartime and George, while never athletic, could be relied on to help keep the lawn smooth with an iron roller. Resourcefully, my father found a donkey to pull the roller while he lay stretched out in a cane chair, describing an idyllic summer in long, minutely detailed letters to his mother in Norfolk.

Three months at Thrumpton were enough to make even my languid father impatient for a recall to duty; it came in September, when he was ordered to join a training camp near York. The discipline here was harsher than at Bushfield; four days after his arrival, my father fainted on parade. Despatched to the local military hospital for inspection, he was diagnosed as suffering from 'effort syndrome'. The specialist was not impressed by either his physique or his attitude to being drilled (my father loathed all forms of team activity, and reacted accordingly). Writing his report, the specialist offered a personal opinion: this N.C.O. would never be passed as fit for action. He urged that the young man should be discharged immediately or transferred to an office post.

Clerical work offered no appeal; George wrote to give his parents the news that he was leaving the army. He begged them not to intercede, or to pull strings; what was done was done. 'I can't help but feel pretty depressed,' he admitted. He had no idea as to what he should do next.

My father's despair sounds authentic; nevertheless, I feel dissatisfied. The specialist's report has survived. It states that he was incapable of strenuous exercise; in the diaries, however, he recorded his cycling trips. During the early part of September, while he was still at Thrumpton, he had been notching up as much as forty miles a day. More tellingly, a letter from one of his Winchester classmates, Philip Parr, congratulated him on the good fortune of his escape, 'knowing you loathe the army as much as I do.' (Philip wasn't so lucky; he was killed on service in Greece the following summer.)

'Effort syndrome' sounds like a bad joke. When I investigate, it turns out to be a new name for the condition known as 'soldier's heart'. First observed in the American Civil War, this was brought on by stressful situations. Soldiers on the Western Front suffered from it; so, later, did those serving in Vietnam and the Gulf War. But there's a difference. These men were on active service, living under the daily threat of death. My father's effort syndrome was a response to the unpleasant, but far from dangerous, routine of daily drill.

'I won't have you saying your father was a coward,' my mother says with the fierce loyalty that can still take me by surprise, given all that she has endured. 'He probably got on the wrong side of his drill sergeant. And you know he hadn't been well.'

'Then why didn't he take a desk job? He had a good brain. Couldn't he have worked for the Ministry of Information, or at Bletchley?'

But I've lost my mother's sympathy. Crossly, she reminds me how poorly I always did at team sports. 'Just like him, you see. I keep telling you so.'

'I had bad eyesight.' My voice is sharp and defensive; I hate being reminded of my unhappy schooldays. 'And it was a completely different situation. There wasn't a war going on.'

This opens the way for my mother to remind me, not for the first time, that I haven't the slightest idea of how it felt to be at war, or to experience training drill. 'You're determined to show him in a bad light,' she says. 'And he can't answer back.'

This is the first of our discussions that has ended in disagreement.

75

My mother, who carried on as a hard-working member of the ATS, even after suffering a nervous breakdown, doesn't want to accept that she married somebody less courageous than herself. Pneumonia had seemed a respectable reason for a discharge; the idea that George suffered from this absurdly named 'effort syndrome' is an embarrassment.

I look at the surviving evidence once more. If he had failed to make a complete recovery, how was he able to go on those cycling trips? If he felt as mortified as his letter to his parents suggests, why was he ready to spend the first weekend after his discharge in a jolly Yorkshire houseparty, eating like a horse and going on long walks? And what about the letter congratulating him on a lucky escape, 'knowing you loathe the army as much as I do'?

Looking at that letter once again, I wonder if it is open to a different interpretation. Was Philip Parr doing his best to make my father feel better about a situation they both understood to be profoundly humiliating? I may do better to stop being censorious, and consider the effect that his discharge might have had on my father. A combination of bad nerves and ill-health bought him a ticket to safety, but the price, in terms of guilt, must have been immense. How can it feel to know that your contemporaries are risking their lives while yours has been spared? How can it feel to read of their deaths?

Who am I, searching for an explanation of the wound in his heart, to say that my father didn't suffer when he was told to go home?

7

LITERARY CONNECTIONS: 2006

The book club that I belong to is meeting tonight to discuss Henry James's disturbing tale of corrupted innocence, *The Turn of the Screw*. ('And I don't suppose you'll bother to mention the family connection,' my father hisses. 'I know everything to do with my family is dreadfully boring, but don't you think your readers might be – just *faintly* – interested?' On this occasion, I'm ready to agree. To hell with those fragile links by which my father claimed kinship to the royal Tudors and Stuarts: it's more exciting, for a writer, to think that Henry James used to spend weeks at a time with May Portsea and her brother, Howard Sturgis. I relish the possibility that their parents' home inspired descriptions of the Touchetts' English country house in *The Portrait of a Lady*, and that May's father was the original for old Mr Touchett, a transplanted Boston banker. 'And so', my father slyly whispers, 'do tell me, darling, just what *is* the difference between your snobbery and mine?')

The meeting ends with a frisson as we drain our glasses and ponder the atmosphere that Henry James breathed into the fabric of Bly, identified by him simply as an ugly old house in Essex. 'Make him *think* the evil,' he wrote later of his projected reader. 'Make him see it.' Suggestion was all that was required.

Later, as the tube train moves away from the station at Lancaster Gate, I watch the bright posters slide past the windows, urging me to visit Spain, to read the *Guardian*, to invest in a new online account. I see the words, but my inner eyes are focused far from here. Remembering the scene in James's novel in which the intense, imaginative governess confronts the ghost of her drowned predecessor, I, too, am staring across a muddy lake. No tormented Victorian female stands there; instead, I'm watching a burly young man. He stands at ease, his feet hidden by the rushes. Fiercely, I wish him out of view; smiling, hands on hips, he holds his ground. He takes up a fishing rod and flicks the line out carelessly, far enough to catch my clothes with the baited hook if I don't move back into the shadows, out of sight. Behind him, under the tree, I glimpse another male figure, thin and languid-limbed. He walks forward, stretches out a proprietor's hand, drops it on the fisherman's shoulder. The fisherman leans back slightly, and his mouth opens in a grin.

I know who these ghosts are. Like James's governess, I lack the power to will them away. They, not I, are the masters here. Shuddering as I come back into the rattling carriage, I catch the nervous glance of a fellow passenger and manage a tight smile.

All is in order. All is bright and bland. Who ever saw ghosts on a London tube?

A few days later, I'm lying in the bedroom where I've slept since the age of fourteen. A four-poster bed hung with heavy white curtains holds us close as we whisper into the tender skin of each other's unsunned flesh, driving the past and its bad faces away from troubled eyes. This is a newfound and late-come love, still strange to me, and wonderful. But I'm not yet used to the fact that the House can show one face to me, another to him, the newcomer. He looks from the window and sees a heron keeping supercilious watch from the top of a tree, a file of long-necked cygnets paddling through the lake's summer coat of emerald weed. I see the shadows of late afternoon and twist them into the shapes of the dead. They're waiting for me behind every concealing bend in the landscape, the two male figures, heads bent close together. Each time I walk through the narrow passages into the back of the House, I hear their laughter in rooms that I know hold nothing but sunlight.

'They're gone,' he says. 'You know it. They're twelve years gone.'

I pull away from his embrace to stare across the pillows. 'They never leave. They just move out of sight.'

Later in the night, filled with joy, I reach out my arms and say what we both know to be true, that I love him more than any man I've ever known. In this room, that's unwise. My eyes are scarcely shut before the window brightens like an angry moon. I look through the diamond panes. My father's pale blue eyes are there, looking in at me. Far away, I hear a startled nightbird screeching in the fields.

'What?' He's trying to hold me still. 'There's nothing there. It's only a bird.'

I'm out of control. Words won't come. Wailing, I shrink under the soft pink quilt and pull it down over my head. Knees to chin, I huddle in the dark body-scented hollow at the centre of the mattress. It's wet with tears.

His hand reaches down to stroke the top of my head, conveying a calmness he surely can't feel as he asks what it is that has scared me so. I have no words. I can't tell him I conjured up that ghost myself, to witness the moment of my betrayal, to warn me not to give my love elsewhere. Here, in this House, only one man counts. And he isn't, while I'm so quick with fear and guilt, dead at all. Whistle and I'll come to you, my lad. Betray me and I'll come to you, my daughter. He never left. He hasn't died at all.

The first novels that I wrote in my twenties featured beautiful houses, tyrannical fathers and stories of obsessive passion. It didn't surprise me, when I began to assemble a file of my father's writings, to discover that these, too, had a common theme. At school, he had written about a beautiful old house destroyed by fire. Convalescing at Middleton Park and fretting about the dangerous politics of his fellow invalids, he used his favourite house as the setting for a story about the importance of tradition. ("'Changes are evil things,'" the house-owner says, sounding like Charlie Byron delivering one of his sermons against progress.) Another story, 'The Fountain', records the sorrowful feelings of a young man who visits a derelict house (the owners have been unable to maintain its upkeep); yet another describes how an impoverished squire dies of a broken heart when the demolition team arrive to raze his ancestral home.

My father was writing these tales of neglect and destruction at a time when the future of the English country house looked bleak. James Lees-Milne, acting on behalf of the National Trust's recently formed Country House Scheme, was doing his best to persuade embattled owners to hand over their increasingly decrepit homes to the Trust, together with an endowment for their maintenance. Many, requisitioned for use as hospitals, schools, or by the military, were past the stage of preservation. It's a curious fact that only three historically important houses were damaged by enemy action during the war; most of the wreckage was inflicted by indifferent occupants. At Alton Towers, bored gunners took pot shots at the glazed conservatories; at Blickling, airmen pillaged the mausoleum; at Castle Howard, a homesick schoolgirl started a fire and gutted the central block of Vanbrugh's haughty masterpiece. Evelyn Waugh's image of the decline and loss of a great house, in *Brideshead Revisited*, spoke to my father's darkest imaginings. In his own writings, over and again, he played out the story of his worst fear, the loss of the House he loved. Thrumpton had not been selected for functional use during the war; on the other hand, it was operating with a skeleton staff, and the Byrons were getting old. Without care, a large house can descend into a state of irretrievable ruin in the space of a few years.

Reading the slender sheaf of my father's typescripts for the first time (hidden away in a drawer, they had never been mentioned), I wanted to scoff, but found it impossible. The style was old-fashioned and ponderous; the intensity of feeling was remarkable. I knew the emotion, and the style, from my own first writings. It was a shock to discover that, quite unconsciously, I'd used the same outmoded voice, expressed the same concerns.

It doesn't strike you, darling, that you're too like him to be objective?

I wish I could get those words of my mother's out of my mind.

My own writing career began almost by chance. In 1971, I was engaged as an under-secretary in the syndication department of the *Evening Standard*. Reluctant to admit to my family that most of my working hours were spent visiting the postroom or making cups of tea, I presented myself to them as a celebrity interviewer. Lists of stars who were staying that week at Claridge's or the Savoy were sent to the office every week: convincingly, I described Gregory Peck's interest in ranching, Eartha Kitt's taste in jewelled slippers. Asked where my interviews were to be seen, I mentioned the *Tanzanian Times*, the *Wellington Gazette*, anywhere, in fact, where my parents were unlikely to have friendly correspondents.

The senior secretary – she was three years younger than I – cheerfully shouldered the work of us both and covered up my mistakes (I had already been sacked several times for gross inefficiency). Left to lounge at my desk with a heavy electric typewriter, the first I'd ever used, I put it to work. 'Shadows under the Cedars' was the result.

The book was to be unguardedly autobiographical, a poignant account of the vanishing life of a privileged minority. I wrote rapidly and with no trace of irony, about summer picnics on newly mown lawns, about crooling pigeons, sunlit gables and starlit skies. By the end of the first chapter, I knew that I was producing a masterpiece. Proud and confident, I left the pages exposed to view and sauntered out to munch a ham sandwich on the Embankment while contemplating a glorious literary future.

Returning, I found that the three young male journalists who inhabited a smoke-shrouded room next to the secretaries' office had spent a productive lunch hour. 'Shadows under the Cedars' had acquired a new title: 'The Recollections of Aunt Matilda'. Reading my way slowly through their account of Aunt Matilda's birthday party and her distress at discovering a dead mouse in the tea urn, I felt sick with dismay. I struggled on with 'Shadows' for a week, but without conviction. On a Friday evening, at six o'clock, I walked down to Blackfriars Bridge and dropped the typescript in the river.

A year or two later, while chastened by the usual experience of rejection slips, revisions and, following the thrill of first publication, a mortifying absence of sales, I knew that I wanted, for better or worse, to write books for the rest of my life. There were some low moments (my first and distinctly unappreciative review was produced and slowly read aloud to a table of twenty acquaintances, including myself, by our tittering hostess, a former schoolmate of mine): nothing dispirited me more than my father's withheld praise. My mother, doing her best to make up for this, gallantly declared each new book I produced to be a masterpiece.

Having seen my father's stories, I can understand more easily how he felt. Of course, it pained him to see his daughter's novels being published while his own writings lay in a drawer, unseen and unknown. Privately, he took out his old stories, typed them up, with small amendments, and marked them as 'revised versions' before putting them back in the drawer. Publicly, he punished me by silence. When I gave him my second book, a gothic romance featuring a Lord Ruthven as an aristocratic vampire, he returned it unread after hearing me mispronounce the name. ('Riven, my poor darling, not Ruth-ven. But why should it matter? I must be terribly boring to want to get things *right*.')

Carrying On, an old-fashioned modern novel, was the first book that I was certain would please him. The story was of a man in thrall to a beautiful house. Confident of a warm response, I presented the book to him in his own library, when it was filled with weekend guests. I was aware that I had not yet given him much cause for pride. This was to be my public compensation.

My mistake had been to describe the house as shabby. The page at which he opened the book mentioned a sofa of threadbare chintz. My father read the phrase aloud, gave me one long look of bewildered rage, and snapped the book shut. Holding it away from him, as if the pages smelt of vinegar, he strode out of the library doors into the garden where, in full view of the startled guests, he tossed my novel into a flowerbed. Returning, he asked my mother how much longer we were going to have to wait for lunch. I never heard him mention the book again. A friend of my parents, keen that I should sign her copy, imported it in a brown paper bag, afraid that the contents might be discovered.

'You said this book was going to be about your father, not you,' my mother says sharply, when I remind her of this occasion. 'And I don't remember him saying anything against your writing. He was always praising you.'

'Not to my face, he wasn't.'

Evincing discomfort, she begins to tidy the objects on her desk, laying out pencils in a row, making a neat pile of her unanswered post. 'What about the Henry James book? Even you can't fault him about that.'

I was amazed, at the time, by the enthusiasm with which my father greeted my first attempt at scholarship. I hadn't, despite the family connection, imagined that Henry James's elaborate style would appeal to a man whose favourite authors were Noël Coward and Lord Lytton.

It didn't.

The book looked at a circle of writers, of whom the youngest, the most affecting and the most beautiful, was Stephen Crane. The place where my father marked his own copy of the book was the page that showed Crane as the newly celebrated author of *The Red Badge of Courage*. Lightly moustached and large-eyed, his face was appealing, even in a faded black-and-white reproduction.

Crane came to England in 1897 with Cora, his common-law wife, who had previously managed a brothel in Jacksonville, Florida. Cora fancied the life of an English lady; she persuaded her lover to rent Brede Place, a manor house not far from Henry James's new Sussex home, in Rye. Brede Place was tumbling down; Crane's lease required him to put it into order. This was the time when his commissions began to dry up and his health to give out. It's no great exaggeration to say that Brede Place killed Stephen Crane; its demands wore him out. He died of TB, aged twenty-eight.

'Of course your father loved reading about Crane.' My mother frowns, impatient with my slowness. 'Think how rundown this place was when we first moved in. Think of them planting daffodils all along the drive at Brede. It was one of the first things we did here; such a job!' And she tells me something I never knew, that Crane's story had so entranced my father that he drove off to Sussex and talked his way into being given a private tour of Brede Place. Back home, he bought every book by Crane that he could find: *Maggie: A Girl of the Streets*, took an honoured place on the shelf of favourites, right between *Earls of Creation* (James Lees-Milne) and Noël Coward's *Collected Short Stories*. Privately, I muse on other aspects of Stephen Crane, the vulnerability and eagerness for which Joseph Conrad loved him like a son, the large, beautiful eyes and light moustache drooping over full lips. But my mother may be right: what attracted my father even more than Crane's looks was the idea of a man who committed his energy to the salvation of a house.

She may have missed the point. Reflecting on other aspects of my father's life in 1988, the year when my book about Henry James and his colleagues was published, I think he was most intrigued by Crane's situation: his pride, his lack of money, his dependence on the kindness of benefactors. These things would have spoken to him. My thoughts turn back to the image of two figures by the lake, my father's hand resting on the shoulder of the burly fisher boy, his proud dependent. But making connections doesn't always bring mysteries to light; here, they threaten to add confusion.

8

SHADOWS UNDER THE CEDARS

The search for my father's life after his discharge from the army takes me to Lamas in Norfolk. Keen to live near Alex, their married daughter, Dick and Vita bought a house here in 1941, after selling their London home; at the beginning of 1943, my father joined them as he started clerical work at the Aylsham branch of Barclays Bank. (A member of the cousinship had pulled strings to secure him this lowly position from which, it was hoped, George would swiftly be promoted.)

Alex's daughter still lives in this area. A conscientious guide, she can drive me through the narrow lanes along which Alex used to guide their tall 'governess' cart on weekly visits to the Lane House at Lamas. Recalling these trips, my cousin describes the fright it always gave her as a small girl when Dick, having waited patiently to play his trick, sprang out with a shout and wave of his stick from behind a roadside oak tree. He didn't, by this stage of his life, have much else to occupy him. Tucked away in the snug little study at the side of Lane House, he retyped his recollections of the years, long gone, when life for a young diplomat had been full of promise.

'Here we are.' A narrow, roughly surfaced lane jolts to a stop at the side of a red house. Peering through the branches of a gigantic copper beech tree, my cousin and I can see the cliff over which the two of us, as little girls, used to plunge in a wooden boat towards an emerald ocean. We've grown; the land has shrunk: the cliff bordering the Lane House garden is a shallow slope, the ocean is a small square of rough turf. Beyond, a dark hedge shuts out the old view across wheat and cornfields; behind us, as we turn to press our noses to the dusty windows of the house, there's no such evidence of change. The Lane House staircase is narrow and dark; the kitchen has gaunt, ramshackle cupboards and a cracked floor of red concrete, laid down for economy in the war. The study, without a fire, looks musty and damp. My father spent hours arranging flowers in these dim rooms; bright branches and blossoms helped to keep despair at bay.

In 1944, the year my father turned twenty-one, he noted the date, twelve years earlier, on which his uncle became the tenth Duke of Grafton and owner of Euston Hall. Nineteen forty-four was the year in which the Duke, having lost two wives, married a jolly divorcee who welcomed younger company. Lamas was no great distance from Euston; my father, to his delight, was encouraged to pay regular visits. Invited by the new Duchess to offer suggestions as to whether diamonds could be worn with a country suit and which size of paper to order for stationery, his heart swelled. He had always prided himself on knowing how things should be done. In the absence of the Duke's eldest sons (Hugh was in India; Oliver was keeping out of the way while he adjusted to the idea of a new stepmother), George felt that he had been given a role. In his mind, to judge from the tone of his proud, excited letters home, he was almost a son of the house himself. At a time when Charlie Byron was once again dithering about the future and keeping his nephew at a distance, this was a solace.

Euston was not in good shape in the Forties, the time my father knew it best. One of the rebuilt wings was housing 150 boys from Barnardo homes; the gardens, laid out by the diarist John Evelyn, were neglected. Flaking paint, chipped plaster and threadbare curtains contributed to the air of gloom.

George noticed none of this. Advising the new Duchess on how to behave, talking to old employees who remembered the days when his mother had been a young girl about the place, gathering peaches in the hothouse, ready to be packed in tissue and despatched to Vita's ailing mother, he felt in his element. All that irked him was the contrast between Euston and Lamas. Why should his mother, so aristocratic in appearance and title, be obliged to live so humbly? Why should he himself be condemned, from time to time, to kneel like a parlourmaid on cold stone, lighting fires and blackening grates? They were FitzRoys, too, and bred for better things. Life was not just.

In fact, as my mother remembers, George's parents loved their little Norfolk home. The Lane House was not distinguished. It had no grand history. But it was their own. My father's disdain was more wounding than he knew: his mother gratefully recorded in her journal that it had been '*so* nice' when a visitor remarked that she thought their house delightful.

George's new alertness to the ducal connection was reflected in his reading habits. This was the time when he started to show an interest in the history of the Stuarts. Immersing himself in a biography of Charles II, he took proud note of the fact that the king's long liaison with the Duchess of Cleveland made him into a direct ancestor. The connection was remote; nevertheless, this was the time at which George came to see himself as (almost) royal.

I can't resist reading my mother an extract from her husband's wartime diary.

'Listen! He's talking about the Duchess.'

'Bloody woman,' my mother says. She takes a bite out of her Lincolnshire sausage as fiercely as if she had the Duchess of Cleveland's white neck clenched between her teeth, not a plump column of pork. 'Go on then.'

Gleeful, I read the entry out to her. *'It is refreshing to feel that at some period of history one's family* – that's the Duchess – *have milked vast quantities of wealth from the country.* And it gets better! This bit's about why it matters to buy your shoes in Jermyn Street, and to have your hair cut at the Savoy. *I am always convinced, more and more as time goes on, that it pays to get the best, and nothing but the best.* Was that what he was like when—?'

But my mother has gone, her breakfast abandoned, shuffling rapidly away and out of reach. Malice has made me forget the need to be courteous. I'm talking, after all, about the young man she chose to marry.

Well-made shoes and a smart haircut were my father's protective devices during a period of insecurity. He hadn't made friends during his time at training camp or in hospital; he was not making more headway at the local branch of Barclays Bank where he was now employed. But how, when he referred to his superiors as 'dreary little men' and regaled the clerks and secretaries with the interesting history of his bloodline, can he have expected to be treated as one of themselves? 'I, who am so lonely,' he wailed, when his fellow employees set off for whisky-steeped nights of jitterbugging at the local aerodrome. 'I, who so long for companionship.'

Life in London was more congenial. Just as the diary is leading me to pity him, I turn a page and find George speeding away from Norfolk in his little Morris car, fashionably yellow string-gloved fingers clasping the wheel and gear shift, lips pursed in a whistle, all ready for a weekend of socialising. He writes about his special table at the Savoy and going to dances at the Dorchester; he describes the joy of lying stretched in a hot, lily-scented bath, before he set off from the Chelsea home of one of the well-housed cousinly tribe to see a 'simply killing' new Rattigan play. The army discharge papers present him as suffering from exhaustion and neurosis; how am I to reconcile them with these accounts of dinners and theatres and dances that went on until dawn?

The diary for 1943-4 ends with a ten-page index of people he has mentioned. He seems to have acquired a vast circle of friends: I'm puzzled that so few of them kept up the connection. I've tracked one of them down, however, and persuaded him to meet me. He's a man in his early eighties, burdened by a title as magnificent as his girth. We're lunching together in a large, old-fashioned restaurant near Piccadilly; I'm having difficulty in distracting his attention from a pert-bottomed waitress who's been assigned to take care of our table.

'You were saying? I was never close to your father, I'm afraid. You're going to find this is a bit disappointing.'

'I'm sure not.'

I'm impressed by the elegance of his suit, and puzzled by his air of courtly blankness. The diary led me to suppose that this might have been one of my father's closest friendships. It's plain that this man doesn't know what he's doing here. His eyes stray again: I cough.

'I think you used to go to the same dances? The Leek-Melvilles? At the Dorchester?'

'I'm sure we did. Still – your father wasn't really one of us, you know.' He smiles kindly, softening a possible blow to my pride.

'You mean, because he didn't have a military record? Did that make him the odd one out?'

He dissects a crimson slice of beef with care, pops a potato in his mouth, and nods approval. 'We didn't think about things like that, my dear.' (He's already told me twice about his year of service in France.) 'It's possible that he might have felt it.' He leans forward, brightening as he finds something to tell me. 'I know! He had a camera hanging round his neck. That's what I remember. He was always taking photographs of us. It was rather odd, you know. One didn't take snaps of friends in those days, not in public. But I can't remember a word he said. Letters? No, he wasn't a letter-writer, was he? I wish I could be more help but – two o'clock? Is it really? No, I won't have cheese. Or coffee.'

Talking about my father hasn't given him any visible pleasure; my impression is that he is relieved to bring the meeting to a close. But he *has* helped, more than he knows. I'd wondered what my father's role had been when he rejoined this smartly social world, so remote from his daily life at the Norfolk bank. I'd guessed that he felt like an outsider, painfully aware of his lack of an officer's rank. A camera gave him a form of control; even if he didn't know these people intimately, he could shape the groups, command the smiles. When conversation turned to military matters, he switched off, to become the recording eye. Cameras keep life at a safe distance.

Our talk leads me to wonder how deeply my father felt his lack of a military record at the time. I'd missed something: now, from this new angle, it jumps out. *He wasn't a letter-writer, was he?* His schoolfriends, going off to squad training and active service, were good about staying in touch with the one they'd left behind. They wrote to him. But here's the thing: my father, the master of correspondence, the man who couldn't let a letter pass unanswered for a single day, my unstoppable father *never wrote back*.

The most striking example of these one-way correspondences to have survived among my father's papers was with John Persse. All I know of Persse suggests that he was an affectionate young man, lively and popular. His housemaster's reports, while harsh about his academic limitations, praise his brilliance as a mimic. Persse was my father's closest friend at Winchester. In 1941, they were stationed together nearby, in the training camp at Bushfield;

in 1942, they met again. They clearly enjoyed each other's company. And yet, after my father left the army, he shut Persse out. 'Write, curse you, write!' his friend entreated, but my father never did. Persse grew angry, then wistful. On the verge of being sent into action in 1944, he wrote to ask what he had done to cause offence. Two months later, Persse was dead, shot down as he went to help a wounded comrade. My father, expiating his guilt, showered reminiscences upon the dead man's family until, with the politeness of desperation, they begged for silence.

Discomfort about his army discharge could explain my father's strange failure to maintain contact with such a good friend. His vaunted connection to Thrumpton offers another possibility. All Persse's letters allude to Thrumpton; all describe his eagerness to visit this wonderful place. Clearly, he'd been led, ever since their days together at Winchester, to believe that Thrumpton Hall was George's family home. The little house at Lamas had never been mentioned; neither, in earlier letters, had the Seymours' home in West London. Living close to Winchester, the Persse family had been unfailingly hospitable to John's school chum; by 1942, John was showing his hurt at not being offered a reciprocal courtesy.

Was this the pitiful reason why those last, plaintive letters from Persse received no answer? Was my father so afraid of admitting the truth: that Thrumpton was home to him only in his dreams, that all he could offer Persse was a dark back bedroom overlooking a Norfolk lane?

'I don't like the way you keep running him down.' My mother brushes out her hair, still a reddish-gold in her eighties, with fierce straight strokes. 'It isn't fair. He paid for that lovely portrait of his mother by Oswald Birley out of his own pocket, you know. And he was only twenty-one.'

'Snobbery. He'd just seen the painting Birley did of the Duke, at Euston.'

'Goodness, you can sound unpleasant,' my mother says with

feeling. 'Well, then, what about all those landscapes of Thrumpton that he had done for Charlie Byron and Aunt Anna?'

Triumphant, I fold my arms. 'Well, actually, if you really want to know—'

She covers her ears. That won't stop me.

My father came across Major Drummond-Fish on one of his visits to Euston, where the artist had just completed painting a series of views of the house and estate. Offered a new commission at a time when he was short both of money and a place to stay, the ageing major gladly agreed to do the same for Thrumpton. The Byrons were not consulted; my father, on this occasion, simply acted as though the House was his own. When the paintings were finished, he invited the Byrons, together with their tenants and employees, to admire the results at a private exhibition in their own library. A few of the more discerning farmers had, he noted with approval, shown real taste in preferring his own favourite view, across the lake. He then had the paintings packed up and taken to Lamas, where he hung them, close enough to touch frames, facing his bed. Here, in the privacy of his room, he possessed the House entirely, from every angle. Just so, perhaps, one of his revered ancestors might have hung up a painting of some shapely odalisque, for private delectation. No voluptuous naked female could give my father what the House had never failed to provide: an image of permanence, security and consolation.

Not even the House could comfort him, in the summer of 1944, for the steady flow of reported deaths of the young men he had looked upon as his closest friends. In August, his parents sat him down in the front room of the Lane House and told him to prepare himself for a cruel shock: Oliver FitzRoy, the cousin my father had thought of as his twin brother, had been killed in action shortly after his twenty-first birthday.

The news came when a shrinking workforce was leading to

rapid shifts of location for employees of Barclays Bank. My father had just received orders to move from Norfolk to the branch near Liverpool Street in London. He went to no parties during this period and stayed away from company. For once, there is no mention of the ritual haircut. Dazed by grief, he walked the streets all night, hoping that a bomb would fall and put an end to him. 'Half of me has died,' he wrote in his August diary: the following month, after news of a further spate of deaths, he made a bitter little note on the worthlessness of his own survival. 'They are all gone now,' he wrote.

It's hard to withhold pity during this stage of my father's life. Dick and Vita were not emotionally demonstrative; his married brother and sister were absorbed in their own young families. Abruptly ordered to move once more, to another Norfolk branch bank at Fakenham, he lodged at a nearby rectory and spent his evenings playing card games with the vicar's small children. Every weekend, he took a bouquet of flowers to old Ismay FitzRoy and listened attentively to family gossip. Here, at least, he could feel that he was appreciated; conscientious George had always been her favourite grandchild.

Family letters show that Vita, Anna and Ismay had been busily scheming for George's future behind his back. The possibility that he might one day be allowed to live at Thrumpton had been raised once more; Anna Byron dropped excited hints to her nephew that he should prepare himself for news of great expectations. The news, when it came, was very different. Charlie Byron did not like plans to be made behind his back. The House was not a FitzRoy home; sharply, he reminded his wife and her sister that he had connections of his own to consider. A savage row broke out; harsh words were spoken, tears shed; hopes dashed. 'Poor George!' Vita noted sadly. 'When we knew his grief [we thought] he'd really be entitled to *anything*.' Recently, she had been fretting about her daughter Alex's loss of a nursemaid; the new drama put the smaller mishap into perspective. 'I feel quite livid with CB (Charles Byron),' she wrote with indignation: 'What a man!'

This upset took place towards the end of 1944. By the spring, old Lord Byron was ready to eat a little humble pie. Their only gardener had just left; the footmen and the chauffeur had already gone; the cook's threat of a forthcoming resignation was the final straw. Servants could no longer be found; might dear George be willing to consider helping out a fond old uncle who still hadn't *quite* decided who his eventual heir should be?

George felt, to judge from the ecstatic tone of his diaries, as though invited to walk back into Eden. Fatigue forgotten, despondency gone, he set to work scything nettles, mowing the lawns, hacking down undergrowth, losing himself in manual labour until, late in the afternoons, he slumped in a trance beneath the lakeside willows, watching the lines of the House he adored dissolve into the dusk. Sitting at his little desk in the Fakenham rectory, he had written of loneliness and a sense of isolation closing in on him like a vice; now, in a moment of epiphany, as he sat out beside the lake on a summer night, he understood all that Thrumpton meant to him and that without it, he was lost. 'God send I never have to leave,' he prayed.

Everything, in that season of luminous beauty, seemed to take place in a dream. No guests were staying. In the drawing room, behind drawn blinds, his aunt played *Liebestraum* on the piano; sitting in the garden with Bingo, the old poodle, asleep at his side, his uncle Charlie dozed the days away in a deckchair. At dinner one night, laying a line of cherry pits across his plate of fruit, George played a private game of divination. The cherry stones promised marriage before the end of the year, and riches. 'I wonder?' he wrote in his diary. 'I *wonder.*'

Preparing to travel back to Fakenham and the bank, he snipped a branch of orange-scented *philadelphus* from the shrub beneath his bedroom window and wrapped it in wet cloths. For a week, the cloying fragrance filled his little Norfolk bedroom with memories.

Three months later, he received two dismaying letters by the same post. One, from his aunt Anna, pleaded for his forgiveness; the other, from his uncle, sounded a more aggressive note. The fact of the matter, Charlie Byron wrote, was that the time had come for things to change. The House had become a burden, too heavy a one for two old people to bear. It was too late for argument: the advertisements had already been placed. The House was to be sold.

Shock numbed my father's mind. When he tried to describe his feelings in his diary, his hand trembled. 'It has been my life,' he wrote; it had represented all that he loved most. Nothing could fill such a gap. 'I am completely and utterly heartbroken.' A day later, his mind was made up: 'This *shall* not be.'

Time, my father wrote three days later, was his greatest enemy. He knew now that his uncle and aunt's plans were well-advanced. They had already made a journey to Essex and taken stock of Langford Grove, the tall, hard-featured house in which Charlie Byron had spent his early life and which was still owned by him. It was not easy to see how they could move back there in the short term, since army troops were still occupying the main rooms and the gardens had been destroyed, but the Byrons were resolute and optimistic. Upkeep costs would be far lower, they believed, and it would be delightful for Charlie to return to the landscape of his early years. Besides, the eighty-five-year-old rector of Thrumpton piously informed his distraught nephew, it hardly mattered where you lived if you had the kingdom of heaven in your heart. This was not my father's view of the landowner's position and obligations; infuriated, he struck back with a list of all the houses he had seen which were tumbling down after being abandoned. Did they not care if Thrumpton was ruined? Lord Byron's answer was to let his nephew know that Earl Spencer of Althorp had already requested particulars and was arranging a visit of inspection. This information caused his nephew a fresh stab of pain: to picture a stranger prowling around the rooms, handling familiar treasures before negotiating a satisfactory sale price, was as painful as the thought of its becoming an untenanted wreck.

Action had to be taken, and swiftly. Hearing that his uncle and aunt were paying a September visit to the Lake District, George took a fortnight's holiday from the bank and dashed north to offer them his latest idea. Might they, he asked, consider installing him at Thrumpton as their tenant if he allowed them to remain with him as honoured guests? And where, his uncle demanded, was the money to come from? Did George intend to become a *borrower*? This was just what my father had been planning – he had already been in touch with a mortgage company to arrange the sum. His uncle's tone and stare were so dismaying, however, that he lost his nerve and claimed not to have thought matters through. Crushed, he retreated to his room.

Two weeks of determined argument and skilfully deployed charm produced the compromise my father had fought to achieve; worn down by such persistence, Charlie Byron agreed to defer the sale for a year. If George could find a solution before the following summer, Thrumpton might yet be saved. In the meanwhile, the advertisements were withdrawn and Earl Spencer was informed that the House was not, at present, on the market.

Luck, now, was all my father needed.

9

※

FALSE TRAILS

The occasion is one my father would have relished, a reception in the Lord Chancellor's opulently refurbished River Room, held in 2005. This is a gathering of Nottinghamshire gentry for the post-humous publication of a book by one of their own. Conversation is more animated than I'd remembered; we've all, with varying degrees of competence, become businessfolk, reshaping our homes as confer-ence centres and wedding venues. Rivalry wears a friendly face; we swap notes on websites, civil licences, the merits of in-house catering, marketing strategies.

I'm struck by the change of attitude, the sense of renewed energy and goodwill. Ten years ago, attending an official dinner for the future generation of stately home owners, I heard nothing but resentment. The old couples were clinging to their heritage; the middle-aged heirs didn't hide their frustration. Looking down the table and studying the faces, hawkish even by candlelight, it wasn't hard to pick up the sub-text beneath the well-bred chatter. My neighbour, a portly, pink-faced

Yorkshireman, leant across me to refuel his glass of claret while he explained how unjust it was that his father was still ensconced in comfort at the Hall while he, his wife and their three children made do with a house that had once belonged to the estate manager. The old man was a fool, he said, hopelessly impractical, caring for nothing beyond his right to enjoy expensive holidays abroad and to dine at White's Club or the Savoy when he came down to London. The estate was going to the dogs, all because he refused to transfer control.

THE TIMES   SATURDAY MAY 25 1968

THE STATELY HOMES

From Mr. G. F. Seymour

Sir,—I was glad to see there was support for Lord Montagu when he raised the threat to British stately homes through taxation in the House of Lords last week.

There was talk of the desirability of more grants to aid the owners of such houses. I have so far managed to maintain this fine Jacobean house which is in the first category of listed buildings without seeking a grant, and have felt that the amount of money available to the Historic Buildings Council was so limited that it ought only to be given to those who could not maintain their houses without such aid.

Things are, however, growing more difficult with rising costs, the 10 per cent surcharge on surtax last year, the special levy on unearned income this year and S.E.T. I would suggest a fair way to help owners of beautiful and historic homes which are of sufficient importance might be by reducing taxation for them both of income and capital.

At present so-called unearned income attracts surtax above £2,000. I believe that people engaged in maintaining such houses do as much, and often more, to earn their incomes than many who are in receipt of salaries. Keeping up a house and garden which until the war employed a dozen servants indoors and half a dozen gardeners with the help of a married couple and one gardener is no sinecure. By their efforts such people are helping to preserve one of the chief attractions this country has for visitors from abroad.

Furthermore, as Lord Montagu said, death duty is penal and obliges many who would like to struggle on to give up. A book entitled *The Great Houses of Nottinghamshire*, published less than 100 years ago, lists 37 such houses of which this is one. Today only 13 are occupied as homes while at least 10 have been demolished.

If the wish to help is really there the Chancellor of the Exchequer could do much to prevent such sad decisions as that recently announced by the gallant owners of Sawston Hall in Cambridgeshire "that the last budget was the final straw which must compel them to sell up and go".

The number of taxpayers affected by such relief and the amount of revenue involved would be minimal and an investment for which I am sure posterity would be grateful.

These houses once lost can never be replaced.

I am, Sir, your obedient servant,
GEORGE SEYMOUR.
Thrumpton Hall, Nottingham, May 20.

My father was anxious to publicise his generation's concerns about the future of the country house.

Lear was the ghost at that particular feast, a tough old king who hadn't yet relinquished the reins. He'd pay for having kept his children waiting; that much was clear. My father had sketched out just this scenario in one of his unfinished stories, rationalising his plan to keep control of the estate until he died. I winced when I first read it and saw the depth of his mistrust. That evening, sitting down to dine with the impatient and resentful heirs, I understood his fears.

Times have changed. Stringent regulations for the transfer of property and soaring maintenance costs have forced the stately home owners to change their attitude. House tours and farming tenancies don't bring in enough income to cover maintenance expenses; it's fair to guess that, ten years from now, even the wealthiest private owners will be running their homes as businesses, converting courtyards, derelict barns and estate cottages into craft centres, farm shops and office space.

I'm glad. These houses were never intended for sole occupation. They suit large occasions; they need to be alive with warmth, light and people. The weddings and conferences help to pay for their costs; they also give energy back to rooms designed for crowds and show. Better still, since little divides a family so savagely as a withheld legacy, the owners have begun to look with kinder eyes on heirs who can offer professional skills for free. From viewing them as a threat to their own security, the older generation of owners have come to see their hardworking sons and daughters as allies and even, when they prove their worth, as friends.

Commerce is the thing that marks the change. A heritage home is divisive; a business forms a bond. Mutual interests, shared expertise and a perception, at last, that trust can be a wise investment, have reaped rewards. Warmth has replaced hostility, a cordiality born of a determination to see these splendid, history-drenched estates through, and help them to survive. There are cases, I'm sure, where Goneril and Regan will still have roles to play, where my father's terror of the old folks' home and oblivion will be fulfilled; tonight, standing in the crowded River Room with its windows looking across a darkly glimmering Thames, I see no sign of this. Goodwill abounds, fathered by recovered confidence.

I have an ulterior motive for coming to this occasion. I'm looking for the face of another of the acquaintances so carefully indexed in my father's wartime diaries. Since then, he has become a celebrated right-wing journalist and editor. He enters the room late, a dapper, white-haired man. He's smiling as I approach him, but with a wariness that suggests that he can't quite place me. I introduce myself, with care, as my father's daughter. I explain that I'm writing a book about him.

'You used to meet my father in London towards the end of the war,' I say, prompting his memory. 'I was hoping you might be able to tell me what he was like then. He was quite a friend of yours, wasn't he?'

His smile, while still in place, is straining at the corners of his plump lips. I'm causing embarrassment.

'I think you've got the wrong person, my dear,' he says. 'I don't remember him at all.'

'At the Orchid Room,' I say, insistent, knowing I'm right. 'The Bagatelle?'

'Ah, the Orchid Room.' Something's stirring, but not, it seems, the memory that I seek to revive. 'So sorry I can't help,' he says. And, while not quite turning his back, a shuttered glance indicates that further questions will be pointless.

I'm beginning to wonder how much trust I can place in my father's wartime diary. The first old friend remembered my father only as a skinny young man who always had a camera in his hand. He may have been delivering one of those coded messages at which the English aristocracy excel (taking snaps of your chums wasn't socially elegant in the days when photographers were always assumed to be working for the press). Were those carefully indexed names only of people near to whom George Seymour hungrily loitered, using his camera as an excuse for his presence? Why is it that he's been so completely effaced from their memories, if not because he never enjoyed the friendship that his diary seeks to record?

I find, to my surprise, that I'm angry with these smiling, smooth-cheeked old men. I've plenty of reason to hate my father, but his achievement matches theirs. They've no cause to be disdainful. They fought for their country; he gave his life to save a house.

After leaving the River Room party, I go to dine with my younger brother. We sit in the corner of a small restaurant in Soho and talk, as we always end up doing when we're alone, about our father. Sharing the memory of what we endured is, as we both know, dangerously addictive. We'd like to break the habit, cut ourselves free from the past; we haven't as yet managed to do so. We don't meet often, alone; when we do, we can be sure there'll be a third presence at the table.

'It's an odd thing to say, I know', my brother says, as though reading my thoughts, 'but do you ever have the feeling that he's still there?'

'A ghost?'

'I'm talking about dreams,' he says. 'Dreams when he comes back, as though he'd never gone.'

I stare at him across the table. 'Comes back where?'

He looks exasperated by my stupidity. 'To the House. Where else do you think he'd be?'

'Always?'

'Always. Why?'

'Because I have dreams, too. Bad ones. Is yours like this?' Almost whispering, we swap images and discover that our dream, our terror, is the same. No death has taken place, only a journey to some distant place. Now, our father is back for good, restoring everything, making sure that his home is just as it was twelve years ago, when he appeared to die. But there's no possibility of his dying in this dream. There's no way out, no end. Past middle age, his son and daughter are back behind the bars of childhood.

Dismayed, we look into each other's eyes, searching them for reassurance and finding none.

'Who knows, perhaps you're going to exorcise him for us,' my brother says, kindly, as we say goodbye on the crowded midnight pavement, trapped in a jostle of bare arms and edgy hips outside a new dance-club. 'I hope so.' And, although he is not often physically demonstrative, he adds a brief hug. 'We'll get clear of it all one day.'

Later, sitting at my desk in the bleak hour before dawn, I rest my chin on my hands and stare into the laptop's grey screen. A photograph of my father stands propped on the windowsill beyond

My father shows off a dapper suit under Dick Seymour's furlined coat, a relic from diplomatic days.

my desk. He's posed at the garden entrance to his House; he's wearing, to entertain the unseen holder of the camera, a mangy fur-lined coat that once belonged to Dick Seymour. He's laughing at the lens and holding the coat wide, like a stripper in a burlesque show.

Encased within, he's immaculate in a three-piece suit, the country gentleman at leisure, down to his well-polished shoes. Sunlight has faded his features out, made a ghost of him in the twelve years that he's stood at my window. I don't see him clearly any more.

If you wish to know me, look around you. That's what the proud epitaph stolen from Sir Christopher Wren proclaims in Latin on the stone that marks my father's burial place in the garden of his House. Look, then: what's on show? A noble old building weathering its prime; a garden filled with trees chosen for the future, not the present; a park of sunny outspread fields, well-proportioned hills, restful inclinations, springing woods. *All my creation*, he liked to say, mocking his own hubris. The claim was not absurd: he gave his life over to ensuring that this beauty should outlive him and remain secure. A heroic endeavour, surely? Passion or obsession, the result is there for all to see. It outweighs the price that we, all of us, paid. It must. It has to show its value.

My brother writes to tell me of a new dream, bred like a bad child from our last meeting. In the first scene, he saw our father striding across the hill above the House, a dog trotting at his side. The season was high summer. My brother watched as the walker stopped and turned, shading his eyes as he stared down. Below him, the land lay under a spell, sunlit fields dotted with sheep, the cricket pitch, the silver line of the river snaking away behind a row of feather-leaved willows, the sturdy tower of the village church, all in place, as it had always been. It's an image, we agree, of the precarious serenity he fought to safeguard.

The second part of the dream comes near to my own night terrors. There's no sign of our father here, only a view of the western stretch of the lake, lit orange by a neon sky. Mud swirls thickly under the water's surface; black bubbles force their way up. They burst, exposing, just for a moment, a glimpse of slippery substances twitching and quivering below, as if in pain. These are things that must not be seen.

I know where this dream comes from. Like my brother, I remember the time towards the end of our father's life when he decided to deal with his estate's last unclaimed area of land. Bonfires smouldered through the nights, devouring the remains of a jungle of twisted creepers and stunted trees that had smothered the western end of the lake, obscuring it from view. They burned through the length of a windless summer, while long-armed machines scooped out the gathered filth of a century and the stink of dredged mud seeped through the cracks in closed doors, contaminating everything we touched.

My brother offers an analysis. At a time of life when any other man might have felt it wise to undertake a little self-examination, George Seymour preferred to exorcise his land, to decontaminate his property. Better to cleanse a muddy lake than to risk taking a look into his own murky depths.

10

※

WELSH CONNECTIONS

'No!' My mother's hands grip and twist the plastic handles of her floral shopping bag as we turn into the melancholy retail park where, two hundred years ago, George Gordon Byron and his cronies came sauntering down into scrubby meadowland to watch a display of cockfighting. Above us, the square bulk of Nottingham Castle looms from the rain clouds; around us, dark figures scatter across the glistening tarmac, fleeing towards the large lit doorways of the stores. I turn off the engine. We sit in silence, waiting for the rain to stop.

'We mustn't forget to buy coffee,' I say. I'm feeling wretched at the distress my questions about her marriage have caused her. 'And camomile tea. Oh Ma, I am sorry.'

'If you were sorry, you'd stop writing,' she says. Unexpectedly, she reaches out to touch my arm. 'You're so tense!'

'Of course I am. I hate upsetting you.'

'I know.' She stares ahead at a row of shopping trolleys, snugly huddled under a plastic canopy. 'Can't you understand how strange it feels for me? Your father and I worked so hard to get the House back to rights. And we did love each other, you know. In spite of everything.' She sighs. 'I keep trying to remember the good times and then I start seeing him. He always looks so cross.'

'Perhaps he doesn't like us to be managing so well without him.'

'He certainly was bossy. Just like you. You'd have thought I was brought up in a pigsty to hear him lecturing me on how to behave.'

'And to look. Do you remember how you had to have your hair set every week, in that style like a Greek helmet?'

As I say it, I remember being taken into a hot many-mirrored room with my mother and watching active but unfriendly fingers force a miniature version of the helmet to sprout in lacquered curls around my glowering face. Worse even than the strain of meeting the hairdresser's interrogative stare with a satisfied smile, was the lack of speech. All around me, well-tended ladies twittered bright floods of repartee; thirteen and wordless, I sat shuttered in self-consciousness.

She flushes. 'I liked it done that way. And some of the clothes he chose for me were lovely. What about the apricot silk dress from Worth? You must have liked that?'

I can't remember it. All I see, thinking back, are the tweed suits of sensible cut, adding twenty years to her age. 'Was he always like that, so controlling?'

'There you go again, always against him.' But she says it without rancour. 'Not when we first met. Everything I did and said was perfect. I must say,' she adds wistfully, 'I did enjoy it. Being adored.'

Packing our laden shopping bags into the back of the car twenty minutes later, I return to the subject. First, I press a bar of chocolate into her willing hand. 'I can't write the book without saying anything about your marriage, you know. It wouldn't work.'

Peeling off the wrapping, she breaks the bar into squares and pops one in her mouth. 'Nice nice,' she says, with a child's pleased smile. 'Not like those awful violet creams your father was always eating after we went to bed. He kept them in a locked drawer, greedy old thing. He thought I didn't know.'

I ask if he ever told her about reading the cherry stones at Thrumpton. 'It was just before he met you. And the stones told him he was going to make a marriage and grow rich within the year.'

'Just like him to be so superstitious. Remember when we went to the circus at Olympia and he wouldn't come out of the fortune teller's tent?'

I remember it as a night scene by Edward Hopper, lights fading from the carousels and slides, music grinding to an end, my mother, brother and I clustered glumly in a doorway staring at the drawn blind behind which my father, then in his mid-forties, sat transfixed by an old woman's warnings of grasping hands and indifferent hearts. She was, he had no doubt, speaking of the future of his home, warning him to keep fast hold of it.

'As for being rich,' my mother says. 'I suppose money might have helped. But he wasn't so badly off, you know.' Always vague about finance, it's possible that she never understood how little his four hundred pounds a year amounted to in 1945. 'He did keep wanting to know how much income I had,' she adds. 'Too boring.'

I watch the familiar gesture of a piece of silver foil being smoothed and refolded, occupying her hands while she considers. 'We used to laugh about all sorts of silly things,' she says after a long pause. 'I hope you're going to say something about that. We did have fun.' An unexpected giggle spurts out of her, so girlish that I turn in my seat to catch a glimpse of her face. She's pink, her eyes screwed up with merriment. 'I was remembering the time when we were in Hyde Park late one night after dancing at the Orchid Room,' she explains. 'We were kissing in your father's car and a policeman stuck his face up against the window. He told us he'd been standing there and shouting at us for half an hour. We never even noticed!'

'Did he tell you about Thrumpton straightaway?' I ask as we drive slowly home. 'He must have been in such a state about it being sold.' And that, I think to myself, is why he would have been so pleased to meet a pretty and rich young woman who, even if she didn't return his love at once, seemed glad to be courted. I've checked out the dates. They fit.

'Sold?' My mother gives me a disgusted look. 'The things you ask. Whoever said it was being sold?'

I'm so flustered that I almost overshoot the turning into the courtyard at the back of the House. 'It's in the diary. Uncle Charles had decided to go back to Essex, to Langford, you know, after the troops moved out of the big house there. Thrumpton was put on the market for sixty thousand. George was frantic. It happened just before you met. He must have told you?'

'Not a word.' Halfway out of the car, she stops and gives me a glance that expresses more amusement than annoyance. 'So that's what you've been thinking all this time, that he married me for my money! A nice thing.'

I don't want to offend her, but I can't dismiss the idea of a connection. The Byrons agreed to take Thrumpton off the market for a year in September, 1945. My father had a year in which to come up with a solution. 'I'd do *anything* to save Thrumpton,' he wrote that month. 'I realise now that it means more to me than anything else in the world.'

Did *anything* include persuading the daughter of one of England's wealthiest men to marry him and provide the funds he lacked?

I'm looking at a picture, painted in 1930. In the foreground, two skinny teenage girls kneel on the floor, playing chess. These are my mother's sisters, Gaenor and Pip. Behind them, near to the fireplace, my grandmother sits at the piano, chin held high: Bronwen, her eldest daughter, known always as The Beauty, plays a viola; Elizabeth, the musical prodigy of the family, draws her bow across a cello's waisted heart. Across the room, their brother turns his back; a tennis racket swings from his hand like a hunting crop, hinting at the impatience he surely felt at having to pose for a family portrait. Facing him, perched on a long window-seat, my grandfather is identifiable by the baldness of his head and the plumpness of his crossed thighs. 'I suppose Pa's fond of us, in his way,' my mother wrote to my father at the time of their engagement, 'but he's a queer person.'

The Irish artist John Lavery has painted this domestic scene in deep, glowing colours that pull the eye towards the centre where, in a short lemon-yellow frock, a child stands. Her feet are neatly pointed like a dancer's. She's watching the game of chess, but the artist has placed her apart, separate. She could have been curled up by one of the two dogs or sprawled beside her sisters in the foreground, but Lavery has made a focus point of her solitude.

This is my mother. Eight years old, she stands firm as a young warrior in the drawing-room of Chirk Castle, a fourteenth-century fortress in the Marches, the borderlands that divide England from Wales. This, until the year she marries my father, will be her home. She will be the last to leave, helping Margot, her mother, to fold curtains, store books, check the inventories, say farewell to the house that always seemed to be their own. Her parents were only a couple in the most formal of senses by 1945, but Margot took care to return to Chirk that year. She knew her husband; left to himself, Lord Howard de Walden would have cared only for the preservation of his library, his writings, and his hawks.

Writing her memoirs years later, my grandmother claimed that Tommy chose her as a bride because of her hands, which were large and capable. They needed to be.

Erudite, absent-minded and notoriously dishevelled in person, Lord Howard de Walden made up for an unglamorous appearance by living like a Renaissance prince. Invited to join the Olympic Fencing team in 1908, he transported his colleagues to Athens on the *Branwen*, his private yacht; the Royal Welch Fusiliers' regiment under his command in the First World War was equipped to fight with medieval daggers from his own collection. Lacking a country home of his own and learning of a family link to the property, he rented and repaired a beautiful, haunted house in Essex until the ghosts – a mighty hound that raced around the dining table and vanished into the wall; an old man who sat on visitors' beds; an army of spectral knights who came clattering up the drive on moonlit nights – grew too obstreperous for the tenant of Audley End. In 1911, he undertook another romantic project: the restoration of a Welsh castle that the resident family could no longer afford to maintain. This was where my mother was born in 1922; by that time, the Howard de Walden family looked on Chirk as their home.

Lord and Lady Howard de Walden enjoyed
dressing up for pageants at their Welsh home.

My mother has taught me to venerate my grandfather and the home he brought to life. I like her youthful memories of being led around the hilltop gardens by the hand of Rudyard Kipling, of being talked at ('never with; you couldn't!') by Shaw. I love to think of her galloping bareback over the Welsh hills on her father's Arab mares. ('There you go again! Bareback! You know perfectly well that we always used saddles.') *And* of my grandmother calling her tribe of daughters home by hooting Brünnhilde's cry across the Ceiriog valley. ('Well, *that's* true.') I relish the story of an intrepid aunt setting off to nurse in the Spanish Civil War (wrong side, unfortunately) before marrying a philandering aristocrat whose baby-smooth cheeks and confident smirk won him a few film appearances (famous titles, undemanding roles, always playing himself, the charismatic cad).

Hearing how five-course banquets were borne across a courtyard from an underground kitchen, I'm amazed again by the ease with which my mother has adapted to a different life. Doesn't she mind wearing velour tracksuits and secondhand shoes when she looks back on those years in a many-towered castle, set high on a wooded hill, with maids to unpack for her, to press her clothes and draw her bath?

I should know better than to wonder; the key to my mother's survival and good humour is that she never occupies her mind with what's gone. It may be that the last memories of Chirk are so bleak that they blot out earlier pleasure. I can't imagine how it felt, aged twenty, to escape a court martial (her misplaced chart pins had sent an American convoy, quite harmlessly, to Scotland instead of Devon). Broken and lost, she came back to Chirk, to recuperate from a nervous collapse in an abandoned house. This isn't a time she talks about, but I've heard enough to know my mother suffered. I've heard her describe sitting alone at meals with her father, staring at the bald dome of his head as he bent forward, oblivious, diligently tracking a line of text in some obscure manuscript. Once, unable to bear the silence, she shouted at him. He flinched, as if a stranger had broken in on his dreams, but he didn't speak. She says it was a mercy when Margot returned from Canada, a warfree zone to which she had agreed to take those grandchildren who could least be cared for by their busy parents.

My mother as a small girl, posing in her tutu; and as a teenager (on the far left) at a fete in Chirk village, 1936.

Back in Britain, Margot looked at her youngest daughter's trembling hands and listened to her frightened laugh; furiously, she lambasted Tommy for selfish indifference before taking control of the situation. My poor mother: hustled off to a local agricultural college to learn the rudiments of farming, she found her *métier* just in time to be deprived of it. A girl must have a season; Margot insisted on it, even when the girl in question was in her twenties. Measured and fitted into a fluid sheath of flame-coloured silk, another of emerald green, my mother was launched, bright-eyed and apprehensive, to find a mate and make a life of the kind for which she had been bred.

In later years, my mother developed a comfortable shape. By the time she had turned twenty-two in the summer of 1945, worry and a poor diet had stripped her of flesh. Large-eyed, and thin as a weasel, she was pale-skinned, her head crowned with a mass of copper-gold hair. (Think Moira Shearer; you're not far off.) She read with voracious indiscrimination, spoke a little French and German, spelt atrociously and was financially innocent. ('Unless I can see money or know it's there, I feel insecure,' she admitted in an early letter to my father.) Her nervousness was hidden by an insouciant manner. She didn't, beyond a couple of tender flirtations, of which one had been with an unseen military pen-pal, have any sexual experience. This was a dove, I'm ready to conclude, who was ripe for being caught and plucked.

My mother shakes her head. 'You make me sound such a ninny. I wasn't looking for a husband. My father may have rented Chirk, but he owned lots of farms in Wales. I'd talked to him. He was going to let me have one of them at half rent. I had everything planned out.' She looks past me, her eyes bright with affection for the picture of something I have never seen. 'I'd have kept a few goats. Hens. A donkey. Pigs. It was going to be just outside Wrexham, near Chirk.'

Life on the land she'd loved. I remember reading the letters that

Robert Graves and Siegfried Sassoon wrote to each other in the closing months of the Great War, two poets planning out a farming future. Unchanged landscape comes to symbolise a lost idyll in wartime. Old-fashioned paintings of pastoral scenes sold well throughout the 1940s; fields of corn helped mask the stench of war: of sulphur, and of death. Of course my mother wanted to farm: what could life offer that was more tranquil, more reassuring?

'And your father,' she says firmly. 'He was just as keen, you know.'

Remembering the wartime diary's notes of visits to the manicurist, and of a certain flower-scented hand-lotion reserved there for George Seymour's personal use, I can't help smiling. 'Just read his letters,' she says, indignant. 'He was just as keen as me. The letters will tell you how it was.'

I tell her that I have been unable to find them. 'But he kept yours in his desk, every single one. All tied up in ribbons and put safely away.'

'So are his,' she says swiftly.

'Oh?' I'm sceptical. I've searched through every cupboard and drawer in the House, but they're gone, those voluminous screeds of adoration which demanded instant response, out on the ash heap or in the fire. She can't remember a word from them now, or even from her own.

'Listen!' I quote one of my favourite lines, when she informed her husband-to-be that her mother thought him '"oh! A perfect pet! (Although she doesn't say what sort.)"'.

My mother looks delighted.

'Did I say that? Did I really? I'd no idea I was so funny!'

11

READING ROMANCE

In November 1945, my father went to a London dinner party and found that he had been placed next to a slender, hazel-eyed girl with pale freckled skin and red-gold hair. With the writer Ludovic Kennedy sitting on the other side of her, she had little time for an arrogant but shy young man with a small head, round spectacles and neatly slicked hair. Nevertheless, she smiled. My father, smitten, noted in his diary that he had fallen for Rosemary Scott Ellis, the youngest daughter of Lord Howard de Walden, and that she had agreed to dine with him at the Savoy. (This was not such an extravagant invitation as it sounds; London's best hotels offered low-budget meals to keep their restaurants filled during the frugal war years.)

I want to like my father at this crucial stage of his life. I want to see him through my mother's (by slow degrees) admiring eyes. To do so, I must overlook a gloating note in his diary about a FitzRoy family wedding at which ('ha! ha!' he wrote) he sat in a grander pew than some of the envied ducal cousins. I need to forget that the future of the House lay so near to his heart, and that he must have known that he was in with a chance to save it, if he could but charm this millionaire's daughter into backing his passion with substance.

I know that there must have been an element of calculation, but the diary tells a different story. From that first meeting at a dinner party, my father lost all sense of decorum. He did not behave like a cunning opportunist. He behaved like a man under a spell, or overwhelmed by love.

He could think of nothing but Rosemary. When they went dancing, he was tortured to see her smiling at another man. When she casually addressed him as 'darling Georgey' and suggested that he might care to visit her Welsh home, he accepted by return of mail and told his diary that he would treasure the endearment until the end of his life. When she cancelled a dinner date the following week, he announced that he was ready to kill himself with grief. When she consoled him with an invitation to a drinks party, he sent her a copy of *Antony*, his favourite book, together with a declaration of unconditional love.

Her answer, to his dismay, was a rebuff. 'I must admit I do think of other things than you,' she told him, and warned him that her feelings were less passionate than his own. 'But if because of this you must go into a monastery, I pray you, don't consider it.' The following week, however, she reminded him of his promise to visit her in Wales: 'I am ordering and beseeching you to come here,' she wrote, and added that he had best bring his riding things. (She rode every day; my father did not dare admit that he had never yet sat on a horse.)

'I hope you're not going to criticise me for sending him back that awful book about Antony Knebworth,' my mother says. 'I did try to read it, but really!'

The reason for my mother's air of indifference was simple: she was in love with another man. Shortly before Christmas, this other suitor told her that he was about to propose to someone else. If his first choice turned him down, he was willing to marry my mother. Passing the news on to my distraught father, she told him not to give up, as she was also fond of him. 'I do like being truthful,' she added.

A week later, her lover's engagement to his first choice was announced.

'And what if he had chosen to propose to you? Would you have married him?'

'Don't be so difficult,' my mother sighs. I'm answered.

The fickle lover's engagement was announced on 15 December. The following day, my mother lunched with my father at Claridge's. She wore her favorite rust-coloured suit; a matching beret was pulled aslant on her red-gold curls. My father, enchanted, told her she looked ravishing. They went to the Tate gallery and discovered that they both hated the Pre-Raphaelites. Later, they had dinner at the Mirabelle.

'We did live it up, didn't we!' My mother is beaming at these remembered pleasures.

A night of dancing ended in a passionate embrace across the small front seats of my father's Morris Minor (this was the occasion on which the policeman knocked vainly at the driver's window). A week later, flushed with love, they drove out of London on the winding road to north Wales. There were storms along the way when my mother refused to wear a diamond brooch on which my father had spent most of his savings.

'That was mean of you.'

'Well!' My mother sips her wine and gives me a little sideways look.

'Not good enough?'

'You've seen me wear it. Perfectly nice.'

I'll never be able to make the word 'nice' sound so lethally dismissive.

★

It's mid-October 2005. I've persuaded my mother to visit Chirk Castle, and to act as my guide. She hasn't been there for over forty years; I've never seen it before. I need to imagine the impression it might have made on my father when he arrived here on a chilly night in December 1945.

'Where's the sweetshop gone?' cries my mother, gazing with distracted eyes at a village restaurant that announces itself as the Chirk Tandoori. I'm staring past it at the war memorial, and the clean-cut bas-relief of a soldier marching, head bent, into action. I can't believe it.

'Eric *Gill*? For a village memorial?'

'Why not? He used to come and stay. Pa asked him to do it.' Of course. What could be less remarkable than that Eric Gill should come to Chirk for a weekend and turn a small commission into one of the finest war memorials in the country?

We drive on a winding road up a hill – 'Mountain! Welsh *mountains*, Miranda!' my mother admonishes me – so that I can admire the Roman aqueduct spanning the broad flanks of the Ceiriog valley. Returning, we pass between gates as proudly delicate as peacock tails, opening the way to a drive that twists like a strangling rope around the castle hill. Mist swirls in and wreathes back, to show a flock of black sheep cropping grass, a view of distant slopes and, rising above the trails of wispy cloud, a square, four-towered castle of grey stone. Sedate as a hearse, we cross the narrow drawbridge on which, during the war, my grandfather parked a horsebox to keep invaders out. Below, grass smooths the banks of the old defensive moat. ('I remember it filling up with snow,' my mother says with delight. 'I jumped in and lay there for three hours, quite snug, with a little hole to breathe through. I cried when they came and pulled me out.' She was five years old.)

This wasn't just a house. It was a world. As I register the splendour of its scale, my mother, smiling, walks back into the past. I climb the winding stair to my grandfather's refuge, a stone room with six-foot embrasures and broad views across the Ceiriog valley. My mother talks eagerly to the curator about a keeper's pet owl and the laundry room where she kept two angora rabbits. I peer down narrow slits through which oil was poured on to the heads of medieval intruders; my mother has found the walk above the castle chapel from which she dropped paper streamers upon the bald head of a visiting minister. I'm down in a dungeon, contemplating the life of Henry V's twenty French prisoners, kept in windowless gloom fifty feet below the tower where my grandfather, centuries later, would hide from view. She's walking along the Long Gallery, recalling the elaborate family pantomimes in which she, as the youngest child, invariably took the smallest part.

Sitting in the Chirk Tandoori that night, while rain beats against the windows, we replay our favourite moments from the day. Mine was climbing an airy flight of stairs to the upper drawing-room, still lit by candles and the silvery reflections of the long glasses on its walls. I didn't need to close my eyes to see the little girl squaring up to the artist in her lemon-yellow frock, centre stage. Nothing had changed.

'And yours?' I ask. I'm sure she'll pick the garden where she walked beside Rudyard Kipling, listening to the stories he shaped to fit the setting. I'm forgetting that her last companion at the castle was a haughty tabby cat. The moment she chooses is the one in which, stalking out of the mist and along the gravel path, a grey tabby advanced to whisk a bushy tail around my mother's calves, before vanishing behind a wall of clipped yew.

Her eyes are shining at the memory. 'He was welcoming me home, wasn't he!' And she reaches forward to pat my hand. 'I'm glad we came!'

I've asked my mother whether, back in 1945, she was told about the deferred sale of Thrumpton. Her memory is only of the fact that my father talked about the House with a tenderness that touched her heart. She had just become aware that her family were about to lose their own home. Chirk, which had never belonged to them, was about to be reclaimed, in its newly repaired and improved state, by its owners, the Myddleton family. This was to be her last Christmas at the Castle.

Of course, as she is quick to point out, she had no expectation then that my father would inherit a splendid house of his own. All she can tell me is that the misery of leaving Chirk allowed her to understand, at once, the intensity of his feeling. This was a bond, and a strong one.

The proposal was made, accepted, and announced to the family within hours of the young couple's arrival at the castle. (The letters and diaries are annoyingly reticent, stating only that George made an offer and was accepted.) My grandfather, descending from his turret, gave a cautious nod. He could rely on Margot, who was arriving from London the following day, to establish how they should react.

'She [Margot] seemed *quite* pleased,' my father noted hopefully in his diary; in fact, Margot was not pleased at all. Aching from his introduction to riding, and sleepless from a night of embraces on the drawing room sofa ('nothing more,' my mother says sharply), George had been briskly ordered to account for himself, his income and his prospects. It was delightful to see him so aglow with love, Margot remarked acidly, but how, at the modest age of twenty-two, did he plan to support their daughter? My father had no immediate answer; prudently, he kept Thrumpton out of the picture at this stage. He described his bank work; Margot's expression chilled. Rosemary was extremely delicate and sensitive, she informed him; a nervous breakdown had weakened her stamina; with no experience of handling her own finances, she needed a husband who would shoulder responsibilities, cherish and protect her. Was George Seymour, a mere bank clerk, that man?

Margot's scepticism acted as a spur to my father's love. 'Precious Rosebud, I will love you and take care of you as long as we live, *forever,*' he wrote before he left. En route to join his parents for a quiet family Christmas in Norfolk, he found time to dispatch two telegrams and

To dearest George,
with love from
Rosebud
1945.

An exchange of photographs: Rosemary to George . . .

. . . and George to Rosemary. My father was proud of his elegant hands, and liked them to be admired.

three long letters to his fiancée. They had been apart for just two days.

My mother's elusiveness had given her the lead in the relationship during the first two months; now, my father began to establish control. He did so by one of his most effective techniques: the letter. My mother had always enjoyed writing spontaneously: she was not used to writing to order, or to a required length. 'There! I've written *five* pages!' she told her fiancé with evident pride; the following day, she was reproached for such clear evidence of her indifference. Love, for my father, was judged by the volume of words in which it was expressed. Two pages of heartfelt passion were worth less than four of modest intensity. To let a day pass without writing was proof of a cold heart.

Keeping pace with my father's own almost relentless flow of letters was hard work; my mother remained saucy and unsubdued. 'I still adore you,' she wrote a week after their engagement, and added that her cat did not feel the same way. When George sent her, unsolicited, a large and solemn studio photograph of himself, she told him that she had given it to her maid, who thought he looked sweet. ('There's another conquest you've made, you Casanova!') This could be dismissed as girlish teasing; my father was more seriously alarmed by a letter that announced the arrival of a new country neighbour ('26, with a vast house, servants galore and lots of farms'). Her mother, Rosemary added, thought him quite perfect. She did not say for what purpose, but it wasn't hard for an anxious lover to guess. George was already conscious of his fiancée's passion for farming and her attachment to Wales.

'Who was it?' I ask, inquisitive. 'You don't mention his name.'

'Can't remember,' she says, a touch too briskly. She couldn't – could she – have made him up? I can't guess. The more of this story I write, the more I realise how little I know about the sharp-witted, strong-willed old woman who has been my chief companion for the past two years.

12

NEARER, MY HOUSE, TO THEE

Retrospectively, it seems as though fate was on my father's side. At the time, however, he was disagreeably conscious of having come up against a character as forceful as his own. Rosemary could be managed; her mother was another matter.

Margot had been frank with him at their first interview. She did not regard a junior bank clerk, however glorious his family connections, as a suitable consort for her daughter. Rosemary's heart was set on farming; it followed that George, too, must look in that direction.

Margot spoke with her husband; the result was the offer of a shared tenancy of one of his finest Welsh properties, Croes Newydd. Rosemary had already been encouraging George to think of himself as a man of the land ('my great big, strong, tough farmer to be'). Now, she urged him to consider the charms of Croes Newydd and the pleasure they would have in running a farm together. Her mother, meanwhile, made it clear that if he did not apply himself to farming, their consent to the engagement might be withdrawn. (She had already insisted that it should remain secret for three months.)

On 13 February 1946, five days after his twenty-third birthday, my father took the plunge. Resigning from his job at the Fakenham branch of Barclays, he ended, for good, his days as a paid employee. With no future prospects, he was terrified.

'Promise you will never leave me,' he wrote anxiously that night to Rosemary.

'Woman is said to be fickle, but I am *not*!' she reassured him. This was comforting, but he was disturbed to note, a little further on in her letter, that 'darling Mummy' had been demanding an answer about the offer of a Welsh farming partnership. Rosemary was unsure about spending her first married years in a house which was not her own. 'I don't fancy the idea of sharing,' she admitted. Neither did George, but he was in no position to turn down the offer of a free home and a source of income. At that precise moment, he had neither.

This was the week in which a promising letter arrived from Thrumpton: his uncle had formed a new plan that might, conceivably, be of interest to his nephew. If George could spare the time from gadding around nightclubs and meeting members of Rosemary's illustrious family – Charlie's Byron's notes were always spiked with malice – perhaps he would care to pay a visit.

He went at once, and was received with warmth. 'We had a most excellent dinner,' he noted (my father loved his food), 'bonne femme soup, roast pheasant, vanilla ice bombe with hot chocolate sauce, and cherries in brandy!' Champagne was produced, and toasts drunk to the happy couple, before the new offer was made. Smiling benignly, Charlie Byron announced that he had thought things through. While conscious of the claims of his own distant relations on the House, he felt that it was only right that George, with his great love of the place, should enjoy it, in due course, as a life tenant. Later, George must understand, the House would have to revert to the Byrons. For the present, since George was unemployed, perhaps he and Rosemary would consider running the Home Farm at Thrumpton – and acting as companions to a fond old couple. He wanted, did he not, to be a farmer? He wanted to live at Thrumpton?

Charlie, in other words, had finally recognised the convenience of having a dependable, affectionate nephew around to work for the estate and act, if necessary, as general supervisor. No Byron cousin was likely to show him the same devoted care. My father accepted the proposal at once. Nothing, he told his uncle, would please him more.

Breakfast the following morning was taken after prayers. Charlie Byron, encased in what had once been a dashingly fashionable teddy-bear coat, retired to meditate on the Sunday sermon in the lavatory. Anna clasped her nephew's hand and led him down the drive. Her pride was evident and glowing; halfway to the village, she stopped to boast that she had been the mastermind behind the scheme for George's happiness. Proudly, she pointed between the trees to the home she had singled out for him.

Her satisfaction was well-founded. I, like my parents, have only happy memories of the house where, a few years later, I was born. A friendly, unpretentious building with ample gables, an eighteenth-century barn and a spacious garden, Thrumpton Lodge was where I would have liked to grow up, had I been given the chance. For my father, it was ideal; only a low brick wall separated him from the House he now looked forward to inhabiting, when the time came; in the meantime, he could enjoy all the beauty of Thrumpton's benevolent atmosphere, introduce Rosemary to his favourite walks through familiar scenery, and have the added pleasure of feeling that he was doing the old couple a favour in lifting some of the burdens of ownership from their shoulders.

There was only one problem, and Anna was confident that he

would solve it. The present tenants of Thrumpton Lodge were family friends who had no plans to leave; Charlie had already made it clear that he was not prepared to serve notice on them. What, then, was to be done? Aunt Anna tapped George's arm with a gloved finger. He could be such a persuasive boy when he set his mind to it, she said archly; this was the time to show off his negotiating skills.

I have no records to show what form of emotional blackmail was deployed on the tenants whom my father visited at the London flat before the day was out; I do know how impossible it was to resist his will, when he set his mind on an objective. Perhaps he simply wore them down; perhaps they were charmed at the prospect of helping a young and homeless couple. All I can discover is that his ends were obtained. They ended by agreeing to cut their tenancy short; their house would be his by late autumn.

'A triumph!' he wrote to Rosemary from London late that night. 'A complete triumph!'

It's hard to disagree. Nevertheless, the shock to my mother when she paid her first visit to Thrumpton two weeks later was considerable. Nothing in George's lyrical descriptions had led her to expect the House's air of wan neglect (she still shudders at the memory of pea-green painted walls, dusty piles of prayerbooks, moss-grown drives, broken windowpanes, and rats). This was not what she had grown used to at Chirk, or what she had anticipated for her married future.

'But you can't just say that!' my mother says anxiously. 'Of course it was run down, but that doesn't mean it wasn't beautiful. You ought to say how thrilled I was when your father took me for my first walk on the hill, and we could see the House below us. You must say something! Not just that I thought it was shabby.'

This was the moment at which my mother's fondness for the solemn, old-fashioned man she had chosen to marry deepened into love. Enthusiastically, she began to lay plans for a herd of Ayrshire cows, to ponder where they would keep horses, and what sort of hens would make the best breeders. The flirtatious tone of her earlier letters gave way to real tenderness. Together, she told George, they would make a splendid team. 'It will be such fun! Such fun together, won't it darling.'

'I meant it, you know,' my mother says, blinking her eyes and hunting for a tissue. 'It was so touching. I'd never met anybody who loved a place so much. I never have. Well – you know how he was.'

We both know how he was. I'm glad to look into his diary and find this insecure and unfulfilled young man – he was just twenty-three and looked less in his round schoolboy spectacles – declaring that he had found happiness at last, with the prospect of bringing together the two things he most adored. 'I must be the luckiest man in the world,' he wrote.

Love, however overwhelming, placed no curb on my father's snobbery. It gave him a sense of singular joy on 4 March 1946 ('the very great day') to see that the official announcement of their engagement took top place in *The Times* gazette, 'at the head of the column!' It tormented him that the announcement came too late for his name to be added to my mother's invitation to a ball at Buckingham Palace. My father became as avid as Mr Pooter, one of his favourite fictional characters, for details of this elegant occasion. (It horrified him that my mother did not make a special visit to the hairdresser or even have a manicure.) To whom had she sat next at dinner, he wanted to know? What kind of china and glasses had been used? And what had the young princesses worn? But my mother, who took little interest in such details, could only remember that the food had been tepid. He was comforted a few weeks later when the two of them shared a dinner table with Princess Elizabeth – among twenty others – for a dance. George seized the opportunity to take a good look at his royal neighbour.

She was pretty, he conceded, but not a patch on his Rosebud, '*by far* the loveliest woman in the room.'

Love coloured everything. He had, until now, shown no taste for classical music; now, when he visited his parents for an occasional weekend, they were amazed to hear Liszt and Bartók crackling down the staircase from the portable player in their son's room. The very mention of ballet, in later life, was enough to curl his lip; three weeks before his wedding, seated in the stalls of Covent Garden for a performance of *Sleeping Beauty*, George was in a state of entranced joy. 'It was *heaven*: the music, the dancing, the decor all lovely – and my adored Rosebud sitting beside me looking like a dream.' He wanted the world to share his awareness of her beauty; if not the world, his entire family. Thrilled by the chance to show his prize off to his grandest relations, he paid twenty pounds for tickets to a charity ball at Euston Hall and fancied they might be asked to stay the night. No invitation came, although my parents were the last to leave.

The visit to Euston spurred him to enliven their long journey home with reminders of his royal connections. Rosemary's family were fine, to be sure, but who could cap the glory of claiming Charles II for an ancestor? (A considerable number, if we are to be honest, after a span of seven generations; to my father, however, the cherished connection had grown close enough for him to thank goodness, for Rosemary's sake, that he had not inherited the king's lax morals.)

My father was in ecstasy; his fiancée was in a state of nervous exhaustion. 'Those endless visits to relations!' she groans. 'Aunt this and cousin that – it never stopped. I never knew a man with so many cousins. And all the worry about how I dressed: I'm sure the FitzRoys couldn't have cared less which hat I wore to church.'

'It was the way he showed his pride. Come on, Ma, you know he was wild about you. And your family: what did they make of him?'

'They thought he was all right.' She fidgets. 'He hadn't read much. At Chirk, we were always talking about books and music and things. George didn't have a lot to say, except about family history.' She pauses to think, anxious not to sound too harsh. 'I mean, there was Thrumpton, and the wedding plans, and his new car – such a wretched thing. An Alvis.'

I know about this. 'You made him buy it. You certainly paid for it. It's always described as yours.'

She looks baffled. 'But I didn't drive.'

'Then you bought it for him. It's not a crime to have been generous.'

'Horrid car,' she says with feeling. 'It never stopped breaking down and you know how useless your father was at mechanical things. That's why he found it so useful later to—'

Breaking off, she gives me a sideways look. 'You know. Have a friend.'

The difficulty about holding these conversations with my mother is that I never know which way she'll want them to go. It's apparent that she's in the mood today to discuss the years in which we lost him. I'm not.

'I'm longing to know more about the honeymoon,' I say.

'I'm sure you are.' Her tone is drily discouraging.

'I didn't expect to find you going off to a film on the first night of your marriage. Do you remember? You were staying at the Savoy as a present from your parents. That must have been fun: I'd love to stay there.'

Babble babble. I'm prattling while I bait my trap, hoping she'll fall into a web of compliments and tell me: why. Why did my parents go to a silly costume drama (the young Gene Tierney and Vincent Price in *Dragonwyck*) when they could have been behind doors and locked in each other's arms, bruising their lips with newly legitimised kisses? Standing above her in the half-light of the curtained library, I stare down, willing her to read my thoughts.

Her fingers are plaited together and she's looking at them intently, circling her thumbs around each other. There's earth under her nails and the cheerful red varnish has chipped away from the rims. Her hands have looked this way for as long as I can remember.

'Shall I open some wine? We could have a glass before supper.'

'I don't want any,' she says in a low voice, then glances up at me. 'I haven't objected to your writing this book. I haven't tried to stop you, have I?'

'Not yet!'

She doesn't smile. 'You don't have to put in everything. I've read your biographies. You didn't say what Henry James did in bed, or Mary Shelley.'

'They weren't around to tell me, but you . . .' Eagerly, I rattle off a quote from one of her own letters, forgetting that this is a sure way to antagonise an interviewee, let alone a mother. 'You called him "my clever, mathematical, neat, precise and altogether perfect person", and that was just two weeks before the honeymoon! It's not passionate. You must admit that.'

'Letters don't tell you everything.' Her voice is still so low that I have to bend to hear her. 'All that side of things was lovely. It always was. Can't you just leave it at that?'

No, I can't, I want to shout. I need to know. Lovely, in what way? Lovely, because of what? But she's slipped away from me, back behind the door she keeps closed on anything unpleasant. I'm my father's daughter in my volatility and imperiousness; each time we talk, I see more clearly that she is hers in the way that she protects herself from intruders and their judgments.

Staring down in thwarted silence at her bent head, I remember the time I first made love and how, full of glee and complacency on a summer day, I tracked my mother through the garden shrubberies to boast about it. Nothing much had happened – the affair was over in less than a month – but I glowed with foolish pride that afternoon. My body was hot with remembered pleasure;

my mind shimmered with the memory of tangled limbs, smothering kisses. Kept down for so long in a state of lowered confidence, I had my parents beat at last. I'd discovered things they could never have dreamed about. I told it all in triumph as she stood there, looking smaller than myself, trowel in hand. The words came rushing from my mouth as I searched my mother's face for – what? Wonder, I suppose, wonder and envy.

What I did not anticipate was the outstretched hand, the gleam of sudden secret pleasure in her eyes. And wasn't it marvellous, she said, when—

Horrified, I cut her off and backed away. I wanted her to be abashed by my revelations. I wanted none from her, a middle-aged woman, an untouchable in the hard eyes of youth. I didn't see, as I do now, the generosity and warmth of her response.

And now, when I want so badly to uncover her sexual feelings, there's no way to get at them. The door has been tight shut. It was lovely. It was always lovely.

I'll have to continue my interrogation another day.

They were married at St Margaret's Westminster in June 1946 ('509 guests!' my father noted, rejoicing at the lavish number of wedding cheques he had received). Since foreign travel was still prohibited, their prolonged honeymoon was taken in Britain. In Wales, they spent a fortnight at one of Tommy Howard de Walden's properties, a seventeenth-century house called Plas Llannina. The summer was a scorching one, too hot for excursions until the end of the day, when they strolled along the beach towards New Quay, past the spot where my mother remembered having seen Augustus John stretched out on the stony shore like a beached whale after emptying a decanter of whisky with her father, his host. Coming back, they peered into the semi-derelict applestore where Dylan Thomas lived while he began to dream up the story of Milk Wood. With the oil lamps lit, they sat reading each other chapters from old-fashioned novels about fox-hunting—

'Seriously?'

'Why? Any objections? You haven't become one of those activists, have you?' my mother inquires with sudden suspicion.

'It sounds so unlikely.'

'Not at all.' My mother is her jaunty self again this morning. 'It just goes to show how little you really know about your parents.'

Snugly tucked up in a big double bed, with the oak door shut against the creaks and whispers of a house more haunted than any other my mother can remember, they opened the window to gaze at a full moon above the sea and to listen for the bells that, so the stories went, rang up from Llannina's submerged church to warn of coming storms.

'And don't forget Valentia.' She sighs. 'Such views: I've always meant to go back there.'

My father's diary tells me less about the little rainswept island lying to the west of County Kerry than can be gleaned from a couple of internet sites; one entry does record that my parents spent time 'very pleasantly' in their hotel room. Does 'pleasantly' hint at unmentioned pleasures? I can't tell and my mother can't – or won't – remember. It's easier to pick up the note of outrage in his account of a visit to the skeletal ruins of a Kerry mansion, burnt out by a careless smoker on a wild weekend in the twenties. My father was too upset to eat his supper that night. Emotion, as he unfailingly reminded us in later years, went straight to his stomach, proof of his exceptional sensitivity.

Hints of troubles to come surfaced in August, when my parents were in Norfolk with George's parents, enjoying the last sleepy days of a glorious summer. ('They seem so entirely happy,' his mother noted, adding that she was glad Rosemary seemed to be a fit and energetic young woman. George's health must be carefully watched,

My parents needed identity cards for their honeymoon off the coast of Ireland in 1946.

Vita warned her daughter-in-law. This project of farming was all very well, but poor George was too delicate to undertake more than the lightest tasks. Advising and overseeing were his real strengths.)

A letter from Charlie Byron cast a sudden chill upon the pleasant experience of admiring a last magnificent clutch of wedding presents. (My father had been shameless in advertising his need for furniture and paintings of a kind appropriate to his future home.) Capricious until the end of his days, Charlie was reviewing his plans once again and wondering if he had been too generous to his nephew, too hard on his Byron cousins. Perhaps, he wrote now, George imagined that the Home Farm and the Lodge were being given to him for nothing? He had better take note, now and for the future: no special privileges were being offered. He would be expected to come to financial terms with the land agents – 'and ME!' the old man wrote in shaking capital letters, forgetting that the proposal for George to run the estate farm had come from himself.

Vita was alarmed by the letter – perhaps Charlie was planning to leave his home to those Byron cousins, after all? My father was irritated, but not unduly worried. Charlie had changed his mind before and would doubtless do so again; at the end of the day, the only surviving Byron claimant was a Catholic and Charlie Byron would not even let a Catholic through his door. True, my father would have preferred to hear he was going to inherit the House outright, but a life tenancy still secured his future. Charlie, he told his mother, was just playing games.

Overall, as my father settled into his new life as a young farmer with a pretty little manor house in the village he adored, his situation was enviable. Rosemary's relaxed attitude to money was due to her possession of a substantial amount of it, to be shared with him; her parents were both fond and lavish. They had helped to find a young Scot who was willing to oversee the Home Farm; three girls from Chirk village were persuaded to come and form a domestic household at Thrumpton Lodge. Anna scurried around to find them a chauffeur, a dairyman and a day-labourer. The final feather in my father's cap was the news that Margot Howard de Walden's personal maid wanted to return to her Nottinghamshire roots. Word arrived that she had settled in a nearby village, on hand to sew, press clothes and pack cases. The level of elegance at Thrumpton Lodge was now, as George joyously noted, almost ducal.

At twenty-three, then, my parents were fitted out for a life of unusual comfort. When my mother, misty-eyed, talks of her farming years, I want to know how many farmers' wives had a chauffeur-driven Daimler in 1947; unkindly, I comment that she reminds me of Marie Antoinette tending vegetables behind the Petit Trianon.

They kept no diaries during the four years they lived at The Lodge; my mother remembers these as the happiest of her married life, marred only by a requirement to dine with the old Byrons at least twice a week. This, as George's uncle began to slip into senility and Anna grew correspondingly fretful, was not a cheerful experience.

My mother believes her memories. She remembers creating a pretty garden at the Lodge ('I put in those borders!') and a cheerful home. ('All the family loved coming there. The Lodge was such a cosy place.') The meagre documentation that has survived shows this to have been a period of dismay, confusion and enforced economy. Can both be true?

The main agent of change was the unexpected death of Tommy Howard de Walden within months of his youngest daughter's marriage. That June, Rosemary noted how ebullient her father seemed, as if he had already managed to put the memory of Chirk behind him. In September, she worried that he was looking tired. In October, he was taken into the London Clinic for an operation. On 5 November, a date she has ever since associated with misfortune, her father died. He was sixty-six. The given cause was jaundice.

George Seymour had married a young woman whose income greatly exceeded his own. In the late autumn of 1946, at the beginning of the coldest winter in living memory, when snow buried the hedges from view and the roads around Thrumpton were blocked off as impassable, bad news came in. Tommy Howard de Walden had never liked lawyers; convinced that they were out to rob him, he had put off the unpleasant business of dealing with them. As a result, scant provision had been made for his five daughters. My mother and her older sisters were no longer heiresses; instead, to his dismay, my father found himself married to a young woman whose means were almost as modest as his own.

'I will take care of you *forever*,' George had promised Rosemary at the beginning of the year. He had not imagined that this would involve economic support. Eleven months later, preparing to celebrate a family Christmas at Thrumpton Lodge to which he had proudly invited his parents, his married siblings and their children, my father had to beg for a delay in paying the fuel bills. His plans to buy three young pigs for the Home Farm were cancelled.

I have said that I would not want to be in a wartime trench with my father; I'm proud to see how well he performed in less dangerous circumstances. The Christmas plans went smoothly forward; Vita praised her son's generosity as a host and scolded him for buying such lavish presents: a pair of crystal vases for herself and a really beautiful cocktail frock, off the peg, that might have been made just for Rosemary. Vita had no idea that her son had paid for these Christmas gifts, and the traditional turkey, by cancelling his order for a new suit – his own was threadbare – and recalling the deposit.

'I'm a fool about money,' my mother had blithely announced in one of her early letters; my father now began to discover that she was, indeed, an innocent. Arithmetic had never been her strength;

she understood only that her bank statements must always show her account to be in credit. Asked by her husband to perform some simple feat of addition, Rosemary gladly offered a prompt answer. Unfortunately, she had halved the sum instead of doubling it.

George could not, it was plain, rely on his wife for the keeping of ledgers and cash books, by which he hoped to control their rapidly shrinking funds. All accounts, bank details and household reckonings would, from this time on, lie in his province.

I was scornful when I first encountered the Telephone Ledger. Begun a month after my grandfather's death, the ledger-book was maintained, with only one break, until a few years short of my father's death. I looked at it, initially, as a potential hiding place for awkward secrets. 'Black Boy' sounded promising; so did three entries for 'artificial insemination'.

Closer inspection showed that the ledger had no shocks to offer. The Black Boy was the name of a pleasantly old-fashioned hotel in the centre of Nottingham; the entries on artificial insemination referred, not to procreational difficulties between my parents, but to the herd of Ayrshire cows they had purchased, at £70 a head, during the first ambitious weeks of taking on the farm.

The entries told me little that I did not expect; there was no surprise in finding that each call to a person of illustrious birth was fully recorded, with titles, while those of less genealogical interest were briskly noted by their surnames. The unexpected aspect was that the entries had been maintained, with a note of the length of time spent and subsequent cost of every call, over a period of fifty years. The ledger brought into question the haste with which I had dismissed my father's service to Barclays Bank (such meticulousness, such dedication, could not have gone unremarked). The ledger showed me that, despite the capriciousness with which my mother had once held him in thrall, my father now controlled the marriage.

★

My father's entire life had been driven by his passion for Charlie Byron's home. I wonder what was in his mind in 1948, when he made a visit to another Byron landmark in the neighbourhood. Newstead Abbey was where his uncle's celebrated ancestor had spent his youth; since then, it had become a desolate ruin. Was my father thinking about Thrumpton as he peered through the Abbey's grimy windows at dusty wooden floors, peeling wallpaper, sheeted furniture? Was he wondering, for the first time in a lifetime of obsessive love, if a neglected, inconvenient old house, in which his children would never have the right to live, was worth the wait?

My father's feelings were about to be severely tested. The following year, in a glorious June, Charlie Byron died. It was not, at this point, apparent just how little he had done to safeguard his family property.

13

❧

THE FULFILMENT OF A DREAM

My father had been anticipating only a lifetime's tenancy of the House he worshipped; outright possession was the unlooked-for gift magnificently extended by a devoted aunt. Anna took frank delight in the naïve expectation that she was free to dispose of her late husband's home as she wished – and to exclude his surviving relatives from any part of the House's future.

In the autumn of 1949, Anna went to a meeting with the family lawyer and two trustees appointed by her husband to act for the interests of the estate. Gently invited to explain how Lord Byron had dealt with his correspondence, she grew flustered. Charlie was always prompt in answering handwritten letters; it was the other kind he didn't like. And how, the principal lawyer asked, did Lord Byron respond to this other kind? Had he answered these letters later? Anna shook her head. Had he answered them at all?

The answer was reluctantly given. She had noticed that all official-looking letters lay on his desk for a certain time, unopened, after which they disappeared. Did she know where to? Anna was growing impatient: after all, there were so many places! Good heavens: drawers, boxes, the backs of cupboards. When space ran short, she added helpfully, Charlie often stored tiresome-looking letters behind the House's heavy cast-iron radiators. Should she start a search?

The lawyer shot a discreet glance at the trustees and shook his head. This was when Anna learned that Charlie had unwittingly thrown away eight years' worth of dividends. A search would be a waste of time; their present value was nil.

Worse was to come. Charlie Byron, an inveterate procrastinator, had failed to act in the best interest of the House's future. The tax bills raised by his death were enormous; they could only be met by a sale of the Estate, the House, and its contents. Anna must not be too alarmed, the lawyer reassured her. She would not be homeless. Lord Byron's principal home in Essex had recently been demolished after a fire, but a smaller house on the same estate was available for her use – if she remained a widow. Dazed, Anna listened to the one condition over which Charlie had taken real care: all of her future benefits were to be cancelled if she remarried.

George's affection for his aunt was sincere; his first instinct was to comfort her. But what reassurance could he offer?

Little correspondence survives from the period following Anna's dismaying interview. All I know is that the University of Nottingham put forward an offer to buy the House as an investment, and that my father persuaded the trustees to reject it.

'And then?'

My mother shoots a wistful glance at a pile of creased cloths stacked on the ironing board. 'It's almost eleven,' she says. 'I wanted to go shopping this afternoon.'

'I'll take you. What happened after the University backed out? I've nothing to do until lunchtime but listen.'

She sighs. 'But you know all this. George must have talked

about it. The trustees knew how much your father adored the House, and that he'd been told he was going to have it. They made us an offer: fifty thousand pounds and a year to find the money. If not, the House and the estate went up for auction with the contents.'

'But you didn't have anything like that sum of money.'

'Of course we didn't. We had to borrow.'

I'm trying to picture it. Fifty thousand pounds, in 1949? Fifty thousand pounds, for an underheated, underlit, decrepit mansion which, following the auction of contents to pay the Inland Revenue, would be empty of all but a small clutch of Byron heirlooms preserved for his relatives by the old man's will? Why not sit tight at Thrumpton Lodge and wait for a friendly and more prosperous buyer for the Hall who would be delighted, surely, to have them as tenants and neighbours?

'Weren't you terrified? How did you think you were going to pay such a sum back?'

'Oh, I know!' she says. 'But think of owning the House, of its really being ours, not just somebody else's home!' (She's thinking, transparently, of the Welsh castle her family had loved, not owned.) 'It was something we were going to enjoy doing together,' she explains. 'A real adventure!'

It's rare to look into the face of a woman in her eighties and see the girl she once was smiling back at you. This, as I know, was the first great test of their marriage; I expected an admission that she felt coerced, trapped by my father's obsessive love for the House. But what I see across the ironing-board is what I glimpsed when she was describing her first visit. Today, the same eagerness brightens her eyes and spreads a flush of pink across her cheeks. She loved the House as much as he did; she was with him all the way.

As an addict to the House's charms myself, I can understand a commitment of passion. Feebler justifications follow, about how people in the village would have felt betrayed if Charlie Byron's nephew had turned his back on them. I'm not convinced; another family might have done just as well by the House, employed the same people, grown to feel the same protective love for the estate. But my mother is persistent; she reminds me of the fate that overtook Clifton Hall, the nearest large house to Thrumpton. Clifton's land, conveniently close to the boundaries of Nottingham, had been requisitioned by the state during the war, and then retained for residential development; Clifton's owners, by 1949, were already planning to sell up and leave. They were not alone: fine old family houses were being abandoned at an unprecedented rate during the late 1940s; some of the most glorious had been uninhabited since the war. Nobody, in 1949, would want to take on a derelict mansion, or so argued my father, seeing himself as a knight riding to the rescue. Nobody would care to save the House he loved. Except himself.

This was not, of course, entirely true; the National Trust, formed in 1894 to save areas of outstanding beauty, had enlarged its scope during the 1930s, in order to acquire and protect significant houses at a time when many of them were being demolished. Since 1942, when the Trust consisted of four dedicated amateurs, a typist and her fifteen-year-old assistant, James Lees-Milne had been visiting embattled owners in the Trust's old Austin car, or on his motor-bike. In cases where the house seemed worth it, and where there was an endowment in land, money or chattels to be offered for its future maintenance, he and his colleagues would negotiate an arrangement.

The Trust's achievements were impressive. Nevertheless, an overseeing body with a duty to justify its work by making these houses more accessible to visitors, was at odds with my father's mission; in this case, I'm on his side. The Trust, increasingly, has come to view its properties with the eyes of a Victorian school-master. All furniture and paintings must be in keeping with the date of the House; all works of art must be fiercely preserved, even if it means keeping them bathed in perpetual gloom; all owners, once they have ceased to contribute to the maintenance, must accept that the Trust knows best. If the Trust decides that Kedleston in Derbyshire is better off without the fountain that Lord Curzon put there himself, Lord Curzon's descendant has no option but to agree with them.

Lord Curzon's descendant was not pleased when the fountain was taken away because it was not chronologically appropriate to the building; my father, in later years, used this example to explain his own dislike of the Trust. Had he known it, Lees-Milne was on his side. He, like my father, saw the old squirearchy as the ideal system of management: benevolent, eccentric and enlivening. But what Lees-Milne recognised, as my father did not, was that the days of feudal patronage were numbered.

My parents, having decided to see their venture through, were fortunate. They found a relative of my mother's who was prepared to help raise the required sum from a group of bankers. The sting in the tail came in the terms: ten per cent interest and full repayment in less than a year. Ruthless steps had to be taken to meet such conditions: two-thirds of the land belonging to the Thrumpton estate was sold, together with the main farms and all but a handful of the tenanted properties. A shrewd investor, eyeing the line of Nottingham's expansion, would have kept the flat farmland that offered the greatest potential for future development; my father, predictably, relinquished this outlying and least pretty part of the property in order to preserve the small heartland of cottages and houses that clustered nearest to the House, safeguarding its beauty, but adding little to its income.

Cutting costs now became the central issue. The Daimler was exchanged for a more modest Humber; there were no more impulsive trips to London, no evenings at the Mirabelle and no lunches at Prunier, unless by invitation. When it came to the business of shifting a houseful of possessions into his new home, my father decided to save money and do the work himself. This, as he noted dolefully at the end of the year, was a miscalculation: after a month of heaving furniture on to trailers and pushing wheelbarrows of books along half a mile of pitted driveway, his back had been permanently weakened, while his wife was sporting sprained wrists and a twisted ankle.

Anna, significantly, sent no assistance from the House. The move took place in May. The hedges were foaming with blossom; the river was alive with ducks and coots; the neglected garden was a jungle of colour. Thrumpton had been her home for almost thirty years. At the point of departure, she looked back on all she had done: the laying-out of flower borders, the copying of ancient documents, the endless sorting of letters, maps, diaries, indentures and contracts, reaching back in time to the House's earliest beginnings. This was how she had occupied her time; this, her husband had always told her, was a wife's work.

Perhaps she felt anger against him for having contrived that she should only be allowed a home on his Essex estate if she remained a widow. Perhaps she felt resentment at the newcomers, usurpers of her territory. Perhaps she had entertained hopes of staying on at the House, as my parents' cherished guest. Perhaps . . . Who knows? For whatever reason, Anna Byron made a bonfire and burnt, on a sunny afternoon, as many historic documents as she could find. It took about three hours for her to destroy almost every trace of the House's former owners and their work; it took her rather longer to dig up every shrub, bush and herb that she had planted, ready for transportation to her new home in Essex. My parents arrived to take tea with her that day and found the flowerbeds stripped, the archives reduced to ash and cinders. Anna didn't, my mother remembers, look in the least ashamed; her expression was one of nervous defiance.

(This is the accepted version; I've also heard that Anna tipped all the papers, disordered, into the cellars of the House; that my parents, unable to cope with a sea of uncatalogued documents, gave up in despair and threw them out themselves. There's no way of knowing which way the House lost its history; all that can be said is that it's gone.)

One of the few documents to have survived from this period is a bound catalogue of the four-day auction ordered by the trustees and held in November 1950. I read it as another testimonial to my father's passionate wish to keep the House as he had always known it. In the margin, with a red pencil, he marked the lots most closely connected to its history. The presence of a number of dealers pushed up the prices; he retrieved only a third of what he had hoped to save. The hardest task, my mother says, was trying to rescue the splendid library assembled by Lucy Byron's uncle especially for the House. Porters had swept the leatherbound books from the shelves and bundled them on to trestle tables under a canvas awning, poor protection on a day of driving rain; jumbled together, they were sold in casually arranged lots. The result is that the House now boasts enough one-volume gothic novels (from sets of three) to fill a couple of sentry-boxes.

'What about help? Did you have any when you moved in?'

'Not enough.' My mother sighs. 'Life before the washing machine! I never seemed to stop washing or dusting. Let's see: your father found a rather frightening woman who came with a rabid Alsatian. She told your father and I that we could do the work ourselves. So she didn't last. And then there was a most peculiar cook who tried to stab me with a carving knife.'

But when, perplexed, I ask the reason (my mother is good-natured and singularly undemanding), she can't remember. Neither does she appear to hold a grudge for the assault. 'They were a funny lot, the people who came and went in those years,' she says dreamily. 'I wonder you don't write about them instead.'

My father planned to do so; his comments tell me more about him than about the person he describes. 'Mrs Easom's cat shot.

Departure of Easoms.' Omitted is the fact that my father, annoyed by the cat's prowling ways, shot it himself, claiming to have mistaken it for a rabbit. 'Mrs Zauner, temporary cook, stuck in tub.' This is shorthand for a farcical incident that ended with a visit from the fire brigade to extricate Mrs Zauner, a large woman whose love of Hitler earned her a rapid dismissal, from one of the House's narrow, old-fashioned bathtubs. The list, a long one, is confined to employees who flitted across his path, and fled, or were despatched; the bedrock, slowly assembled, was a small and loyal workforce who never told tales out of school and never questioned my father's capricious ways. They receive no mention. Were they less eccentric, and thus less easily characterised, or was it the case that long connection turned them into extensions of himself, no longer identifiable as individuals?

I'm trying to imagine those first years of occupation: the carved staircase draped in dustsheets, stone passages inadequately carpeted by cracked brown linoleum, plaster swelling and peeling from the pale pea-green walls, the biting cold of winter winds stabbing through cracked panes of glass so frail – a few remain to cause a shuddering chill – that they shiver at a touch. I look at the book in which, always meticulous, my father noted the lists of tourists to whom they opened the House, week after week, from 1952. I can easily see him, thin shoulders hunched against the cold, sitting in the doorway with a roll of tickets that still, fifty years later, looks almost untouched; I see my mother, wrapped in a heavy coat, conducting tours around rooms which, although efforts had been made to brighten them, can't have seemed to justify the twenty-four old pence that was asked for entry. The rewards were small; after the euphoria of receiving three hundred visitors on their first open day (the incoming revenue repaired three wooden shutters and gave the dining room a one-bar electric fire), numbers dwindled rapidly to twenty, ten and often, in bad weather, to none at all.

My parents ranked low among an heroic band of older sur-
vivors. James Lees-Milne, touring the countryside on behalf of the
National Trust, was welcomed into houses that had lost their roofs,
or had their windows blown out by bombs. Some of the ancient
owners were surviving with only a supply of water that had to be
fetched, by themselves, from an outside well. Several large houses
had no electricity whatsoever. Had Lees-Milne visited Thrumpton
at the time my parents took it on, he would have told them they
were lucky. This house had not suffered from wartime occupation;
although neglected and in poor repair, the foundations and roof were
secure.

Above all, the new owners were young. Many of the house-
owners visited by Lees-Milne were in their seventies and had lost
their heirs in the War. My parents were in their late twenties, filled
with energy, determination and hope. My father, although he lost
the knack in later years, proved clever enough at investing to build
up enough money by the mid-Fifties to pay for a nanny, a nursery-
maid, a cook, a chauffeur and a gardener. I admire what my parents
did; nevertheless, these, in the dour Fifties, were not straitened
circumstances.

The House was the grail my father had pursued throughout his life.
It came as a shock to find he held an empty cup. The glorious
aristocracy, about whom he knew so much, did not perceive the
new owner of Thrumpton Hall as one of themselves. He achieved,
with persistence, occasional triumphs, but a letter to the Duchess
of Devonshire, complimenting her on the excellent conversion of
Chatsworth's kitchen into a restaurant and inviting her to
luncheon, brought back only a well-phrased note of regret at the
fullness of her diary which, alas . . .

Such rebuffs were felt as wounds. The Duchess got off lightly;
other displays of indifference to his treasure and himself were stored
away for vengeance. One grand connection, having neglected

either to visit or to issue invitations, was punished when my father bid against him at an auction, deliberately driving up the price of a cherished family portrait that he had no intention of buying for himself. Asked by the irritated purchaser what the devil he'd thought he was playing at, my father giggled, twirled his umbrella and replied: 'Fun!'

My father's impish sense of humour (he was a good raconteur) earned him some reputation as a wit; the problem was that he had no sense of where the boundary lay between sport and malice. Jokes of the kind he practised on his relation in the auction room lost him more friends than he won by telling the stories.

From the point of view of social achievement, the capture of the grail was disappointing. In another respect, it brought liberation, although not of the kind that could have been easily predicted from George Seymour's earlier life.

From the date, almost, at which he acquired the House and its estate, a rift began to appear in his personality. On the one side, the more predictable one, he easily adopted the trappings, traditions and obligations of squireship. One of his first acts was to restore the Hall's Victorian habit of holding a Christmas party for the children of the village, complete with games, a handsome tea and carefully wrapped presents. He sat on committees, supported the county, and fought small wars on behalf of the village's preservation, with tireless zeal. As a proud patron of the living, with rights over the church, he subjected each new vicar to a searching interview. A little too conscious of the need to set an example to his own small flock of tenants, he never failed to attend the Sunday service, impeccably dressed, or to read the first lesson in a voice of sonorous certainty, whether condemning the profligate or blessing the pure in heart. Disdainful in his reception of newcomers to the village, he was tirelessly thoughtful of the needs of the older inhabitants, whose nostalgia for the past tallied with his own views. If my father had not been such an autocrat, he could easily have become a beloved paragon, a model of old-fashioned patronage.

Few can play Dr Jekyll's role without chafing at the traces of being constantly good-mannered and conscientious. Hyde is always there, biding his time for the moment of release. An imaginative mind might guess that the moment of Hyde's escape wasn't too far ahead from the family portrait which my father commissioned in the mid-Sixties.

In concept and setting, the picture is as conventional as the place in which it hangs, in the family library. (Tellingly, it faces the smiling portrait of Vita that my father had proudly commissioned when he was twenty-one.) This painting is set in the House's most formal room, an ornate saloon on the first floor. I sit at the piano, off to one side, tidily dressed in a white shirt and dark skirt. (My father, who disliked short hair, had decided that his eighteen-year-old daughter looked best in a shoulder-length wig.) My mother, implausibly dressed for an afternoon scene in a smart blue cocktail frock, also wears a wig, a replica of her best Greek helmet style. She sits bolt upright on a sofa, ankles crossed, hands folded, looking on with apparent interest at the scene that occupies the centre of the painting.

Here, two players confront each other across a backgammon board. (My mother's enthralled gaze convinces nobody who knows her; backgammon registers itself with her only as an irritating sound of clattering dice.) My brother, a fair-haired schoolboy, faces both the artist, and his opponent. He leans forward a little, intent upon the game, meditating his next move as he poises his hand above the counters.

In the family painting by John Lavery of my mother's family at Chirk, she had occupied the central place, all lines converging upon her. Here, the lines meet on the image of my father, the second player at the games board. The picture had been his idea, and was paid for by him. But – was it by choice? – his back is turned toward the viewer. All that can be remarked is the fall of the jacket from his shoulders, the slight stoop of his head over the board. He is at the centre, but the face of the dominant figure in this family portrait is entirely hidden from view.

Artists are often prescient. George Gissing, in his fictions, predicted the troubles that lay ahead in his own life; Millais, painting Lizzie Siddal as a drowned Ophelia, looked forward to the model's early death; Shelley, mourning his fellow poet Keats in *Adonais*, foretold his own watery end. Did the young artist who lived with us while he worked on our family tableau catch a glimpse of another, secret self, yet to emerge, and choose to hint at it with that resolutely cloaked view? Did he intuit that, as time unrolled, the hidden face would become a cipher, that the act of concealment would become the most significant feature of what seemed, at the time, to be a conventional representation of a country family, at ease in the interior of their home?

George FitzRoy Seymour enjoyed posing for this portrait of him as High Sheriff of Nottinghamshire, on his favourite staircase.

I don't know. Neither can I do more than guess what the same handsome young artist was thinking when my father, glorying in his new role – all jokes about Robin Hood were banned for that year – posed for him again a little later, as High Sheriff of Nottinghamshire, in full, magnificent regalia.

My father liked the portrait of old Lucy Byron, standing on her grand carved staircase, looking down on the viewer. The artist was invited to paint him in the same position. The clothes – black silk stockings, silver-buckled shoes, velvet suit and foaming lace jabot – both mock and honour their wearer's pose as the aristocratic owner of a stately home. My father had a redeeming sense of the absurdity of his pretentions. It's likely that this portrait was intended, in part, as a joke. What interests me more now is the strained expression upon his face.

These paintings were done in the late Sixties. By then, my father was struggling to unite two quite different forms of life: one as a conventional squire and family man; the other, as a fun-loving, risk-taking Jack the Lad. This second aspect of his complex nature was, at the time he became High Sheriff, still under wraps.

PART TWO

The House: Possession

1

⅌

I HATE AND I LOVE
(THE LISTS MY FATHER NEVER MADE)

Depressing Things

A time-consuming letter, replete with carefully composed items of news, is mailed to a former friend who (unaccountably) does not answer, thus gradually prompting the revelation (after three further epistles have been written and despatched) that the friend in question has been dead now for some number of years.
Oh, how depressing!

Discovering that the only place at which one's favourite variety of chocolates (violet creams!) could reliably be purchased will in future no longer be stocking them ('insufficient demand').
Oh, how depressing!

After encouraging guests to enjoy a hot bath before dinner, finding that one's own bath runs cold (this misfortune compounded by the impossibility of disclosing the fact).
Oh, how depressing!

Discovering, during a perfect summer's afternoon, that clouds of smoke from the newly constructed neighbouring power station have obscured the sun and cast the garden into deep and enduring shade.
Oh, how depressing!

Rare Things
A person of impeccable taste.

A well-fashioned pair of shoes that fits uncommonly narrow — aristocratic! — feet.

A woman of wit.

A young person who is not bored by the company of an older man who has come to possess youthful tastes. (*Alas!*)

Annoying Things
A postal clerk — the last collection having been made just before one reaches the post-office — adamantly refuses to have further letters added to the outgoing sack. (*Bureaucracy!*)

Guests who produce sheaves of holiday snapshots, and yet fail to admire the house in which they are fortunate enough to be staying.

At church services, the use of texts other than those derived from King James's Bible.

Women who refuse to allow men to sit together in the dining room after dinner. (*Barbaric!*)

Any detailed response to one's simple and courteous inquiry as to how a guest has slept.

Splendid Things

The lace collar of a young Prince, painted by Van Dyck.

A magnolia grandiflora that has just unfurled its petals.

A full-length coat of sable.

A loved, and impeccably maintained, old family house.

A Ducati, unthrottled. *(The Duke!)*

Disagreeable Things

A certain gentleman – who (in modesty) shall here remain nameless! – having gone to enormous trouble to restore his family monuments to positions of appropriate prominence within his local church, subsequently discovers that the congregation, instead of showing their gratitude, complain that their generous benefactor had not first secured their permission.

The faint odour, from beneath a woman's clothing, of unclean linen.

Nylon sheets . . . Morris dancers . . . Medieval music.

Conversations about Proust (or any other French writers).

Unpolished wine glasses upon a dining table.

Things Worth Seeing

Fred Astaire movies.

'Race of the Aces' at Snetterton!

Valmouth (the musical), with Fenella Fielding as Lady Parvula. (*Heaven!*)

Other people's carved staircases (for purposes of comparison to one's own superior version!)

Pleasing Things
A guest who appreciates the amount of work that must go into the maintaining of proper standards in hospitality.

A newspaper article (about oneself) or television appearance (by oneself) when remarked on and admired by persons of discerning judgment.

A trim woman, fully conscious that she looks well in her clothes, walking briskly along a Mayfair street to keep – one can only suppose! – an appointment most agreeable in nature.

A friend who, spending time in one's company, deigns never to consult his watch.

The least sign (from one's children) of any recognition (however slight!) of all that one does (and continues to do) entirely without complaint.

Embarrassing Things
A conscientious host, discovered while thoughtfully drawing the curtains in the bedroom of guests, who appears to them (quite without justice) to have been spying.

One's adolescent daughter, having put on weight, so that her clothes, once appealing, now appear unpleasantly tight.

One's wife, oblivious, on a public occasion, that her slip is showing, or that she possesses traces of lipstick stains upon her teeth.

Surprising and distressing things
A conversation with one's daughter which leads her on to criticisms of oneself, the precision of her analysis suggesting that she has been pondering these (supposed!) flaws for some time.

Upon the birth of one's first grandchild, discovering that it is impossible to feel pleasure at this sudden intimation of one's mortality.

Learning that one's children dislike one's most intimate friend.

Things That Have Relinquished Their Power to Charm
An enchanting house, from which its rightful occupant has been compelled to depart.

2

❧

FAMILY SNAPS

'Miranda is so completely happy up there,' my grandmother wrote to my father in 1952, the year my brother was born. Vita, while staying at the House, had visited the nursery – the same that had once served as my father's – on the top floor.

I don't remember this occasion. I do remember crying when I was taken away from a more comforting room, my home for the first year that we spent there, in the lower part of the House.

To a small child, the House was not welcoming. When I described my father's early days there, I was drawing on my own fear-laden memories. The Byrons, with no children of their own, had made no provisions for reassurance or comfort. The top floor of the House, when I arrived, was as it had been in the 1920s, a chilly, desolate region, shut off behind doors.

Later, after the birth of my brother, our parents tried to brighten the garret-like rooms and narrow passages. My bedroom walls were papered with garlands of roses; the nursery acquired a tall bookcase, an electric fire, a rocking chair and a big, old-fashioned doll's house with rooms large enough for a small child to hide in. To a visitor, climbing the stairs from below, the children's wing must have seemed cheerful enough.

A birthday note delivered from the top floor.

'We'd have kept you nearer if we could,' my mother says. 'But there wasn't any room, not with a nanny and nursemaid. And you were happy. Don't go pretending you weren't. You never stopped reading! Whenever I came upstairs, you were always sitting by the bookcase.' I ask her if she remembers the time – I can still see her turn and go crying down the stairs – when she asked if she might take me into the garden at some hour that had not been previously arranged. The nanny, even though she did not particularly like me, grasped my hand and squeezed it. ('Whose little girl are you?'

Squeeze. 'I'm Nanny's little girl. I want to stay with Nanny!')

'Nasty little thing,' my mother says. And she does, for a moment, after fifty odd years, still look distressed. 'Why would you ever say something like that?'

I've no idea. I only remember the pleasure it gave me to see that I could cause pain to a parent, somebody who seemed, at that thwarted age, so beyond my reach. 'I think', I say, 'I wanted to punish somebody. I was so scared.'

'Scared!' My mother puts on her sensible face, the face of a woman who has no truck with terrors. 'What nonsense you talk! What did you think was going to happen?'

'I didn't know. That was what frightened me so much. I never knew.'

Three terrors ruled life on the top floor: ghosts, fire and floods.

The ghosts, as I now know, were imaginary. Then, however, I had complete faith in my father's story of the pregnant housemaid who hanged herself from a skylight outside the little room in which he, a quarter of a century later, would sleep. My father had been subjected to this story himself; the room in which he had shuddered was now mine. (No record, other than the testimony offered by my father, suggests that a hanging actually took place.) Like my parent before me, I felt the ethereal housemaid's soft skirt brush the back of my neck each time I went down the four steps beneath the skylight; like him, I heard her weeping in the night, whenever the wind was up, and trembled.

I had other companions as well, of my own making. I believed in a sharp-faced, skinny-tailed devil who pressed his face to my window each night after the curtains were drawn, hoping that I might have forgotten to shout, before I jumped into bed and pulled the sheet up over my head: 'Get thee behind me, Satan!' I believed in witches who hid in the garlands of roses strewn across my newly papered bedroom wall. (Poor sight helped to foster this delusion.)

I believed in the power of the moon to strike me and lay me under a spell.

If, during the long night, I wanted to visit the lavatory, I had first to pass through the hanged housemaid and then, after opening the door on to the high carved staircase, dodge past the long, treacherous moonspokes that barred the way to the top floor's only watercloset. Bedwetting, although frowned on, often seemed preferable.

*But pictures present a different story; here, I look
extremely cheerful in my new party dress.*

Fire, fear of it bred in him by his uncle, was my father's greatest terror.

Years later, laughing, he told me about Sammy FitzRoy's visit to the House in 1928, when he himself was five years old. Sammy, Anna's wild younger brother, was in unusually subdued spirits:

never lucky, he had just burned down a house – his own mother's – by dropping a lighted cigarette. Charlie Byron, frantic with alarm, imposed a smoking ban during his stay at Thrumpton; Sammy, for the first six hours of his visit, was the model of abstinence.

A pre-dinner glass of sherry brought on the crucial return of the urge. Sammy felt for a cigarette, remembered orders, shook his head, looked firmly around the room and announced that he was in need of a rest. An hour later, climbing the stairs to bed, my father encountered his uncle Charlie kneeling outside Sammy's bedroom door, nose to the keyhole, hands clasped, as if engaged in prayer. (Which, as a devout clergyman, he may well have been.) This performance was repeated, every evening, for a week before Sammy, bored with frightening an old man out of his wits, called for his car and left.

I'm not sure whether my father realised how close his own behaviour came to that of his uncle. I witnessed him undertaking precisely this ceremony whenever my brother or I invited any smokers to stay. If caught hovering outside one of their bedrooms, he was unembarrassed and unrepentant. The House, and its safety, came first.

The burning of Nuthall Temple was the first fire I heard about. Described by my father with horror – what could be more wicked than the wanton destruction of a family home! – it took on the proportions of a mythic devastation. A gaudy oil painting by Frank Brangwyn (or someone who admired his style) hung on the flight of stairs leading to the top of the House. It showed flames belching out of a black fortress, with figures streaking across the canvas in front of them, orange-tipped by the firelight. This, I supposed, was the Temple.

I had never visited the site of the Temple. All I knew was that it had burned to the ground in the course of an afternoon. If a stone temple could be destroyed in a couple of hours, little imagination was needed to guess how quickly a house like our own, comprised largely of wood, plaster and brick, could be reduced to ashes.

Fire threatened our lives. Fire kept our household warm. The windows of the House looked out upon country fields, but this was also coal country, ten miles from the notorious pits of D. H. Lawrence's Eastwood. Sometimes, sitting beside my father for the half-hour before bedtime when he would read aloud from *The Pickwick Papers*, I might see a glowing lump of coal jump the low brass fender and land upon the library carpet. My father always noted it in time, but what, I wondered, if nobody had been watching? What if the fireguard were one time forgotten, or if it should fail to prevent the leap of a smouldering fragment?

Mrs Bardell shrilled with fright at Mr Pickwick's innocent invasion of her bedroom; I couldn't pay attention. Fiery tongues were already licking their way across the carpet to the bookshelves and out towards the closed door. The encyclopedia in the nursery bookcase had informed me that fire burns through a seasoned plank of timber in just four minutes. In four minutes, the flames would be past the library door and enfolding the fruit-crowned wooden pillars at the foot of the staircase that climbed all the way up to the last oak door that shut off the nursery wing and the sleepers who lay trapped inside it.

We, my brother and I, would burn in our beds.

Not true, my mother says. We children were never in danger. We had The Chute.

The Chute, hacked out of a thick interior wall on the recommendation of the local fire department, led directly from my bedroom into our nanny's bedroom cupboard. Here, it was imagined that Nanny, neatly dressed and ready for action in any emergency, would receive her little charges with open arms and carry them down a blazing staircase to safety.

I had no faith in this scenario. Nanny, a gaunt, anxious, passionate woman with the improbable name of Ruby Rose, often expressed the wish that she might have a little boy of her own. She didn't feel the same way about girls. My brother was clear-eyed and pink-skinned. He had a mischievous smile and a mop of flax-yellow hair. I knew which of us Nanny Rose would save.

Our parents were not unloving; they certainly had no wish for their children to burn. Further precautions were eventually taken. An iron bar was attached to the nursery windowsill. Inside the window, a hemp rope lay coiled, neat as a cobra within its wooden box, long enough to stretch three storeys down to the flagstones at the foot of the House. Today, I wonder whether either that box or that rope could have survived a fire; at the time, all we objected to was the sensation of coarse hempstrands rubbing our tender thighs and clenched palms raw as we practised the descent, drilling against our father's stopwatch. (Later, despatched to a school that rated pupils by their ability to saddle up a horse or hurl a ball through a ring, I shone at the gym exercise that required skill in rope climbing.)

My father's terror of fire conflicted with his aesthetic views. He was terrified of a fire; still, he could not bring himself to get rid of the old flexes, plugs and fittings that had been part of the House for over seventy years. They reminded him, he said, of its golden age. At the time of his death, most of the electric fittings spat blue flame when they were connected to plugs. Edwardian flexes, long stripped down to naked wire, trailed potential firelines across the wooden floors. One bulb, still burning dimly at the dark end of a passage, had 1926 printed on the underswell of its globe.

Water held even more terror than fire. In books of mythology, I read about Neptune, who struck the earth with his trident to raise the floods. Rivers raced across the plains, and waves lapped the mountain peaks, until all was a shoreless sea and fish swam in the branches of the trees in the woods.

Water rose from the dreams of my childhood like a smiling thief,

Our parents were not unloving: here, I help my mother to steady the old-fashioned perambulator which holds my younger brother.

stifling each room in turn with clammy outstretched fingers, filling the cupboards and drawers with the stench of river mud, burying the House as deeply as the trunks of tall willows that are sealed from sight by a sudden tide of winter floodwater, the whole reflecting, at its loveliest hour, the salmon blush of early evening, of twilight at Thrumpton.

Fire, like ghosts, lived in the dark world of nightmare. Water was real. Each winter, as the river spilled over its banks and joined the lake, water seeped up from the earth and into the warren of cellars beneath the House, spreading a net of slime below the polished floors of orderly rooms. This was the season in which the smell of death taunted the ceremonious life of the House with the impolite stink of rotting fish.

This, in earlier times, was when the House's owners took long, quiet holidays on the Riviera, for the protection of their lungs.

The life of our ritual afternoon walks was changed by floodtime. To the west of the House, the flat fields lay under a surface of grey silk, a shroud for the puffed corpses of rabbits that had been either drowned or poisoned by hostile farmers. Walking carefully on the hillside above this seasonal lake, my brother and I avoided looking at the bobbing bodies. Instead, we admired the high clumps of yellow bubbles that danced across the surface of the floodwater. We thought of these billowy products of pollution as pretty playthings. Watching the waters spread, we imagined the House as an ark, ourselves as its crew.

Once, escaping from the House, the two of us strayed off the village road, down to the river, and into flooded pastureland. Trying to turn back, we found we could not stir. Greedy river currents sucked and swirled around us, pouring grey water into the funnels of our small rubber boots, holding us fast, as if under some spell. Wailing, we reached towards the high bare hands of the willow branches at the edge of the field, begging them to bend and to save us.

Eventually, the pasture-owner waded in and scooped us up, a howling child pressed each to a broad hip, as he strode back to land and up the drive to the House.

Afterwards, we talked about our escape. Would our father have ventured into a flooded field to rescue us? We were unsure.

In the event, we found we had never been missed.

Water was at its most bewitching in the landlocked Midlands during the deceivingly brief season of high summer and parched fields, when a stroll beside the river brought cooling thoughts. This was when my brother and I wandered down to the far end of the park. Here, at the foot of a cliff of red clay, lay a secret world: a small marina, complete with lock, bridge and a sweetshop selling aniseed balls and fizzy lemonade. Here, hours slipped past as easily as the trickle of licked ice cream while we watched the lock gates swing closed and the watery pit begin to surge, bringing a bargeload of cheerful river-travellers up to the level of the path. Red-checked curtains twitched forward to mask the cabin rooms from sight; saucepans rattled; glasses clinked. Hungrily, we watched the bargees chug away, adventurous and free.

Watching life on the canal, I imagined it winding away to flamingo-bordered, cobalt blue lakes, and to undulant turquoise seas that might spread their lapping waters to the earth's far continents. (Fed with Fifties-style colour postcards from the travels of our parents, my brother and I pictured the larger world in bilious enamel tints.) Digging a hole, after the flood had receded, in the gravelled laundry yard at the back of the House, I was hoping, quite soon, to reach Australia.

I sit on my father's knee for a family snap with Dick and Vita, who is trying to hold my brother still.

Familiarity with the power of floods, increased by our adventure in the farmer's field, bred a respect for water that bordered on terror. I didn't mind paddling when our parents took us on summer visits to the seaside; I screamed if anybody tried to coax me further than the water's edge, out to the point where the sand sheered away and nothing lay below but the sucking depths, cold as the clasp of mermaid's hands.

My introduction to swimming as a pleasure came with the arrival at the House of Slav, who was both fond of children and good at swimming.

Slav was an Ethiopian. He had been castrated and sold, so he told us, as a slave in the market of Addis Ababa. Bought by an Englishman for unspecified use and taken to Southport, he escaped at the earliest opportunity. We never heard what happened next. Slav did not like questions about his past. What he did like, he made abundantly clear from the very start, was the personal freedom of physical nudity.

Slav arrived on a bicycle, one summer afternoon, clad only in a khaki shirt and, in a temporary concession to propriety, a thin pair of shorts. He knocked at the back door, introducing himself by his first name – we would know him by no other – and asked for work. He took pains to emphasise that he expected in return little more than his bed and board. My mother was doubtful; my father, keen for cheap workers, was enthusiastic. Slav was hired, on the condition – this was laid down by Nanny Rose – that he would always wear, at a bare minimum, a loincloth, while working in the House. My mother, after some thought, produced the remnants of a silk dressing-gown that dated back to her family's visit to King Farouk. Egypt, surely, wasn't too far from Ethiopia? Slav wore his loincloth dutifully, but without any show of pleasure.

The presence of our new employee caused talk in the neighbour-hood. My father had, until this point, been regarded as faultlessly conventional. The arrival in the household of such an outlandish figure brought his reputation into question. Did gentlemen employ such people for normal reasons? What, precisely, was Slav's function?

This, so far as I am aware, was the first taste the neighbours were to receive of my father's waspish humour. A Baron de Charlus might have appreciated it, but this was the Midlands in the late Fifties and such sense of humour as the majority of my parents' country neighbours possessed was uncomplicated by wit.

On a fine July day, a lunch was held. The dining room blinds were drawn; my father, masked by dark glasses at the head of the table, proclaimed a headache. Plunged into a yellow gloom, the guests exchanged desultory chat and did their best not to stare too eagerly every time the door from the kitchen swung open.

Time ticked away; nothing out of the ordinary had transpired. Glances were exchanged, followed by knowing nods, indicating that the guests believed they had, perhaps, been led up a garden path. Conversation grew louder and less deferential.

Then, as coffee was announced, my father walked idly towards the window and snapped up the blinds. The gasp from behind must have given him as much pleasure as had the planning of the scene now unveiled. For there, stalking across the lawn, in all his (possibly unselfconscious) glory, strode our tall, beautiful, coffee-brown Slav, a tiny watering-can dangling from his fingers, a shred of yellow and scarlet silk knotted about his naked hips. The pretence of his engagement at a task was quite perfunctory.

In retrospect, and in the light of my father's obsession with physical appearance, Slav must have provided him with an aesthetic pleasure that compensated for the fact that, as time went on, he showed increasing reluctance to actually do anything. Observing him from one of my many hideouts – a clump of bamboos; a laurel thicket; the lower boughs of a densely covered ilex, or holm oak – I watched Slav strolling to and fro across the lawns, doing nothing except, with no personal effort, to look magnificent. Some-times, looking past him to the House, I would see a shadow etched on one of the library blinds. Behind it, my father sat at his desk, writing a letter or, perhaps, simply gazing at the figure on the lawn.

Too young to understand what castration meant, I asked Slav to explain it. He did so, at length and without embarrassment. Castration could affect you in two ways, he told me. For most men, the result was a high-pitched voice, like a lady's. For him, the operation had produced only extreme sensitivity to temperature. This was his reason for not liking to wear many clothes. But what about the winter, I asked? If he grew very hot in summer, didn't it follow that he would grow very cold in the winter? Why, then, did he wear just as few clothes in December? But Slav, who had a proud, capricious streak, grew suddenly bored with the conversation. Closing his eyes slowly and looking, to my admiring eyes, more than ever like a beautiful marching soldier from Darius I's army in my history picture-book, he walked away.

Slav was as sensual in his pleasures as a cat. In winter, he liked to roll naked in snow; in summer, he waded, without a stitch on, into the lake and swam sleekly up and down, his head held high above the water, like a ship's prow. Watching him one day, I admitted that I was scared of water. Slav smiled sleepily and suggested that I get my bathing suit.

Being lifted on to Slav's shoulders and carried down the grass bank, out into the dark water, was the most delicious sensation I had yet known. Even so, I panicked as he pushed my legs away from his chest and out into the treacle-dark lake. Still clasped by strong hands, I flailed and choked and floundered – and found, to my surprise, that I had reached the rushes. Clutching them and kicking while I cried with fear, I raised up my legs to level with the frantic paddling feet of a startled coot.

'You're there!' said Slav, and pulled me back to try again.

One afternoon, two years after his arrival, my parents, my brother and I walked up the village street to watch the home team play cricket on the field they called Twentylands. The pitch lay close to the road, enabling us all to see, as the batsmen paused to change ends, that Slav, wearing his shirt and khaki shorts, topped off, on this occasion, by one of my father's panama hats, was bicycling gracefully past. This was surprising – Slav had left his bicycle, untouched, in one of the old disused stables at the back of the House, since his arrival. Comfortably, my mother suggested that he must be trying to get his weight down. (Slav, although still elegant, was no longer so lithe as he had been on his arrival, possibly because Nanny Rose had taken to baking him a weekly batch of scones.)

Perhaps Slav heard my mother's words and took offence. The House, when we returned from the match, was empty. Slav had left a bundle of possessions behind, but he never came for them. He had gone, without warning, as suddenly as he came. We hadn't, until then, realised how much he had become a part of our lives. Nanny Rose remarked that the House seemed quite empty without Slav about the place. Peeping out across the lawns from my hideout in the bamboos, I closed my eyes to slits, willing one of the long straight shadows to turn into the silhouette of my hero.

My father was quite irritable after Slav's departure.

The hat that Slav had taken away, he explained, was one to which he had been particularly attached.

To my eyes, one panama hat was much the same as another. But there was only one Slav.

I am sorry, both for the reader and myself, that no photograph of Slav has survived. My mother says that he did not care to be photographed.

Everything in the House leads back to the lake.

Up above the top floor, a steep staircase leads to the roof, and a walkway hidden behind the gables. Above it, accessible by scrambling up a gutter, a square platform of lead, bleached pale as birch-bark by a century of sunlight, overlooks the landscape.

The Turn of the Screw is a story I always connect to the House. It does, however, have a flaw. Henry James, bringing the governess back from one of her first strolls outside Bly, the country house to which she has been despatched, makes her look up. She has to do so, in order to see the ghost of the dead butler, Peter Quint, defying her from the rooftop. As a dramatic scheme, it works; in real life, it's implausible. People, unless called to do so, look ahead, not up. A roof is the place to go, not to exhibit oneself, but for concealment.

From the high platform, my refuge through all the years of my father's life, the view stretches out to the distant railway line, where it spans the river, beyond a hill massed thick with beeches. Come back. Follow the slow snake of the river to its bowstring tributary, the lake. Perched up here on the leads, you can watch a world of activity below: herons staking out their watchpoints in the rushes, cormorants balancing on treetops, swans skimming low enough to ruffle their own reflections. From here on the roof, all is visible.

Looking down now, I might see myself being carried out into the water on Slav's shoulders. I might, but I don't. What I see is always the same. I see my father.

He's sitting on the bank, the boy from London at his side. The long plumes of the willows overhang them and keep the bright sun away. My father is reading aloud, from one of the old-fashioned humorous novelists that his own father relied on to keep sadness at bay. The boy is leaning forward, laughing and enjoying himself. My father's arm isn't quite touching his.

Here's happiness and ease. Here's what he never found with us.

I'd be frightened now to look at my own face, or to hear my own voice, when I hid up on the roof, spying on the usurper, hating them both. My screams sounded so ugly that I'd put my hands over my ears to keep them out. It shocks me, today, even to acknowledge that the screams of an angry, jealous child were still coming out of my mouth when childhood had long been left behind.

Euston Hall, the Norfolk home of the Dukes of Grafton.

Dick and Vita Seymour pose, looking a little subdued, at the Legation in Bangkok.
Leo and Alex are sitting on the small carpet at their parents' feet.

An aerial view of Thrumpton Hall and its park, 1968,
looking very much as it does today.

Home life with the Byrons at Thrumpton in 1928. The county boundary was in constant flux; here, they have been shifted into Derbyshire.

My father lines up for drill at Middleton Park, Lord Jersey's Oxfordshire home, during his brief convalescence from a head injury. George FitzRoy Seymour, the author guesses from his stance and leg-shape, stands second from right in the line facing the brand-new (it was completed in 1938) Lutyens façade.

Chirk Castle, my mother's romantic family home in North Wales until her marriage. *By kind permission of Gillian, Lady Howard de Walden.*

Sir John Lavery's painting of Lord Howard de Walden and his family. My mother stands at the centre. *By kind permission of Gillian, Lady Howard de Walden.*

My parents at their
marriage, June 1946.
Just behind them is my
mother's bridesmaid
and best friend, Judy
Montagu.

The Seymour family at Thrumpton, painted by Julian Barrow in 1967.
My mother, seated right, and I, left, at the piano, both wear wigs.

Palmy days: My parents with new friends, Mr and Mrs William Douglas Home, on a QE2 voyage in 1970.

My father's daughter. George Seymour quite liked this photograph of me, wearing my false tresses and accompanied by a suitable escort, Lord Charles Hay.

My father lounges on the right, with Nick on the far left. Between them sits Griselda, a contemporary of mine who shared their enthusiasm for bikes.

Robbie shows off one of his best catches from the Thrumpton lake, a massive carp. My father was the photographer.

George FitzRoy Seymour takes his six-year-old grandson for a first –
and last – tearaway ride on the Duke.

My father's headstone, in the garden at Thrumpton.

3

A QUESTION OF APPEARANCE

My father had hoped for so much from the House. It was his Camelot, his grail, his lost land redeemed, from which all good would flow. But the House couldn't give more than it was. It couldn't confer friendship, or success. This was a source of bewilderment, sadness and disappointment.

Increasingly conscious that the House alone was not doing all for him that he had expected, my father looked harder at possible areas of improvement. Standards must be raised higher. The family, above all, must make more effort to live up to the beauty of their surroundings.

My brother, by virtue of being male, escaped the onus that fell on the shoulders of my mother and myself to be fitting inmates of the House. Intelligence was neither required nor desired; my father himself could be relied on to provide conversational vivacity and wit. Our role was to contribute an appearance of beauty, or, failing that, a show of good old-fashioned elegance.

My mother, in her eighties, wears whatever she pleases. Throughout her married life, she wore what pleased her husband. He, as we were all made aware, had impeccable taste. No matter that it was a taste formed by living in the company of elderly female relations who would have thought it daring to go for a summer walk without parasol, a veiled hat and gloves; he, who had lived, however tangentially, among duchesses and countesses, must surely be deferred to, conceded to know what was right?

'And hadn't you known a few people like that, in your family?' I ask my mother. 'Why didn't you ever stand up for yourself?'

She shrugs. 'You knew him. We did have that one time when you took over. Do you remember what a success that was?'

I'm unlikely to forget. This was the occasion that I think of as the mermaid dress disaster.

I was fourteen, and the BBC were to film a Hunt Ball at the House. It was the kind of moment for which my father had lived, a homage to his home and his achievement. Cleaning and dusting reached an unprecedented level that week; a temporary butler was recruited on the strength of his impressive appearance when dressed ready for the cameras in my father's second-best evening suit, and his skill at polishing silver. A big houseparty was invited; I was given special permission to come home from school.

During the last week of the preceding holidays, I persuaded my mother that she should take my advice, not my father's, about the dress in which she should appear at the Ball. Never having been allowed to buy anything more revolutionary than a khaki belt, I was wild with excitement at the prospect. This was to be the night on which, invisible for too long, she was at last going to shine. And so, reflected in her glory, would I, her daughter.

Walking through the hushed rooms of a London department store, we crossed acres of pale beige carpet to reach a section marked *Evening Wear*. An assistant appeared and was waved away: this was to be our own joint stab at independence.

It was hanging on a rail that smelled expensive. Silver sequins trailed lines over turquoise silk net as prettily as patterns on the surface of the sea; the neck and back plunged boldly down; the arms were bare. This was a dress for a goddess or a mermaid, and who better to be a mermaid than my mother with her red-gold hair and creamy skin? It fitted closely on her generous breasts and hips; this was good. The saleswoman clasped her hands in admiration; I was ready to skip with joy, until the price was whispered.

'Fifteen?' my mother said pleadingly.

Fifty-four pounds was what the mermaid's dress was going to cost; and this was 1962. My mother wasn't used to independence. She never had more than, at most, a twenty-pound note in her purse for a London visit. In 1962, the only way she knew of obtaining more without consulting her husband or going to Drummonds, the grandest London branch of the Royal Bank of Scotland, in Trafalgar Square, was to make a visit to Bond Street. Here, two old brothers ran a silversmith's shop that had benefited from the shrewd tips given out by my mother's grandfather. In return, the brothers gladly cashed cheques for my mother and her sisters on their expeditions to London. Unfortunately, the shop we were visiting was on the opposite side of Hyde Park, and my mother had an afternoon appointment to keep with her hairdresser.

'Oh dear,' my mother sighed, as she began to search for a way to unhook herself from the glorious dress. 'What a shame.'

Assistants who worked on the clothes floor of big department stores still received part of their pay in commissions at that time. Sweetly and swiftly, as she saw her percentage receding from view, the saleslady produced the solution: Mrs Seymour should take the dress home, let her husband see how beautiful she looked, and then see how glad *he* would be to pay the bill!

Of course! We brightened. Once he had seen it, how could he not applaud our choice?

The weekend came. Mr Alan Whicker arrived with his crew. It was decided, for the benefit of the cameras, that the houseparty would assemble for drinks upstairs, in the graceful upper drawing-room where old Lucy Byron had presided over her first Thrumpton ball at the age of sixteen. This was perfect: my mother would be able to make a dramatic entrance by the side door leading from her bedroom (I hadn't yet read *Rebecca*).

The film of the Hunt Ball, when it was finally seen by us, proved disappointing. Nothing registered but the sound of drawled vowels, the angled thrust of heads, the tap and shuffle of dancing feet, the yelps of laughter. Mr Whicker hadn't travelled all the way to the Midlands to celebrate my father's rescue of a handsome old house, but to show blue-blooded bumpkins at play.

We weren't to know this at the time. The room was aglow with bare skin and soft light and the buttery chat of those who are bred to sound bored. Glasses chinked. My father, alight with pride at the celebration of his home, sped from group to group, a dragonfly of joy. Too excited to care, for once, that my forehead was sprouting pimples and that my long feet looked large as boat-paddles in new and uncompromisingly flat gold sandals, I watched the door in the corner, willing it to open before the cameras were switched off.

'I helped choose my mother's dress!' I boasted. 'It's got sequins on! It's beautiful!'

A tall, cold-faced lady bent to waft scent into my face. 'How very brave of your mother,' she said. 'And your father? What does he think of it?'

'He hasn't – oh, look! Look!'

The door swung open. And there she stood, my creation, a white-skinned, wide-hipped mermaid in a dress that clung to her soft body like the flowering tendrils of some tropical aquatic tree. My father, across the room, with his back to the door, was pouring a glass of champagne. Framed by the door, she stood still in a way that was at odds with her usual reticence. She knew that she looked lovely. She was happy to wait for his admiration.

Her husband turned, at last, and stared. 'Oh my God,' he said and then his voice shifted up from disbelief, to shrill rage. 'It's dreadful!' my father cried. 'Absolutely dreadful. For God's sake, go and put something on that suits you. Anything! Anything but that!'

The guests must have been her friends, too, but nobody said a word. My mother turned and closed the door quietly behind her. When she returned, perhaps ten minutes later, she was wearing a pale brown dress in which she looked quite unnoticeable. My father complimented her warmly on her recovery of good taste.

The cameras left her out.

The dress was not, contrary to my expectations, sent back to the store. Instead, it languished at the back of my mother's cupboard, like a turquoise teardrop, unworn and unloved until, in the late Eighties, it left the House for sale in a charity shop, after being ignominiously bundled into a black trash bag.

I still don't understand why my father reacted with such hostility to the dress. Was it because he considered sequins to be vulgar, or the colour too loud? Or did he dislike the fact that it exposed so much of my mother's luscious, creamy skin? The clothes he bought her, I noticed, never exposed her shoulders or her back. It seemed strange that while he had been amused and even delighted by the spectacle of a near-naked employee wandering around his House and gardens for two years, his wife was encouraged to cover herself as thoroughly, almost, as a woman in purdah.

In the same year as the episode of what I came to think of as 'the unfortunate dress', my father sold a small piece of land. Avarice was not one of his vices: when he had paid for the recarpeting of the two main staircases of the House, a surprise was announced. He was going to take his wife, his mother – Dick Seymour had died three years earlier – and his son and daughter on an Italian holiday. No expense was to be spared: we were booked to stay at the Cipriani hotel in Venice, before visiting Rome, Amalfi and Positano. We would eat lobsters and see St Peter's. I had never, until now, travelled further than Scotland and the West Country. The prospect of a European adventure was quite thrilling.

Up in the nursery (I still slept in a child's bedroom on the top floor, although I had now been at boarding school for two years) I practised my phrases – *per piacere*; *vorrei andare a*; *bella vista!* – and stitched together a continental two-piece of my own design. The result, when I posed sideways, the thinner view, was pleasing: a hot pink linen crop-top and low-slung bellbottoms. *Che bella!* I could hardly wait to show my new look off to the world.

The Cipriani was grand, isolated and not, I thought, the kind of place in which to show off my costume. Rome was a blur of humiliation, caused by the sudden loss on Capitol Hill, in a wind, of one of my new and uncomfortable contact lenses. (My father, who had worn spectacles all his life, couldn't bear the ugliness of a woman or girl in glasses.) My grandmother was convinced that the wearing of one lens without the other would ruin my sight for life; spectacle-less and almost blind without artificial aids, I was forced to try out a small and mean-looking patch which had come free in a first-aid pack. James Joyce might have got away with it, or Samuel Beckett. Perched askew on the pink and moonlike face of a chubby fourteen-year-old, the patch looked sinister and ridiculous. I wept and said I had rather go about blind. My father agreed: the patch, he said, did nothing to improve my looks. My grandmother, annoyed at the ingratitude being shown for her (freely provided) remedy, instructed him not to upset me. My father said that it was a pity nobody ever thought about *his* feelings. He, after all, would have to be seen with me. And I looked, if he had to be frank, a perfect sight.

'Gracious!' says my mother. 'I mean, what a lot of fuss! About a patch! As though it mattered! You didn't look *that* bad!'

My mother had suffered from the opposite extreme. She could, as she says, have sat beside her own notoriously vague father with a cardboard box on her head, and have been judged to look in no way strange. Being noticed, in her view, remains preferable to being invisible. I'm not so sure.

We sped down to the Amalfi coast in a sky-blue Zephyr. My father, tieless, in dark shades, tipped panama and striped blue shirt, spun expertly around the dizzy coils of the coast road, whistling 'Volare!' while Vita, bolt upright between my brother and me in the back seat, entwined the fingers of her beige suede gloves, determined not to show her fear.

Luxury, by this stage of the holiday, was becoming an agreeable habit. My father had booked us into the best hotel; after we had admired our balconies overlooking the sea, and lunched on lobsters and cold white wine, Vita announced that she was ready for an afternoon nap in her room, while my mother wanted to write postcards. All smiles, my father proposed to take my brother and me out for a trip across the sparkling bay in a speedboat. At last! The perfect opportunity to show off my new costume! Removing the patch, and with it, my remaining contact lens, I passed the afternoon in a haze, confident that my pink top and smart hipsters had been admired. Clear vision was not required for me to know that I was being observed, discussed and praised. *Che bella!* What a lovely young girl!

Flushed by triumph and the sun, I glowed all the way back to the hotel. Here, over a candlelit supper table, my father told the family what he had heard whispered under someone's breath as I scrambled out of the boat. *Nice girl. Pity she's so big.*

It could have been worse. They could have said I looked like a pig; there's no doubt that I was overweight. What hurt, and sent me crying all the way to my elegant bedroom with a sea view, was the scorn and anger in his voice. So little was expected from me, and still I had let him down. Was it so much to ask that his daughter should appear . . . *thin*?

Che bella! Shades and a large hat help hide the eye patch, and divert attention from the plump form of which I had just become aware.

Minding so much himself, he tried to hide disappointment behind a joking manner. The story of 'Pity So Big' was produced, over and again when we returned home: in front of me, he told it to visitors, guests, relations.

'Can't you shut up about the girl?' an outspoken old cousin once said to him, coming to my rescue. 'It's not her fault she's got a big bottom.'

This, although well-meant, was not altogether comforting. My father paid no attention at all. But it was, he said when I challenged him, just a funny story; had I no sense of humour? Didn't I understand how affectionate he was being when he referred to me in public as Melon-Face or, when I streaked my make-up, as Tiger Tim?

A more confident girl – but what adolescent female has the confidence to doubt a father's view of her looks? – would have ignored or ridiculed him for this obsession with her appearance. Instead, I grew increasingly eager to win his praise. I managed to gain it, in my late teens, but at a price.

My hair had always disappointed him. Instead of being luxuriant, it was fine, straggle-ended and fiercely resistant to my attempts to make it curl. The colour ranged from dark blonde (winter) to light mouse (summer). Always keen on self-improvement, I decided to have it cut in a bob. This, the hairdresser explained as tufts of hair scattered around the chair, would create an illusion of thickness.

I had forgotten, when I presented myself for inspection, that short hair was one of my father's pet hates. After covering his face with his hands and declaring that it was painful even to look at me, he produced five pounds and told me to buy myself a wig. (My mother had already delighted him by agreeing to wear a full wig for all formal occasions.) Bearing his fondness for long hair in mind, I bought a cap of captivating blonde nylon tresses that spilled over my shoulders. My father was thrilled.

'You look really pretty,' he said, with delight. 'Don't ever take it off.'

I didn't. Having found the way to please him, I didn't dare. For three years, I wore my wig night and day.

This was not an easy task. Swimming in the Caribbean sounds like a fate that anybody would be glad to endure (my father, after one of the palmy moments when his investment hunches were successful, had bought a house in Jamaica); swimming in hot water in a shoulder-length wig is surprisingly uncomfortable. An additional problem is the fact that wig-hair doesn't dry in a natural way. I envied the girls who sat chatting to each other on the beach, styling damp hair with their fingers, while I slunk away behind a bush where, unseen, I could safely remove my waterlogged false locks and tweak them into shape. On another occasion, when I was dancing, the wig suddenly flew off, leaving me with a rats' nest of hairpins exposed to view and nothing for it but to crawl through a jigging forest of trouser-legs and silky calves until I correctly identified a small, pale, dead Pekinese dog as my lost head of hair, spread out across a corner of the dance floor.

I was consoled for these trying experiences by the fact that my father, for so long as I wore the wig, was unfailingly complimentary, kind and good-humoured. The downside was that my own hair fell out: the trichologist I consulted when I was twenty was succinct.

'Screw him,' he said when I explained about my father. 'You don't ever put that thing back on your head again. Not ever!'

But my confidence had already been undermined. The week before my wedding, four years later, I bought myself a long blonde wig. Pleasing my husband was the last thing on my mind.

My mother's looking guilty.

'I should have said something. I hadn't realised he hurt your feelings so much.'

I pat her hand. 'You couldn't have made any difference. He had us beat.'

The technique by which this in many ways unremarkable man kept two strong-willed women under his control was simple and invisible; he made us feel worthless. Without value, you have no power. No physical force was employed, no threat, except of his displeasure.

'I don't remember,' my mother says, when I ask her about the charm game.

Memory is being kind.

The charm game, devised by my father on our Italian holiday in 1962, revealed the depths of his own insecurity more profoundly than I realised at the time. Then, the game excited me. The game was my chance to be as cruel as he, and to feel that I was not, after all, the most disappointing member of the family.

The rules were simple, as simple as the way in which the game was introduced among us, and must be allowed to develop, if my brother and I were to benefit. Our father controlled the family budget: if we wanted to enjoy a good dinner, and go to bed feeling loved, then the game's originator must score well. To give him bad marks was unwise.

But somebody had also to be the loser, and our father made it clear who that somebody should be. High marks for him; low marks for her; it never failed to give him joy. (Possibly, he was taking revenge for the first humiliating months of their courtship, when he had been at her mercy.)

We played it first in Amalfi, after my grandmother Vita – she would never have tolerated such a vicious game – had gone early to bed. He laid out the rules; my brother and I didn't even need to glance at one another. We knew what we were meant to do.

'I thought,' my father said, lounging back in his chair, crossing his legs and smiling at us with unusual graciousness, 'that we might start with – charm? Now, how do you think I might score – truthfully?'

We hesitated, debated, looked solemn, and had to tell him the absolute truth: on a scale of ten, he scored nine. (The mark was not outrageous; our father could, when he chose, squirt charm more efficiently than a tom-cat sprays musk.)

We'd done well. He looked delighted, even though he tried to smother the smirk in a handkerchief.

'And now: your mother. Rosemary? Well, darling, I wonder what we should give you.' *Pause.* 'Do you know' – *pause* – 'I don't know that I would say charm, not exactly *charm*, is one of your strongest points. What do you think, yourself? Honestly now.'

Let her damn her chances, out of her own mouth. He knew she'd do it. And she did. Smiling, but not happy, she said that he was probably right and that she was feeling tired. She wasn't allowed to escape so easily.

'And you, Miranda darling? What do you think about Mummy and charm? Do you think she's charming? Truthfully?'

She hadn't spoken up when he mocked my size, and laughed at my spectacles, and sighed regret at my skimpy hair. She'd let me carry the blame for the mermaid dress, said that it wasn't her choice, but mine.

'I'll give her four,' I said, and watched her wince.

Divided, we fell.

4

❧

BETRAYAL

My mother has been asking about my memory of earlier years. She thinks it odd that I've written nothing about my relationship with my father before the age of fourteen.

'You can't', she says reproachfully, 'have forgotten everything.'

'Such as?'

Fluently, she rattles off a list of scenes. the after-tea visits from the nursery to the library downstairs to listen to a chapter from *The Pickwick Papers*, our father's favourite of Dickens' novels; the Christmas party for all the children from the village, with old-fashioned games being played around a candlelit tree; our annual winter visits to the pantomime and the circus; playing croquet in the garden; eating impromptu picnics up on the hill above the House; walking through fields thick with buttercups, down to the foaming weir . . . 'You had a wonderful childhood. I can't imagine anybody being better looked after.' She's plucking at the pockets of her purple velour suit. 'And now, all you remember are the bad things . . .'

I don't know what to say. I remember all the scenes she cites, but in black and white, like old photographs. There's no emotional freight.

It startles me to discover that I have hardly any memory of her at these occasions, but I think I know why. Married to a volatile man with high expectations and a short fuse, my mother had already embarked on the path she kept to throughout her marriage: to comply or keep quiet. When hurt, unnerved or in doubt, she smiled. I do remember her smiling more than seemed reasonable. I can't remember her voice.

I can see him far more easily. The first image to surface is the fluttering, languid movement of the long white hands on which he prided himself; this is followed by the deceptive impression of weakness delivered by a soft and loose-fleshed chin below the narrow, unpredictable knifeline of his mouth. His grey-brown curls are slicked flat to the sides of his head; his pale blue eyes are hidden behind dark glasses. That's how he liked it; he could look out, but we couldn't see in and guess at his thoughts.

'It isn't that I remember only the bad things,' I say. 'It's just that they're more personal. I know they happened, the scenes you're talking about, but they don't seem quite real. It's as though they were part of a stage play.'

My mother flinches as if I'd struck her; nevertheless, I believe I'm telling the truth. The upbringing that had been devised for my brother and myself replicated, as closely as possible, our father's idealised memories of his own first years in the House. Revisiting the past through the expeditions, games and pastimes he arranged for our enjoyment, he left no room for us to receive new impressions. Everything, as we were aware, was a repeated process. These secondhand experiences have left only the faintest of traces behind. I remember them less well than pictures in the books from the nursery bookcase: Cuchulain's head being kicked around some Irish field; a sharp-faced villain being hurled down a precipice, long hair flying up behind him like parachute strings . . .

'So it didn't mean anything to you that we did all those lovely things?' My mother rarely shows emotion. 'Anything at all?'

I must try harder, but none of the images I recover will serve to satisfy her need for reassurance that they, our parents, did well by us. I can see his fingers making a pile of pale shells from the tiny shrimps we caught for his tea on summer seaside holidays. I can remember the erectness of his carriage and the smartness of his shoes treading back towards our family pew after he had read a lesson; the scent of the handkerchief with which he once dried my eyes; the hot sense of shock and shame when he first mocked me for being overweight, for not incarnating that ideal of what he had imagined for his daughter.

I remember the back of his neatly rounded head, as I sat in the car behind the driver's seat, willing him into extinction . . .

'I remember when I moved into my first grown-up bedroom,' I tell her.

Sighing, my mother walks away. I know I should have offered more. There's nothing there to give.

Connected memories of my father begin in the year that I moved down a storey in the House, to a large – and chilly – white bedroom, overlooking the lake, a room which, to this day, is still my own. I was fourteen, young and fearful enough to sleep with my knees tucked up hard against my stomach, away from any nasty surprises. (This was the room in which, in his nineties, old Charlie Byron had died; I'd heard it whispered that he returned to lie there on the bed, from midnight until dawn, in his coffin.) Placed within easy reach of my parents' room, and without a key to lock my door, I found I had acquired a new role. I was to be my father's confidante, a receptacle for the sufferings of a sensitive heart.

Our bonding had not, until this point, moved beyond the occasional and unwanted invitation to enter the intimacy of his dressing room. Here, awkwardly, I stood with my back turned towards the bathroom, anxious to catch no embarrassing glimpse of his pale, unclothed body. The rules were now reversed. Friendship of a new kind was being offered. It included, to my considerable dismay, a father's right to walk into his teenage daughter's room, at any time he chose, before or after bedtime. The given reason, on most occasions, was that he had received a letter that it would interest me to hear (this was seldom so) and on which my opinion would be welcome. (The notion that personal correspondence should be treated with discretion was as alien to my father as the idea that I had any rights to privacy; all handwritten letters were read aloud, analysed and – if they contained gossip or material that had the potential to cause damage – passed along to whoever might help to stir the brew. This, I realise now, was a trick he had picked up from old Ismay FitzRoy, herself an arch intriguer. Letters, in the view of herself and her grandson, were to be shared, not spared.)

I did not especially mind being asked for my opinion. I did not at all like to know that, during any stage of undress, the door might suddenly open to reveal him. He never apologised; my discomfort was ignored even when I crouched on all fours behind the bed with a blanket tugged down over my naked back. He spared my blushes by appearing oblivious to my state. Walking past the rumpled bed to the window, he looked down at the lake, out to the young woods beyond it, and launched into the matter in hand.

'Perfect morning! I couldn't resist letting you know what X wrote. Quite incredible!'

All squeaks of protest were ignored. Astonishingly, my father maintained this habit of casual intrusion during the whole of my first marriage, and through most of my second one. I was never able to convince him that the habit was a strange one, or that a grown daughter had some right to privacy. Neither were my husbands, when we visited Thrumpton for weekends and festivals.

He came with the territory. His House. His Daughter. Theirs not to reason why, but to smile, share and endure. They did so with a grace that, while it speaks well of them, says more about the force of my father's personality.

It was during these earlier, pre-marital invasions that my father began to draw me into his confidence. Staring out of the window while I tried to dress, invisibly, beneath a bath-towel or quilt, he spoke casually of various young women who had caught his eye. Nothing serious, as he was always keen to explain; nothing for me to give him such looks for!

'What a face! I must say, darling, it's a pity you don't try to make the best of yourself. And aren't you going to get dressed for breakfast?'

Enraged both by the invasion of my privacy and by the expectation that I would applaud his good taste in girls, I punished him in the only way I could. He wanted my approval; he couldn't force me to grant it. Stubborn in my silence, I willed him to stop talking and go away.

'Not that he ever did anything,' my mother says with a sniff. 'Talk, that's all it was.'

'What about Carole?'

'Good grief! You're not putting *her* in!'

'Why not?'

On the rare occasions when I had been invited into the nostalgia-drenched sanctum of my father's dressing-room, I always noticed a large portrait quite out of keeping with the rest of his private hoard: the dreary prints of Tudor Seymours; the tiny framed photographs of venerable and plain-faced relatives. This picture could have been copied from a Fifties poster; it showed a deep-breasted young woman with dark hair, gleaming teeth, and parted red lips. The prints and photographs offered no competition; the room belonged to her.

This was Carole, with whom, apparently, my father had engaged in some lively bouts during the early years of his marriage. Incapable of keeping a secret, he confided in his wife. This, he explained to her, was a different kind of love.

'I should say so!' my mother exclaims. 'She was in here with him! On the library sofa! Anybody might have come in! Just as well I didn't. I might have hit them both over the head with a frying-pan.'

In fact, as we both know, my father always waited until his wife went to visit her mother in London for a night before making an arrangement with Carole.

'And what *did* you do?'

My mother sits up straight, looks demure.

'You know! And you're not to go putting his name in! I found that London art dealer. He'd always looked as if he'd like to get to know me better. We did what we shouldn't. It was—'

'Quite nice?'

'Oh, quite! And then I went home from London on the train and told George. He was livid!'

'And did you ever do anything like that again?'

'What do you take me for? Certainly not. As for him, well, if he wanted to make a fool of himself after that, chasing girls young enough to be his daughter – let him! They only laughed at him. Silly old thing!'

It isn't the first time that I've been struck by the way my parents' generation dealt with their moments of sexual weakness. I'm impressed by the fact that what really outraged my mother was the use of the family home. Had her husband gone, discreetly, to a hotel, she'd have let it go. Appearances – of our selves, of our conduct, of the House – were what mattered most.

It wasn't hard for my father to charm girls. At his best, he looked like a cross between wistful-eyed Leslie Howard and a posh playboy. He had charm enough – even when he'd mocked my shape, my hair, my spectacles and my choice of clothes – to make me ache for his admiration. I'd seen others bask in it, watched how he could, when he chose, work magic.

I first felt its power when I was fifteen years old.

Home for the holidays, I was thrilled when he suddenly asked if I'd like to be taken to dinner with him, alone, in the local city's best hotel. (My mother was away for a night, visiting one of her sisters; I wasn't yet old enough to comprehend the strength of my father's loathing for solitude.) After all the talk about the pretty girls whom he took dancing at clubs in London, I was flattered. I'd never had a boyfriend, never been kissed, and never – yet – been asked out to dinner. This was a rite of passage.

My hair was brushed neatly to my shoulders (this was in the pre-wig days). My stocking seams were pencil-straight, shirtwaister belt pulled in until my breath came in gasps. The mirror gave me hope. I didn't look, that night, especially fat or plain. My father even used the word 'elegant' when I came downstairs. He swung open the door of his red sports car and helped me in. He sang along with Ella Fitzgerald on the radio as we glided through the darkness. Arranging my legs sideways, as I had seen film stars do, I felt sophisticated.

'This is rather fun, isn't it?' my father ventured, kindly. 'It's nice having a grown-up daughter! We must do it again.'

That evening, I was given a taste of the charm my father could deploy, when he was in the mood. He asked about my friends at school, made jokes about the headmistress and told me that having dinner with me was the greatest fun he'd had all month. The sense of having glamour draped around my shoulders, like a silk cloak, lasted all the way through the prawn cocktail and well into the main course of scampi with tartare sauce. My plate was almost clean when my father leaned forward.

'It's been wonderful, darling, but now – there's something I want you to know.'

A smudge of sauce on my chin? Anxiously, I dabbed.

'Not you. Me. Don't frown, darling. It spoils your looks.'

I put down my knife and fork and, trembling, folded my hands on my lap.

'What? Please tell me?'

He was dying, I suddenly realised with a rush of love and guilt. I'd spent all those years praying for something dreadful to happen. Now it had, and I could only just hold back the tears.

He told me. Of course, there had been girls before, nothing serious, just a little fun, nothing to worry about. But now, there was a woman. And then he named her.

'She is wonderful, isn't she?' my father said, insisting on an answer. 'And she's tremendously fond of you. I know how much you admire her.'

I felt sick. He was, of course, quite right. The woman he had mentioned was everything I most wanted to be. She had a tiny waist, large eyes, glossy, long brown hair and a low, slightly foreign accent. My parents were friends with both her and her large, quiet, kind-eyed husband. When she came to stay, the woman played tennis with my father and went on long walks around the garden with my mother. I liked the woman for giving them both an equal value, and for bringing a spirit of serenity into the House. It had never occurred to me that she could be my mother's rival.

'But she's married,' I whispered.

Divorce was a word I didn't even like to say. The only girl at my boarding school whose parents were divorced was treated as a tainted alien. I turned my head to one side when I spoke to her, as if divorce was something I could catch from her breath. My reaction to my father's words was entirely selfish: I didn't want to be treated like my unfortunate fellow-pupil. A tear plopped into the little puddle of tartare sauce at the side of my plate.

My father was too absorbed in what he had to tell to notice my reaction. The story, I began thankfully to realise, wasn't about to start: I was hearing about a finished event. Of course, nothing was going to happen, he said. It simply wouldn't have been fair to us, his family, or to the House. That was what he wanted me to know. I mustn't be upset. All thoughts of his own happiness had been renounced. The price had been high, but all would be well. The only real victim was himself, for this had been true love, and hard to sacrifice.

I watched him remove his glasses to blink and, with one of his immaculate handkerchiefs, dab moisture from the corners of his pale, blinking eyes. Stiff with anger now that I knew we were safe and that I myself had been frightened to the edge of tears for no good reason, I allowed his hand to clasp mine. I heard that I was a dear daughter, so sympathetic and loving, *when I wanted to be*. It meant so much to have shared his secret sorrow. Well, time to call for the bill.

Lighthearted again, he sang along with the radio all the way back to the House.

'It sounds,' my mother comments, 'almost as though you were jealous. Not of me. Of her.'

'Oh not at all!' I say. She doesn't look convinced.

'Really,' I repeat, 'not in the least!' My voice sounds, this time, too emphatic.

A few years later, travelling abroad by myself, I spent a couple of nights staying with the couple in question. They had lost touch with my parents since leaving England; nevertheless, they both spoke warmly of their visits to the House and of the careful attention with which my father, in particular, had always seen to their comforts. I listened attentively for some hint of a more nuanced relationship. I heard none. But this was to be expected: why would she want to give her secrets away? It was possible that her husband had never known of the romance.

Towards the end of my visit, however, I found myself alone with her. She was still a graceful and beautiful woman. I could understand my father's passion, and the pain that renunciation might have cost him.

'I wanted to thank you,' I said suddenly, and I told her about the dinner of revelations, and then I thanked her again, for allowing our family's happiness to take precedence over what clearly had been a serious affair.

She looked astonished, and, as I came to the end of my pompous little speech, faintly amused. Hurt, since this had not been easily done, I asked her to tell me what was so comical. Only, she said, that the mildest of flirtations, a couple of lunches, a postcard or two, a birthday present of some nicely bound book, could be so misrepresented by a charming, but rather silly man. She had been fond of my father; the idea that she would ever have dreamed of ending her own marriage, or expected him to leave my mother, was absurd. Quite absurd, she repeated, and shook her head over the version with which I had lived for all those years.

While ready to suspect that she was playing down the impact of her own beauty and flirtatious manner on a susceptible man, I believed her. I do not think now that this was a passionate relationship or a profound one; my father may have enjoyed none of it so much as the moment when he could overwhelm his teenage daughter with the tale of a grand amour, heroically renounced for the family's sake.

The relationship described here was one of several that marked the passing of my father's fortieth birthday. This was the decade during which he took advantage of the new motorway, the first to be built in England, cutting the journey between Nottinghamshire and London by an hour. The proud owner of a sporty little open-top car, he used the motorway like a private racetrack, roaring off to take some merry-faced bachelor girl to supper and to dance at his favourite, old-fashioned nightspot, the Four Hundred, before he returned to the more decorous life of a father, husband and country gentleman. Here, in his other life, we saw an opener of fetes, cutter of ceremonial ribbons and – a new role – a conscientious magistrate who took an entirely respectable interest in the welfare of juvenile criminals.

'That's innuendo,' my mother says sharply.

But it's not. My father's visits to approved schools for boys looks bad in the light of later events. I'm sure now that this work increased his sympathy for young men who had lacked his privileged upbringing, but I see nothing sinister in it. He worked hard. He tried to get their living conditions improved and to put in a kind word when he felt that a remedial sentence had been unjustly harsh. This was in keeping with his self-perceived role as a patron. No boundary lines were crossed.

My mother's singular absence of jealousy during the years when her husband was discovering the joys of flirtation was based on common sense. She was well aware that none of these pretty, cheerful young dinner partners threatened her position. Why would they want to take on a shabby stately home, and the care of a petulant country squire? And which of them, however delightful, could compete against George Seymour's passion for his home? It was just conceivable that he might be prepared to abandon us; he would never desert the House. And the House, without her willing commitment to the role of its drudge and slave, would not survive. She was, so long as she kept smiling, entirely safe.

The flirtations were, however, a form of betrayal, and their existence helped to drain my mother of authority and confidence. The smile, a bright gash of vermilion in those days, stayed in place. Her feelings were never publicly expressed. As a girl, she had watched her reticent father encase himself, for a pageant, in a suit of mail from his collection of medieval armour; now, hooking her girdle tight, she pulled wool sleeves down to her wrists and planted a bright tam-'o-shanter upon her spray-fixed waves, a reminder to herself of the jaunty girl who had once held at her mercy the insecure, obsessive man to whom she now was married.

Flirtations and a taste for fast cars marked the onset of restlessness in my father, and a terror of approaching middle age. Depression accelerated the process. Some causes for this were trivial or imaginary; others were real. The news that one of the largest power stations in England was likely to be built on the doorstep of the House to which he had given all of his energy and love headed the second category.

The Trent, running across the centre of England, has been rated highly by business interests since the days of the Industrial Revolution, when fast-running water was needed to fuel the mechanical enterprises of Arkwright and Wedgwood. In the post-war decades, as power stations and pylons reshaped the skyline of the Midlands, the Trent played a key role in determining their location. Today, watching the shadows of clouds scud across their pale exteriors, and steam puffing up from their stacks in soft white clouds, spectators can bewitch themselves into seeing such architecture as the twentieth century's variation on the castles of crusaders and conquerors. This view was not shared by George Seymour.

The first hint of a threat came in 1963. Two sites had been selected in the Nottinghamshire area, of which we were one. The new station, if it came into being, would be built just beyond the Thrumpton estate, within half a mile of the House.

My father was incredulous. He had only just, after twelve years of ownership, succeeded in bringing his cherished House back to its former glory, from a state of semi-dereliction. The years ahead were the ones in which he planned to harvest the rewards of a lifetime's dedication. The House, the landscape, and the part of the village he loved best, were his. Luck and skilful investments had procured him enough money to support a leisured life; a closely-knit family circle consoled him for a dearth of intimate friends. (Letters written to my father during this period draw attention to the four of us as a unit, tight-packed, like a Roman phalanx. Friends declared that they envied his good fortune in having such affectionate children, such a marvellously competent wife.) All of this, now, lay under threat for how, conceivably, could Thrumpton survive such a transformation? We would have to leave – and without his House, my father knew that he was a lost man.

('I am under no illusions,' he wrote to me several years after this, in a letter which tried to explain his enduring commitment to the House. 'Who, if we did not have lovely Thrumpton to offer to our friends, would give a damn about a middle-aged couple who had achieved nothing, and who lived in some quite ordinary home?' I had not, until then, understood that my own lack of confidence was as a drop to the ocean of my poor father's insecurity.)

From 1963 on, he waged a five-year battle. By 1967, the matter was settled. There was no way out. Fields would be flattened, lanes buried, trees uprooted, making way for an edifice as alien to this drowsy landscape of little hills and wooded bluffs as the outsized funnels of the cruise ships that often, in those less protected times, overtopped the palaces of Venice's Grand Canal. The difference was only that the funnels could always be dismissed. This change could never be entirely undone.

The slow stages of the station's growth were the hardest for my father to bear. Each phase was like a death. The towers came first, sprouting above the hilltop like the decapitated stalks of gigantic concrete mushrooms. I, entranced by their hollow hearts, spent illicit weekends prowling over the internal scaffolding and listening to the booming echoes of their muffled vacancy; my father moved the garden benches to face away from the devastated hilltop, and discovered a new enthusiasm for fishing in the lake. (The lake was one of the few places from which the towers could not be glimpsed.) Leylandii, trees that he had always dismissed as suburban, were suddenly found to have a certain stately grace: no other trees would grow fast enough to preserve his favourite views.

The towers could be managed; the chimney was beyond his reach. Even I, who had enjoyed annoying him by defending the station's right to co-existence with a private family home, grew silent as the column of concrete reached that height for which we had fearfully prepared ourselves – and then doubled. Swiftly, our hill shrank to a hillock, overshadowed by a giant snout from which, we were reassured, an invisible plume of smoke would silently rise and pour its waste, not upon us, but Norway. This, too, proved an illusion.

From left to right, with the towers behind: my brother, mother, father and a visiting friend, Cornelia. From the collection of Warner Dailey.

My father was not stoical about his trials: old acquaintances, fed with too many station tales, fell away like dead flies. He had reason to be wretched. The noise, during the first years, was like living in the middle of some Victorian factory, complete with clanks, explosions of steam, and shrieks of suddenly-vented air, all of it calmly acknowledged by the authorities. The rose-coloured bricks of the House's walls, unpitted through three centuries of rough weather, became newly pocked with black holes. Each year brought further assurances from the station authorities, boasts of a dramatic fall in the level of sulphur emission; each year, smarting eyes and cankered leaves argued how slight that fall must be.

It was the visual impact that most affected the spirits of my father. We had to be sure to warn each new guest to the House not to mention the looming presence of the station. Taken out for a walk or drive in the park, they must look only in the direction indicated by their host. Jokes – a favourite was alluding to the chimney's always visible crown as 'George's Folly' – would assuredly not be well-received.

The power station has increased in size by almost a third during the past twenty years; the tall chimney can still blot out the brightness of a summer day and its red lights – a warning to low-flying planes – still wink down on us like dragon's eyes. Now, however, I see it as a friendly presence. As old laws protecting the landscape grow weaker by the year, and the population of provincial cities and towns continues to increase, it's apparent that the closure of the station would open the area to the threat of new and less contained forms of development of the kind that swiftly blossom around city fringes: shopping centres; car parks; factories; warehouses; housing estates. These would feel no obligation to beautify a location that had already been ravaged. The station, however, conscious of its massive size and the pollution, both visible and invisible, that it creates, has always worked hard to offer compensation. A golf course lies at the foot of the cooling towers; visitors are encouraged to take tours of the site and listen to the overwhelming roar of the turbines thudding at its heart in the sealed box of the powerhouse; around it, new woods and banked plantations soften the impression of a desecrated landscape.

It's sad to think that the remains of a Roman bath-house lie irretrievably buried under the station; still, unlike my father, I admire our modern neighbour. Standing on top of the hill that separates the tall Jacobean chimneys of the House from the concrete towers and cloud-challenging pillar of the station, I find it hard to say which building I prefer. Both are magnificent. Both are of value.

My father was too engaged by his memories of the past to take this view. Watching black smoke-clouds belch out into a bright blue sky to screen the sun and make winter of yet another summer day, he cursed the burden that had been laid upon us by our hideous neighbour. Living beneath the shadows it threw across his fields and his House, he mirrored these dreary eclipses in the darkness of his moods. The only difference between him and the station, it came sometimes to appear, was that one produced energy while the other sucked it out.

5

⚜

ON THE ROAD

Turning sixteen in the summer of 1964, I had reached an age at which to dread the family's annual pilgrimage to the seaside. Bored by the present and apprehensive of the future, I saw charm in nothing, except the make-up counter at the High Street chemist and the slick-haired boys in black leather jackets who clustered like a nest of vampires about the doorway of the local expresso bar, sucking cigarettes in moody silence.

This was the birthday for which I received, to my delight, a two-tone Honda blue-and-cream motorbike, brand new and capable of doing (downhill) seventy miles an hour. My father immediately asked to try it out; I didn't object. He climbed on, revved it up and, with a flourish of his hand as he recovered from an initial skid across the gravel, shot round the corner and out of sight. I smirked with-out tenderness: whom did he imagine he looked like, riding his teenage daughter's motorbike, decked out in a borrowed helmet that made his head resemble an upturned eggcup? Alain Delon?

*I show off my new Honda 50, above the Cromer promenade,
before my father decides to try out its capacity.*

He came back only at sunset, all aglow at the speed with which he'd covered a hundred miles. The following morning, he left the house before breakfast. Returning late that afternoon, he casually informed us that he'd spent the day with the son of a local shopkeeper. The boy – his name was Nick – knew about bikes. They'd been to a garage and picked one out, a real beast, a black Norton. Fascinated, I stared. I'd never seen my father's eyes look so alive or heard such relish in his voice, as though each word were being licked clean by the tip of his tongue. Catching my glance, he shot me a little twisted grin.

'You aren't planning to buy it, are you?' I enquired.

'Oh dear,' he said, pulling his mouth down to mimic my disapproving gaze. 'Isn't it awful? I already did.'

This was the moment at which my father and I entered a new stage of a relationship that already reeked of conflict. I had, until this point, led an unusually sheltered life, while my father, despite that series of merry flirtations, had been acquitting himself well in the role of the model squire. I am willing to think that, in presenting me with a motorbike, he was hoping to enlist my support for his own future escapades.

It didn't work out like that. I, too, was ready to let rip and to escape from the claustrophobic closeness of our family unit. My adventures were not destined to be momentous (even the experience of performing as the only white topless dancer in the black ghetto of Watts during the riots of 1966 came about entirely by accident); all I wanted was independence. But having freedom myself did not mean that I felt inclined to grant it to my father. The further I removed myself from the old, orderly life of the House, the more important it became to me that life should continue there just as it had always done. The last thing I wanted was to end by competing with my father for the rebel's role.

This might explain how it was that in the summer of 1966, just before I set off to explore America by Greyhound bus, I wrote my father a censorious letter. I didn't like the fact that an enormous motorbike now blocked the tiny entrance to my parents' London home. I didn't like the fact he was spending time away from my mother. I didn't like his friend, Nick, who seemed to me both sulky and dull; above all, I didn't like the fact that he was beginning to live a life more suited to his children's age than his own. I made all these things clear.

My letter was disagreeable enough to produce a long and defensive answer. Biking, my father explained, was a necessary compensation for an upbringing that he now perceived as 'most unnatural and oppressive'. A week later, he wrote again, to explain that his 'trouble' came from the fact that he retained 'a zest for doing things more suitable to people much younger than I, coupled with the opportunity for doing them.'

Put simply, he had begun to realise that there was a life beyond custodianship of the House he loved. Mr Jekyll would continue to do his bit as a pillar of the community and holder of traditional values; Mr Hyde was ready to play. This was the stage at which the family portrait was commissioned, the painting in which my father's face was turned away from the viewer.

My mother is looking thoughtful. It wasn't, she says, as uncomplicated as George's letter to me suggests. What he needed, as much as the sense of danger and speed which motorbikes offered, was company.

'You know what he was like,' she reminds me. 'I always found it so odd. He couldn't bear to be alone. You and your brother weren't around as much as you'd been in the past. And I – well, I couldn't always be with him, could I?'

She's right; my father's horror of solitude had become stronger with age. I remember another letter that he wrote to me, in 1969. Four years earlier, he'd bought a house on a Caribbean island, without thought for the fact that this exotic getaway, for a man who wouldn't set foot on a plane, wasn't going to be easily enjoyed. The letter, written on the way home from his last winter holiday there, exuded self-pity. My mother had already returned to England by air; my brother was at boarding school; I, back from my American adventures, was off in London, listlessly employed as a secretary. Travelling home on a Fyffes line banana boat, along with eighty fellow passengers, my father was consumed with despair. The captain was stupid; the passengers were un-congenial; the sea was flat; the bananas smelt. 'I am,' he wrote, oblivious of the irony, 'entirely on my own.' Four months later, the Caribbean house was sold, having failed to provide the long-sought panacea.

Loneliness plagued him; acts of duty filled his days. Appoint-ments, no matter how tedious, were never cancelled: discussions with his land agent revolved interminably around the minutiae of the estate. The old and sick, whatever their role had been in his life, could rely on my father to be a faithful attendant, bringing flowers, books and a surprisingly easy manner to brighten the dreariness of a hospitalised existence. All that virtue and no reward: no wonder he felt low. No wonder, riding pillion with Nick, by now established as his regular motorbiking companion, that he was always ready to turn back the clock, roar out from under the power station's shadow and plunge into an experience of visceral excitement.

As a magistrate with a keen interest in juvenile offenders, my father was a regular visitor to Lowdham Grange, a prison for underaged boys.

A car, at whatever velocity, is still somehow comparable to a home. Four wheels and a chassis marry it to the ground; a bike, by contrast, is an extension of the body and soul of its rider. It expresses his power; it makes him one with the world through which he rides; it allows him to register life, its blur racing past like unspooling film, as he speeds along the horizon's edge. This is the line between dawn and dark, life and death. The thrill of the ride lies in its intensity, the need to live in the moment, never outside it. Here, everything extraneous falls away. Cocooned in his black leather uniform, masked against the night wind, hugged close as a twinned spirit with his fellow rider, my father found the happiness he'd searched for all his life. Here was the elixir of youth that could be drained over and again, and never lose its power, never fail in the effect of its ambrosia.

By the 1970s, biking had become as necessary to my father as the drugs with which he blotted out constant worries about the House and plunged into insensate sleep. Nothing, in life, had turned out as he'd hoped. The House, albeit beautiful, was marred by the presence of the power station, an intrusion that had possessed his mind for nearly a decade. Old friends, settling into their maturity, were unable to share his new enthusiasms. His wife seemed always to be preoccupied with the garden; his son was off at university; his daughter had become a married woman. And he, in 1973, turned fifty years old.

My marriage, the previous year, to a scholarly author rather than to the friendly young viscount on whom my father's hopes were pinned (he had already planned which grand relations to humiliate by demoting them to seats at the back of the church), had not gone down well. The revelation that I was pregnant, a respectable year after my marriage, caused active dismay. Newly cool behind his shades, clad in jeans and leather jerkin, he wasn't prepared for grandchildren; asked to come and celebrate, he wanted to know a good reason why. Surely news of this nature should be concealed, he begged: 'too *boring* for you to have to endure *boring* things like people examining your appearance to see if you have got larger!' (The anguish in that doubly-stated 'boring' was hard to ignore.) Kind though it was of me to suggest that he should visit, he didn't care to see me looking so heavy and, besides, his diary was fully occupied. 'I do realise,' he added in a guilty postscript, 'that all this sounds dreadfully unfriendly and unloving.'

Although disconcerted, I was not surprised; a man who found

it difficult to tolerate the sight of an overweight woman was unlikely to relish the spectacle of a pregnant daughter. It hurt me more, when my son was born, to realise that my father had no plans to come and admire his first grandchild. (His letter of apology mentioned a troubling cold; his diary reveals that he went off with Nick on a two-day bike trip to Cornwall.)

Seven days later, my father finally managed a visit. Wearing an expression of frozen distaste, he asked what I planned to call 'It'. When I told him 'Merlin George', he expressed unexpected delight. I was slow to grasp the reason: I appeared to be honouring his beloved sports car, a green MG. I never disillusioned him. My son's lack of affection for cars – and indifference to bikes – later became a source of keen disappointment to a devoted grandfather.

'I don't feel fifty-two,' he wrote me the following year, adding a rhetorical question: 'Should I?'

The letter brought me up to date on the other life in which my mother played no part. He had just taken Nick to see the musical, *Godspell*, and then on to hear some late-night music at Ronnie Scott's. It seemed that Nick was not much of a jazz fan; he'd shown more enthusiasm at Snetterton, where, awed, the two of them watched, over twenty laps of a two-mile track, the Race of the Aces. Nobody could have failed to sense the thrill of a bike that day, proclaimed my father; it was plain that he was still looking for support from me for his late-found passion.

My own wild days, briefly enjoyed, were over; at the age of twenty-six, I asked nothing of my parents except that they should be conventional. I did not want to hear about my father's adventures with Nick; in fact, the more I heard about his friendship with Nick, the more uneasy I felt. There was nothing there that could be defined as wrong; nevertheless, it seemed strange that my father should be spending so much time with this young man. Frankly, other than biking, I couldn't – I didn't want to – imagine what they might have in common.

Prim in my new maternity and offended by his absence of interest in my newborn son, I wrote to thank my father for his news, and to convey a pious hope that he was not over-exerting himself with all the biking and late nights. His answer covered four pages, complete with a photo of his newest toy, a magnificent, black and gold 750cc Ducati, on which he had just been out for a night ride with Nick. Keen to remind him of his age, I wrote back that I was sending him a present, a charming antique wheelchair that might soon come in useful.

Surely his darling daughter was still just a *little* young to be taking such precautions, my father snapped back by the afternoon post. But how touching that I was so concerned about my approaching decrepitude!

Thwarted, I fell into a sulk.

The two sides of his nature still maintained, during this period, an equilibrium. The thrill of hearing that a neighbour was to bring along an ancient member of the Royal Family to lunch at the House was matched by the joy my father was experiencing upon his glorious new machine, to which he always referred, with a little snort of laughter, as 'the Duke'. My mother, while she had once been a fearless horsewoman, never mastered the art of driving a car and was not keen to attempt a bike. It's a testament to her loyalty that she asked to be taken pillion, and came back declaring that it had all been a most wonderful experience. Any hopes she may have had of displacing Nick were quickly dashed; no further spousal expeditions were suggested. The family had, by 1974, fallen by the roadside.

It wasn't, at the time, clear to me how much hurt my mother was feeling, since I myself had already fled. Under-educated (my father felt university would only corrupt his daughter's fine upbringing) and, consequently, hungry for any scholarly knowledge I could get, I was making the most of my marriage to a man who loved to teach. No love was lost between my husband

and my father since they were both competing for the same dominant role. Paying increasingly rare visits to the House, I felt each time as though I was entering a war zone. Away from it, my father was enjoying his new, more youthful life; when he returned, he was more insistent than ever on the maintenance of order, etiquette and routine. When breakfast had ended, the time had almost come for pre-lunch drinks. Lunch rarely ended before three; at five, the ceremony of tea commenced, bringing us close to the hour for a glass of sherry, or two or three, before dinner. Trapped together by this endless series of meals, my husband and my father eyed each other like two boxers squaring up to a fight. A good weekend was one in which we left before a screaming match broke out. The screaming was mostly done by my father and myself. Neither of us knew the meaning of a controlled temper.

I still loved the House, as did we all, with an intensity of feeling that could make me catch my breath when I stood outside it, relishing the gentleness of its lines, the serenity which never failed to bring me peace. It was only when I walked through its doors that the atmosphere changed. The saddest part of my father's love for the House was that his longing for it always to be perfect, always at its best, had created instead a sense of tormented strain. It was as if the House had become the mirror to his own unquiet spirit.

My father would claim that it was I, not he, who broke up the little family unit when I chose, at the time of my marriage, to invest my savings in a romantic ruin on a hilltop in Corfu. This house, when it was eventually made habitable, became my home of preference, an excuse to escape the relentless insistence by my father that every weekend should be spent under his roof, and structured to his rules. I, after all, being female, was never going to be the heir. My brother bore that unenviable burden of obligation. I didn't have to dance attendance.

The news that my husband and I would be spending all of spring 1975 at the Greek villa, where my mother would briefly join us (she enjoyed flying as much as my father feared it), was broken to my father at Christmas. This was one of the few remaining occasions for which the family still convened at the House, where the stone entrance hall was decked for the season with more boughs of holly than a Victorian chapel.

I had been worrying that there would be a row about our Greek plans. The news, although grudgingly received ('But Easter at Thrumpton is so beautiful! How can you bear to be away!') was rapidly overshadowed.

Nick had also been invited for Christmas. My father's explanation was that he needed a mechanic to accompany him for long night rides on icy roads; secretly, we all wondered what Nick's own family must think about this defection. But Nick himself seemed eager to accommodate my father's needs. He didn't even object when, on Christmas Eve, he was languidly invited to don fancy-dress – we had a collection of elaborate, and very fetching, military uniforms laid away – and wait on the family. Fitted out in a waisted and splendidly-braided jacket, with a peaked cap perched sideways on his dark curls, he looked shyly pleased by the compliments my father lavished on him.

The reason for Nick's obliging behaviour became clear when, shortly after handing round the soup and with a nervous glance at his host, he announced that he had a piece of news to give us: he'd got himself engaged. The marriage was set for early summer.

'Well! This *is* a surprise, Nick dear,' my father said, through lips that had become thin as filleted anchovies; I watched white fingers tap, and then begin to drum, the edge of the table behind his glass. My husband, raising his eyebrows, glanced at me across the table. I shook my head. I had no idea what we were in for, but the look on my father's face didn't suggest that we'd be celebrating this engagement with much joy.

The storm broke an hour later, after Nick had taken off his uniform and retired to watch football on television. The details, for me, remain obscure. All I remember is my father's low groan of self-pity as the door closed behind his friend. The familiar catalogue of complaints began. If only we could all stop being so selfish, realise how hard he laboured to keep the House going, how unappreciated he felt, how neglected, how despised by all these members of the family (furious looks at myself, my brother, and my husband) who regarded themselves as so much more intelligent than himself. Of course, Nick had the right to get married. But if we could only understand how much the bike trips meant to him, how terrible it was for a man who had known so little friendship in his life, to have such a boon companion so mercilessly snatched away . . .

In fact, as was abundantly clear, my father was jealous. Nick belonged to him. The idea that he might have led another life, in which he had been stolen away by some wretched girl who – Nick had cheerfully admitted as much – cared nothing for bikes and wanted him to give them up, was torture. We were invited to agree that Nick should be urged to reconsider and, perhaps, postpone such a hasty match; when we murmured disagreement, my father burst into tears.

I was already seething. I'd hated seeing the way my father praised Nick's good looks in his military attire and stroked his arm with a covert hand while being served his soup; I was infuriated by his response to the engagement, and his eagerness to undermine it. But it was the tears that undid me. I'd seen my father shed them too often. I knew how easily they flowed. Seizing a handful of boiled potatoes, I flung them, hard, at his bent and weeping head. When this failed to shut him up, I dropped on my knees and, while my husband's jaw dropped in dismay, sank my teeth into – what would some enlightened Freudian make of this delicious detail? – a leg of our family dining table.

'Stop it at once!' my mother whispered.

I heard her as if through a mist and didn't care. I was high as a kite on rage that evening, intoxicated by the joy of letting emotion finally flood out and take whatever form it found. Easily my father's match when it came to putting on a display of histrionics, I hadn't the gift for precise timing that allowed him now to rise to his feet, deliver one long sorrowful glare, and then dramatically sweep from the room. Still crouched upon the floor by the table-leg, I smelled defeat. That I hadn't quite shown to advantage was confirmed by the horrified stares of my mother, my brother and my husband.

'You and George!' my mother sighs. 'I don't know what it was about the two of you. You couldn't let each other alone for a moment. Dreadful. He was never so bad when you weren't there, you know. So long as he had his own way; that was all it was about.'

This mild attitude infuriates me so much that I have to walk away from her and stare out of a window while I steady my voice. Hadn't letting him have his way been just the problem, in later years? Had letting him have his way, as she so submissively did, been a form of compliance and endorsement? Wouldn't it have been better, when things got worse than this – and they did – if she had stood up to her husband and spoken out against the way he imposed his new life on us, obliging his family to conform to patterns of existence we could never have anticipated?

But this is unfair of me. I know that, while I relish storms and confrontations, my mother dreads them. There was a scene, just before my father's death, in which she did at last speak to him frankly, but I have never caught more than a shadowed glimpse of what occurred that night. I know only that words were said in the small London house, their second home, where much of my father's other life had been played out in his later years. I know that the scene traumatised her to the degree that she refused ever to enter that house again. (We sold it immediately after my father's death, at her request.) This was, I believe, the only occasion on which she nerved herself to speak to him, not as his subject, but as his wife and equal. To do so, she had needed to be pushed beyond the terror for her own future that conditioned all her earlier behaviour towards him.

Nick was not a lively character, but he possessed a kind heart, coupled with a warm affection for the man who had taken the trouble to teach him how to drive a car (and who had funded the purchase of his own first bike). He may even have felt some guilt about the distress his approaching marriage had caused.

Shortly after Christmas, my father mailed me a joyful letter (our quarrels were always as quickly extinguished as ignited), to explain that his youthful friend had devised a happy plan. My mother was scheduled to visit the Corfu house in May; Nick, never having left England before, had expressed the wish to ride out there in April, with my father and 'The Duke'. The fact that my unpopular husband was to be away in America for the summer offered an added incentive and excuse. A young mother must, surely, be in need of company?

The expedition was, from my father's point of view, a triumph. But I, from the moment that a villager shouted up at my window that two foreigners in black leather were awaiting me at the taverna, was stiff with self-consciousness and embarrassment. Instead of admiring their achievement – 550 miles in a day, my father boasted, beaming, in pouring rain, over the Alps and down through Italy to Calabria – I spiked their cheerfulness with snide remarks. I mentioned my mother's name incessantly; my conversation was angled to slant just above Nick's head, or to wound him with allusions to episodes of which he could have no possible knowledge. If I proved clever enough, subtle enough, even my father couldn't catch me out in any overt discourtesy.

Looking back, across the years, at Nick's hunched back, as he sat out on the terrace, staring at the hills and wishing, I'm sure, that he had never crossed the Channel, I'm ashamed of my viciousness. He had done all the riding, acted as the mechanic, humoured my father's wishes, sacrificed the company of that fiancée whom he, presumably, missed; his reward was to be tarred with condescension until his cheeks must have burned. I could see that he didn't like Greek food, that he felt lost and that he would have preferred to be anywhere other than where he presently found himself. Nevertheless, he was still my enemy.

The trouble, this time, stemmed from my father's disconcerting announcement that Nick and he would like to share a bedroom. The room I had selected for his friend, as he pointed out with accuracy, was less agreeable than his own at the front of the house, with a view across the valley. And for Nick, far from home, it would be a comfort not to be alone. In fact, my father added with a smile, he couldn't imagine for a minute that I would object.

He gave me no option to do so. Lying alone that first night in my own bed, after checking on the room in which my small son slept, I listened to the sounds of laughter and shifting bodies on the other side of the wall, and writhed. All those years, I'd followed the rules of his House; now, in mine, I was being forced to do so again, and to endorse a way of life that reeked of betrayal: to myself, to my mother, to our family.

Later, after his return to England, my father wrote me a long and warmly affectionate letter. He reported what fun it had been to take Nick for drinks at the Ritz in Paris; and, later again, of the misery of going into the cold empty bedroom of the little London house, after Nick had gone off to spend their first night back with his fiancée and her parents. My father had begged Nick not to leave him on his own, but of course, it couldn't be done. '*Did* I feel flat and alone and downcast to think all that super time was over? It was *horrid*.' Still, the journey to Greece and back had been an experience that would never be forgotten. 'It did,' he added, 'seem to bring us much closer together, didn't it?'

Had it? I wasn't so sure. It had touched me to see how care fell away from my father's face when he was on holiday and out of reach of the House, with its relentless need to be cared for and paid for and kept up; it had filled me with confusing and distressing thoughts to know that he and Nick, when we went upstairs at night, walked into a shared room. I had hated the sounds of their laughter, their whispers, their stirring bodies.

Readers will think it odd that I did not immediately draw the obvious conclusion, that my father and Nick were lovers. I had no means of knowing whether this was true or not; oddly, I didn't care. What troubled me was the sense that I myself had been supplanted, that somebody – Nick – had taken a place that was rightfully my own. Not my mother's? Did that mean that I wanted to be sharing a room with my father? The idea shocked me so much that I promptly shut it out.

In truth, I didn't know what I thought. All I understood was that I felt disturbed and uneasy, and that it was the sense of exclusion that caused me the most pain.

6

CHERRY ORCHARD BLUES

It's rare for a son or daughter to possess sufficient understanding of a parent to be able to proffer a fair assessment of that parent's behaviour.

'It doesn't seem to have stopped you,' says my mother. 'I never knew anybody so keen on judging everybody else's behaviour as you are.'

'What I *mean*', I say, 'is, what I'm *trying* to say is . . .'

Italics, here, admit to unease. I'm writing about my father with the benefit of hindsight, and with unlimited access to his diaries, letters and notebooks, writings that neither my mother nor I was privy to during his lifetime. The connections that these personal records are enabling me to draw, between my father's early life and his later behaviour, now appear obvious; I'm being granted an overview that was from nowhere visible back then, at the time.

What we saw then, as my father entered his mid-fifties, was the emergence of what appeared a radically altered personality. The documentary evidence of his life, up until the time of his marriage, suggests to me today that this final phase, though a long time coming, may have been inevitable.

Sickly and spoiled, my father grew up as the cherished darling of an over-indulgent mother, encouraged to develop into a preening young snob by doting grandmothers. At Thrumpton, as a child, he'd assimilated the habits and attitudes of a reactionary octogenarian, so thoroughly, in fact, as to guarantee that he'd be seen as an outsider by his peers, and given a wretched time at school. Later, he'd failed to pass his military training, and his diary reveals that he felt both lonely and unpopular in his banking job at Barclays. Here was a man who had a lot of living to make up for in life. Is it surprising he fell so hard for the sensation of freedom and rebellion afforded by biking? Is it any wonder, as he saw his children slip away, eluding the patriarchal grasp, that he looked for compensatory companions who would prove, if perhaps less challenging, then more dependable?

'And what about the clothes?' I ask my mother. 'All that business of the biking uniform? All that leather, the *black*? What did it all mean? Do you think wearing clothes like that was a redress of some kind, for his not having served in the Army . . .?'

My mother's look conveys such utter lack of enthusiasm for the subject that I break off. For a moment, I feel the sense of obscure depths that she may still adamantly be concealing. Am I imagining it, or is she battling a secret urge to speak out – fully, finally – after all these years?

My mother says: 'I wouldn't know.'

My father, while he did not approve of psychoanalysis, never minded indulging in discussion of family failings, so long as the topic didn't involve criticism of the head of the House. (It was acceptable to reproach him for being 'sensitive', or 'vulnerable', or 'trusting': these backhanded virtues were his authorised weaknesses.) But a quality such as my mother's resilience – in the face of such acts of cruelty as the public humiliation by her husband over her sequinned dress, or his belittling of her in personality games, or his snide and constant comments upon her shape (neither his wife nor his daughter could ever match up to his willowy and near androgynous ideal of the female form): this was drawn from a profound inner security that was unfathomably alien to my father.

'My religion, I suppose you mean?'

My mother's faith is simple and unquestioning. There is an Afterlife. The good are rewarded. Evil, in the end, reaps its punishment. God may drag His feet, but, though dilatory, proves ultimately benevolent.

My father's beliefs were less secure, and consequently more rigidly held, more sternly enforced. His response, when I dared as a child to question the existence of the Holy Spirit, was to order the local vicar to walk me up and down in our park, in full view from my father's writing-desk behind the library window. This purgatory was to be perpetual, or until my belief was restored, after which we could return to the House for lunch. (The vicar, after an hour of our pacing on a hot morning, admitted that he himself wasn't certain about the precise dogma of the Holy Spirit. We were both in need of refreshment; a collegial accord was reached. We did not forfeit lunch.)

'It's more to do with an inner confidence,' I tell my mother today. 'I can detect it already in that painting of you as a little girl at Chirk. You always knew just who you were. Maybe you had an understanding governesss; maybe it was a result of growing up as an accepted part of a large family? I don't know. But that's the quality he never achieved. And he couldn't shake it in you, however unhappy you became. Do you think I'm right?'

'Mmm – perhaps.' (Unlike her husband, my mother has always disliked discussing other people's traits of character.) 'I hope we aren't going to stand here talking about this all day?'

It's hard, listening to her brisk tone, to credit how completely my mother hid all evidence of an independent mind during the twenty years leading up to my father's death in 1994. It was as if she'd drained all colour from herself, leaving behind only the faintest of sepia tints. At meals, she sat in silence; when asked a question, she simply referred it to her husband for an answer. This was a form of loyalty that maddened my father. Enraged by her refusal to offer a point of view on any subject, however provocative, he flung at her the accusation that she acted like an ostrich. It seemed as if he wanted her to lift her head and hold it there high, while he took the opportunity to launch at it whatever he found at hand to hurl.

My mother kept her head down. Safe from sight, she could survive.

Bearing in mind the fact that she was now as much a slave of the House as he had ever been, that the worst thing she could imagine was not that her husband should humiliate her but that she should be separated from her familiar surroundings and her small, safe routines, I don't see, now, what else she could have done. At the time, I longed for her to speak out, or even to let us, her children, speak out on her behalf. She wouldn't allow it. Whatever George did was right was the attitude she decided to take, as a form of self-protection: a silence that spoke poignantly of grim endurance did nothing to diminish the sense of nervous unease that made visits to the House increasingly disagreeable.

It seemed, after Nick's departure in 1975 into married life, fatherhood and a regular job that put an end to the joint biking expeditions, that our family sat as if watching a clock, all of us, anxiously, simply watching. And waiting.

In company (given a proper guest list, meticulously chosen), my father remained entertaining, malicious, witty, and always hospitable, allowing his darker side to emerge only as the final moment of departure threatened, and once again there gaped before him the dire prospect of solitude.

'Where has civilisation vanished?' I remember him wailing as the guests filtered away from a mid-week lunch party, one chosen to suit his calendar, not theirs, at my home in London. Informed that these people had jobs to go to, he was incredulous. *He* was free; why weren't *they*?

Abandoned by his self-absorbed and heartless children, feeling inadequately attended to by a wife who appeared always to be in the kitchen or planting bulbs in the garden, my father would lapse into gloom, an ennui so profound that only his writing table could provide conceivable remedy. My brother, patient, good-humoured and deeply attached to the House, tried to make our father plan for the future: how did he hope to transfer his property without exposing his heir to the crippling maximum penalty imposed on unprepared estates? You would think, having experienced the effects of this at firsthand when Charlie Byron failed to make proper arrangements, that our father would have been eager to do better by his own son. Far from it; my brother was accused of a cold and calculating spirit for even daring to raise such questions. Better, my father droned in one of his favourite phrases, to let the tapestry unroll, by which he meant that he had no intention of doing anything to ease my brother's mind, or lessen the financial burden he would have to bear. Retrospectively, it seems that he intended his heir to endure all the tests of devotion that the House could impose.

Not being the heir, I was freer to speak my mind, and frequently did.

'Thank you, darling, for a shrewd appraisal of my faults, something which it can never be but salutary to hear,' my father wrote in 1976; my reward was a counter-lecture upon my taste for heavy late-Renaissance-style chairs ('the ghastliness of such furniture makes me want to cover my eyes') and another on my style of dress ('those awful monolithic rings and see-through skirts').

I was more deeply affronted by his next swipe, a pointed reminder of the fact that my husband, after four years of marriage, was spending little time in my company. 'My poor darling, you really are a grass widow now,' my father wrote, oozing fake sympathy; 'don't you ever wonder what people must be thinking?'

Licking the wounds of the defeated, I withdrew from this round in our lifelong epistolary fray.

I hated him. I loved him.

Let's look first at hate. Like most of us, my father was enthralled by the glamour of the stage. Few things gave him more pleasure, in the days when Nottingham's new and daringly modern Playhouse Theatre was making a name for itself in the Midlands (this was during the late Sixties), than to ask the cast over to Thrumpton for a meal and a tour. This was fun, with the exception of an excruciating occasion on which he lured over a well-known actor who was playing Lord Byron by promising to lend him a household treasure, the poet's very own signet ring, for future performances. The actor, delighted, visited, took the tour, and held out his finger for the precious loan. A sudden silence fell. The ring had belonged to Byron when he was a schoolboy; the actor, as we all now saw, had large hands. He struggled; twisted; sighed: patently, it wasn't going to fit. 'But look, it's perfectly easy!' my father shouted. Infuriated by the failure of his project, he seized the ring back and demonstrated, triumphantly, how elegantly it fitted his own narrow finger. 'You see!' We did. Flushing crimson, the actor apologised for having such workmanlike digits and regretted the trouble he had caused. My father, oblivious to the embarrassment he had caused, remarked on the contrast all over again, inviting his unhappy guest to admire the blue tracery of veins in the hands of a true aristocrat.

On this occasion, I would gladly have stabbed him through the heart.

And then, let's look at love. In London, he made friends with the girl lead singer from a well-known pop group. Asking me to come and lunch at the ladies' annexe to his club one day, he explained that Grace was to join us (she had expressed an eager wish to see such a place) and that my duty was to help steer her through the subtleties of club behaviour.

The club was old-fashioned and pompous, creaking with elderly men in pinstriped suits and chirping, neatly suited ladies from the shires. Grace, when she entered shyly down the stairs, made quite a stir. For this special occasion, she had chosen her clothes with care: high white heels, a fake leopard coat, a tiny skirt and an even tinier top. Descending the stairs, she began to remove her fur. Eyeing her bronzed thighs and popping breasts with a combination of admiration and alarm, my father hissed at me to give her a hint by putting my own coat back on, quick. I did as asked. Grace kept hers off.

Having reached us and smiled warmly around her, Grace showed that she was perfectly at ease. Sitting down, she adjusted a slipped shoestring shoulder strap, tucked one foot up under a bottom tightly draped in scarlet silk, and took out her camera for a snap. The ladies from the shires forgot their manners and gaped; this wasn't what they were used to: even to produce a pencil and paper was a social crime in this hallowed spot. The head waiter hurried over and whispered furiously in my father's ear, while grimacing at Grace's upheld camera as if its mere presence had the power to blast the club to bits. My father, in turn, rose to his feet. With a sweet smile for us and a glare for the head waiter, he announced that the place was far too dull for such a glamorous creature as his guest. Swept up the stairs on the tide of his indignation, Grace and I were carried off to feast, at twice the price, at a restaurant in which grandly discreet cubicles protected us from comment, and honoured Grace's reputation as a celebrity. Grace was overjoyed: 'He's a lovely chap, your dad,' she said when he went off to hail her a cab home. 'Such a gentleman.' Later, my father told me that the waiter at his club had insisted 'Madam' must put away her camera and wear her coat throughout her stay, so as not to distress the other diners. 'Pompous ass,' he said furiously. 'A sweet girl like that.'

I loved him that day, because he was so transparently concerned only that his guest should have a happy time. He could, when he chose, be kind.

I hated him. I loved him. I longed for the affection he bestowed so generously on Nick and Grace. He could make me laugh until my breath choked in gasps. He's the man whose autocratic ways and vicious sense of humour, as surely as his unappeasable craving for love, have most formed my nature. The note of self-pity that lurks about my conditional clauses, and the inflections that escape from the corners of my whispered asides – '*if* you cared' . . . 'as *though* it mattered' – are part of my father's heritage. Like him, I hunger for praise of the House; like him, I quicken with rage in its defence.

'I never knew a man make such a fuss about such an ordinary little English manor house,' an old acquaintance of his remarked to me only the other day, in a conversation about my father.

Ordinary? *Our* House? At moments like that, my father's spirit approaches as close as the hand that used to brush my shoulder whenever, playing the piano, I picked out some sentimental tune ('I'm just a lamb that's lost in the wood,' he'd croon with mocking awareness of the self-pitying aspect of his nature, parodying his own besetting weakness).

I love and I hate; and his is the familiar voice, whenever I discover myself alone, that whispers to me from the dark.

In 1977, two years after Nick's defection, my father deserves our sympathy. No substitute biking companion has yet appeared. His daughter, meanwhile, has gone off to spend six months with her errant husband and small son at a beach house in Malibu, writing a book about Greek island life, recollecting it in utter tranquillity, while watching the dawn roll in upon lilac waves.

'Your life,' her father writes with justifiable irritation, 'is so beautifully glamorous . . .'

His son, goaded by him into riding about town on a motorbike, is hospitalised after an accident in a city street. The accident was life-threatening; now, there's daily pain and grim talk of a possible amputation. But it's not at all my father's fault; not in the least. He'd never asked his son to get knocked down by a lorry (although he had forcefully pressed upon him a machine quite alien to the young man's nature). What matters most to my father is the resulting emptiness that has descended upon the House; and that its appetite for care remains inexhaustible.

Taken at their London house, this photograph shows the real affection that continued to exist between my parents, and, in the placing of her hand, an indication of my mother's wish to protect her husband.

Living in California, I scarcely gave my parents a thought. Now, looking through the old diaries and letters, I see that a little more concern might have been welcome. Money, by 1977, is in short supply. Often as not, now, when my parents have visitors, it's my mother who does the cooking, lays the table, and washes up afterwards, while my father scurries off round the bedrooms, twitching curtains shut, running baths, refilling water-flasks, vainly attempting to replicate the leisured life of a perished century. Reading stories of ageing and decline by William Trevor and Molly Keane, my parents smile at one another and sigh in recognition. Sometimes, when all the guests have finally gone, their hosts are so exhausted that they fall asleep in their chairs, waking with a start only when their shoulders sense the chill of en-croaching night. They worry about their son's slow recovery; they comfort themselves by buying tickets to see The Roly Polys, a troupe of unusually plump dancers, or Hinge and Bracket, a transvestite revue that mocks gentility (my father's favourite target for mockery). There's a companionship here, and a good humour, that it will fortify my mother to remember in the difficult years ahead.

Times had been growing harder for the privileged owners of stately homes. In 1974, a dramatic exhibition was mounted in London to warn of the speed with which this unique portion of its heritage was being lost to Britain. Visitors to the show, put on by Roy Strong at the Victoria & Albert Museum, stared in disbelief: were there really so many fallen monuments and roofless halls, such a number of tree-flanked avenues leading up to unkempt fields and ravaged ruins?

Articles were written, appeals launched. Some of the larger and more famous buildings attracted public interest and elicited grants, but life for those who owned the smaller and less celebrated houses posed problems that lacked simple solutions. These once stately mansions were not, after all, crucial repositories of the Crown

Jewels. What right had these smart-voiced couples to squander precious land, and then proceed to speak of themselves as noble custodians? Why shouldn't their oversized homes be sold and put to more productive use, as training colleges, for example, or nursing homes?

My father resisted the temptation to apply for a grant, since he feared, far more than the lack of money, being placed under any form of supervision. (Much of his delight in the House stemmed from the sense that he could do as he pleased with it, and be beholden to none.) Instead, he and his wife did what they could to limit the costs of a way of life they could no longer properly afford, but which continued to seem demanded of them by the House. The family cars grew smaller, and secondhand; the heating was turned down, until damp patches upon the walls portended worse problems than high fuel bills. Plans were made to economise by hibernation, during winter months, at the rear of the House.

During this period of slow deterioration, my father's diaries – my mother had no time to keep one – became increasingly laconic. Each week carried a brief notation of the days upon which smoke-clouds from the power station had been worst, and of the number of trees upon the estate that had had to be cut down, victims of a virulent plague of Dutch Elm disease.

Elms, and the sound of the wind sighing through their lush boughs, were one of the glories of Thrumpton's park. Over a hundred of them had been affected by the virus, and now stood, drab-branched and skeletal, waiting to be felled. My mother, in a rare confessional moment, admitted in one of the letters she sent to California that she could no longer bear to walk out into the fields. All day long, the chainsaw whined; trunks sprawled on the land like the severed limbs of fallen giants.

Nineteen seventy-seven was a bad year. After losing in rapid succession two adored black labradors, loyal animals who seemed bred for love, not hunting, my parents managed to locate and purchase a third. They'd owned the dog just six months when burglars, casing the House for some future felony, abducted it. Drugged, and stabbed with a knife up the rectum, the poor, friendly hound was left on a local roadside, to bleed to death. The prospective theft, efficiently executed in the absence of any guard-dog, was carried out the following month.

This was a major burglary, on a scale that felt, to my parents, as if their home had been raped. For me, the devastation did not, at that time, carry great impact. Living far away, off on another continent, I had fallen out of love with my parents, with their way of life, and with the House. If asked for a view, I might have quipped that the House had always been too cluttered and that a few old clocks and antique miniatures weren't worth crying over. Even I, however, regretted the loss of objects that reminded me of the now rapidly vanishing past: I was six when I first watched two tiny blacksmiths tap their anvils against a bell in my great-grandfather's gold repeater watch; I was not much older when I was shown a silver fish that concealed in its innards a secret cargo of toothpicks, a pretty trinket designed to adorn a Georgian lady's dressing table.

The repeater watch was gone for ever; the fish turned up ten years later in a Nottingham silversmith's shop. My father, driving at dawn to a deserted car-park on the edge of Doncaster, discovered, as his informant had promised, that the prettiest of the clocks had been left ready for him, deposited in a brown paper bag between the front wheels of an abandoned Ford Sierra. I never heard what exorbitant bribe had been paid for its recovery, or how the extortion had been effected. All that mattered, to my father, was that the clock had come home.

The burglary brought out both the best and the worst in his nature. The best was represented by the tenacity that had come to the fore back in 1950, when he borrowed beyond his means to rescue the House he loved. Now, when the police made it clear that their obligations did not extend beyond reasonable endeavour, my father undertook to tackle the job himself. He transformed himself into an amateur sleuth. Loitering in the narrow lanes of Brighton, where stolen goods often appeared prior to their journey across the Channel, he was at virtually no risk of being mugged; when he started going alone to the Mile End Road, and asking questions in places where, despite his flat cap and shabby jacket, he could never have passed unnoticed, he was pushing his luck.

My father's determination paid off: goods were recovered; confessions, improbably, obtained. My impression was that, distressing though the burglary had been – my parents were in the House at the time, and were fortunate to have survived the pillage unhurt – the ordeal had soon after devolved, on the part of my father, into a titillatingly farcical treasure hunt.

The burglary also brought out the worst in my father, as I discovered on my return to England and, inevitably, to the House. My father's insistence that all weekends were his pre-requisite, driving me into elaborate lies to cover each time I failed to show up, with or without my husband, had not weakened. He talked about the burglary all the time. The precise details were replayed until, as with the power station, guests and visitors had to be entreated, for all our sakes, to keep away from the topic. There was no power station. There had been no burglary.

We could forestall conversations. We could not inhibit the feverishly elaborate workings of my father's mind.

A detailed inventory of the House and its contents had been drawn up shortly before the burglary. The suggestion for this had come from a homosexual couple with whom, a decade or so before, my parents had become close friends. (The couple's sexuality had, in those years of necessary discretion, been well-hidden – so much so that I, as a schoolgirl, placed the more handsome partner's name under my pillow, hoping that this might induce from him a proposal of marriage. My parents' early endeavours to find suitable wives for this agreeable couple suggest that they lived in a state of similar ignorance.)

Two facts had aroused my father's suspicion. One was that the older of their two friends, a sweet and softly-spoken man, worked for a well-known antique shop, from which insider information might conceivably be bartered. The second was that the couple, emerging at last from camouflage during the late and less inhibited Seventies, began to lead an overtly stylish life, in a house that was reported to be filled with splendid things.

To my father, all now became clear. Accounts of a fine house filled with antiques clinched his suspicions. Their two old friends had been the masterminds behind the burglary. This breakthrough in the case was announced to the family over lunch at the House, on a tranquil summer's day when I was just daring to hope that the subject of the burglary was closed. Beaming, my father announced a plan of action; dumbstruck with dismay, we asked him first to produce any shred of evidence.

But it was so obvious, so excruciatingly obvious! (He thumped his fist on the table so hard that the knives and forks danced from their set positions.) What fools we were! How blind! The couple had never once, since the burglary, asked my father to their house, to stay! What could be clearer? Patently, they had everything to hide!

Hopelessly, we pointed out the flaws in his reasoning. How could the couple possibly expect to hide well-known pieces of furniture in a house visited by mutual friends? Why, when they had successful careers, would they stoop to burgling? Why would they still be issuing invitations to my parents to dine with them in London? *Why?* Only, surely, because they were innocent – and, at this stage, unaware that they had fallen into the camp of suspects.

We were wasting our time. No protests could dissuade my father from his chosen course of action. He took a hotel room in the town nearest to the house in which his friends lived. From there, he went, ineffectually disguised beneath a flat cap and dark glasses, to case the joint in which, he *knew*, his stolen goods were being concealed (if not flaunted!), all that missing booty plundered from his beloved home.

The denouement proved both melancholy and ludicrous. The gay couple, having gone out for the afternoon to visit some friends, returned to find a familiar figure, strangely disguised, with his nose pressed hard to the locked window of their library, a room which overlooked the private, garden side of their house. Trapped, my father muttered some improbable tale of how, having found himself in the vicinity and happening to pass by, he had idly wondered, seeing how lovely their roses looked . . .

The episode was one of complete discomfiture and farce. It did not stop my father from believing, for a single second, that his friends remained guilty. If the stolen goods were not on show, then it was because they had been secreted away, or spirited off to be fenced. The possibility that his conjectures might prove wrong was never entertained. His old friends, baffled by his visit and puzzled by his altered manner, were not afforded the chance to defend themselves or the opportunity to clear their names.

'Of *course* they'd claim they were innocent,' my father stormed. 'Anybody who isn't an idiot can see they're just covering up. I don't mean they did the burglary themselves, but they were behind it. Who else would it be?'

(Years later, I'm tempted to wonder whether this blameless couple, brave enough as middle-aged men to proclaim their love to a social group notorious for its narrow views, had not evoked within my father an anxious mirror to his own secret compunctions? At the time, his eagerness to condemn them as felons seemed both bizarre and inexplicable.)

The discovery, ultimately, that the burglars comprised a group of well-known criminals who specialised in country house robberies, came too late for the salvation of a congenial relationship.

This was sad: that long-enduring friendship was one of the last true ones of my father's to have survived.

Increasingly critical of others, and mortally sensitive to any criticism of himself, my father, as the decade of the Seventies gave way to that of the Eighties, was rapidly approaching what he had always fled and always dreaded: a state of almost total personal isolation.

7

GANYMEDE

The king of the gods once loved a Trojan boy
Named Ganymede . . . and carried off the youngster
Who now, though much against the will of Juno,
Tends to the cups of Jove and serves his nectar.

OVID, *METAMORPHOSES*,
TRANSLATED BY ROLFE HUMPHRIES

It was in 1980, shortly after my father had given up hunting for his lost treasures, that he found Robbie, the young man who became what J. R. Ackerley called 'The Ideal Friend'.

Ackerley, having tried love and found it disappointing, settled for a dog. My father, looking to fill the gap left by dead pets and absent children, found a substitute for both in a sweet-natured boy who was willing to offer the uncritical devotion he needed and had never, as yet, found.

Robbie was not, at first sight, an obvious candidate for my father's love. Heavily built, with bad posture and nicotine-stained teeth and fingers, he appeared older than his age. Shaving and hair-care were low on his priorities; he looked rough as a straw mattress. His eyes were small and flickered shyly when you tried to meet them; his smile was unexpectedly sweet. He was quite muscular. He was also, as my mother reminds me, proud. Nick hadn't objected to dressing up as a footman to hand around our Christmas dinner;

Robbie would have served us with a better grace, but in his own clothes. Probably, he would have wished to contribute something to the feast; always short of money, he had a generous heart.

So far as I know, my father never read Ackerley's writings: if he had, these candid discussions of homosexuality might have struck some familiar chords. To the reader, who has already heard of his sharing a bedroom with Nick, and who is now being introduced to a relationship with another young man that lasted, in growing stages of intensity, for fourteen years, the situation will seem transparent. It will seem more so when I state that my father eventually gave Robbie the bedroom in the House that lay closest to his own private dressing room, that they took holidays together, went biking through the nights and often only returned for breakfast.

This points, does it not, to an obvious conclusion? Even my mother, when we last discussed this delicate subject a few weeks ago, reminded me that my father had allowed Robbie to share with him my parents' twin-bedded room in their London house. She added that she had never cared for the fact that Robbie slept in her bed, and that it was often still unmade when she paid her own next visit.

'So what do you think?' I asked her, and she shrugged. 'I don't see what else could have been happening,' she said. 'Do you?'

The strange truth is, that I'm finding it difficult to set the words down. As soon as I write them, doubts crowd eagerly in. Really, I know that part of the trouble is that I just don't want to imagine my father in bed with Robbie, any more than I wanted to imagine my father in bed with Nick. I wonder, never having been to an analyst, what I should make of this reluctance. Am I too prudish to tolerate the thought that my father slept with boys? Can I honestly believe that this attachment, so close in all other ways, was sexless? Why can't I acknowledge it with the simplicity that my mother seems at last to have achieved? I don't know. Is it the biographer's mind at work, warning me to abhor speculation unless proof can be given? I simply do not know. But I may be the last person who clings, absurdly, to the faint possibility that my father was, until the end, a heterosexual.

I'm clearer on the fact that it was, once more, the pain of displacement that troubled me most. Being ousted, reduced to a lesser place in my father's affections than his friend: this was what hurt, like a bad headache, all the time.

Whatever my father's private life may have been, he wanted the world to know him as a straight man. Robbie was introduced to the small circle of people who encountered him as a friend, never as a lover. We, as I knew even then, were valuable camouflage. If my mother, my brother and I played our parts obligingly, Robbie could be presented as a friend to all of us, an approved addition to a close-knit family. My brother and I were not happy about this plan. How could we be, when Robbie had usurped us?

And my mother? The other question that needs answering at this point is that of my mother's extraordinary restraint. My father kept company with Robbie for fourteen years: why did she put up with it?

'I was weak,' she says now. I don't see it as weakness, but as evidence of how well she understood her husband, a man whose need for love was as profound as his insecurity. They write of people who will walk through fire for the sake of a loved one: she's one of those. This is why, when I see my mother watching her favourite actress, Giulietta Masina, in her favourite film, *La Strada*, I understand the look of enchanted recognition that transfigures her face.

La Strada tells the story of Gelsomina, who leaves home to travel the road with a circus strong man, Anthony Quinn playing the character of Zampano. A taciturn but handsome brute with a terror of solitude, Zampano bullies Gelsomina and humiliates her by his casual affairs; she, loving him and with no other place to go, stands by her man and accepts humiliation as her fate. When, finally, she leaves him, Zampano goes to pieces; in the last scene, he is seen trying to bury himself in the shore where Gelsomina's abandoned body lies.

Time and again I have watched my mother, her dinner forgotten as she stares at the screen. I've seen her hands caress the side of the chair as Gelsomina turns to show us, by her bright little smile, her determination to endure. 'I can't bear it!' my mother cries. But she always wants to watch the film once more.

My mother, throughout this last epoch of her marriage, played Gelsomina's role. Like Gelsomina, she understood that however much my father hurt her, she would damage him far more if she failed to play her part. He needed Robbie, but he also needed her.

They met, so my father explained to me later, in Leicester Square in London, in a cinema queue. My father talked about his bike. Robbie, just turned eighteen, was awed by his descriptions of the Ducati: shyly, he admitted that he had never seen one of these glamorous machines. The cinema tickets were sold out. With nothing further to do that evening and a sulky young wife waiting for him in a Vauxhall basement, Robbie was happy to be offered supper and taken to a London house where, with a fond pat on its ebony side, he was introduced to 'the Duke'. He felt honoured by the friendly manner of a man who seemed both kind and lonely. They agreed to meet again.

Confidences were soon exchanged. My father, anxious not to frighten Robbie away, played down his own circumstances. The House was never mentioned, only an unsympathetic family and a need for freedom. Robbie revealed that his father, four years earlier, had killed himself, and that he had since lost contact with his mother. A girlfriend had pressured him into marriage, a step that he now regretted. He didn't have a job and didn't relish the idea of full-time employment. (His options were restricted by the fact that he could only with difficulty write his name.)

It was my father who suggested that Robbie should train to be a despatch rider. Self-interest played the predominant part. My father liked to instruct; despatch riding wasn't a full-time job; the boy, when once qualified, could replace Nick as his co-rider upon the Duke.

It didn't take long for my father to realise that he was underestimating to himself the role he desired Robbie to play in his life, and that his feelings were reciprocated. Robbie, a confused and gentle young man who had been deeply affected by his father's death, was as lonely as he was himself. Grateful for my father's solicitous friendship, Robbie came, in time, to worship him, as a substitute for his own lost parent, as a tutor, and, at the least, as a beloved companion.

For the first two years, the friendship flourished in secret. Their mutual pleasures were simple. They walked along the tow-paths of the London canals, ate breakfasts at greasy spoon cafes and went to bike shows. My father picked out a few films of a popular kind, at which they both could laugh. Years had passed since my father had felt so merry. Robbie was an easy laugher; he chuckled at everything, even when no cause for mirth was apparent.

Here was the kind of easy companionship that my father had hankered after during his miserable years of employment at the bank. Here, surely, was what his children should have continued to provide? The closer he became to Robbie, the more resentful my father grew of what he perceived as the cold indifference of his son and daughter. We had never been so readily available, so willing to fall in with his whims, so happy to place our lives at his disposal.

My mother, during this early period of the relationship with Robbie, was kept in the dark. While surprised by the amount of time that her husband now apparently devoted to his voluntary work in London as chairman of the Juvenile Magistrates' Court, she was not much grieved by his absences; ill-health, hypochondria, and low spirits had made of my father a querulous and demanding companion. As the daughter of a near recluse, my mother was equipped to make the best of solitude. Unlike her husband, she enjoyed her own company.

My father had now reached his late fifties. He was overdue for a mid-life crisis, ripe for the rebellion that had never taken place in his early life. The timing of Robbie's appearance was perfect; all of the older generation for whom my father retained a ghostly vestige of awe were dead. Nobody was left to gainsay him, or to tell him how best to treat his wife.

My mother, if she happened to hear about Robbie's existence, could be relied upon to defend her husband, and fight off any suggestion that there was anything odd about this unusual partnership. Friends presented a trickier situation.

George FitzRoy Seymour and Robbie.

My father had lost none of his snobbery. He cared, as much as ever, about where he was invited and by whom, about annual invitations to stalk in the Highlands, and the fact that he frequented the same London barber as the Duke of Muttonchops. It amused him to flout convention by inviting a young female pop star to his club, just as it had once given him delight to shock his country neighbours by showing off Slav in his loincloth, as part of the household. Robbie was another matter. He did not wish it to be thought that he was paying a young man for sexual services; he was acutely conscious that rumours would spread if Robbie and he appeared, outside my mother's company, in public. He was, for this reason, unnerved when Robbie casually proposed that the two of them should take a walk together, sometime, around Piccadilly and St James's. When my father began to offer alternatives – a visit to the Tower of London was held out as an enticement – Robbie displayed his most annoying characteristic: extreme stubbornness. Nothing would satisfy him now but the promise of a long and leisurely day during which my father would show him a glimpse of his other, more old-fashioned world, and share with him – Robbie loved picnics – a sandwich in Green Park.

Green Park was the least of my father's worries. 'Avoid Boodle's' he wrote despairingly in his diary. The reference was to the club from the ladies' annexe of which he had defiantly stormed when warned that his young companion must hide her skimpy clothes under a coat and put away her camera. Like all the old-fashioned gentleman's clubs, Boodle's invited its members to be treated like schoolboys: to eat nursery food, to dress ever so nicely, and to behave as Nanny would wish. Robbie had heard my father mention the club as a place for which he felt a particular affection. As a favoured friend, he was keen to pay a visit. Untruthfully told that strangers were forbidden to enter, he requested to be allowed to admire it from the doorway.

His prodigal daughter wasn't there to relish the spectacle of her father's anguish; today, I find no difficulty in imagining it. Sauntering down St James's Street with his friend 'Georgie' (he disliked the name George, finding it far too formal), Robbie kept his hands jammed into the pockets of his jeans. Hurriedly informed that they were passing the sacred door, he climbed the step, stared in, let his stomach take the air and gave it a prolonged and cheerful scratch before announcing that he was ready to move on. This would not have been a protest against the splendour of his surroundings, or an indication of the fact that he had intuited my father's anxious state of mind, but a modest declaration of his lingering independence.

The diary reveals that the mission was successfully accomplished. They had met nobody my father knew. Robbie remained unconscious of having caused even a moment of anxiety – and thoroughly enjoyed his day out.

The year 1982 saw two strands of my father's elaborate life become entwined. It's possible that Robbie was starting to feel hurt at being kept apart from his friend's family; it's as likely that my father could no longer face daily life at Thrumpton without him. He invited Robbie to stay, for a week of biking. He didn't tell him what to expect, what sort of a House. He did, imperiously summoning me to come and visit at the same time, try to ensure that his friend received a warm welcome. I was told that I would be meeting a somewhat illiterate young man with a sensitive nature that would respond quickly to slights. I heard the tenderness with which my father anxiously offered this brief description. Just as with Nick, I felt my body shake with jealous rage. I knew what to expect now. Another cuckoo: another usurper.

Robbie, as I later learned, had arrived a day earlier than myself, riding the bike that my father had given him when he passed his test. My mother's recollection is that she offered the unwelcome visitor a friendly welcome, a good lunch and an invitation to carry her basket of stems and cuttings while she pruned the garden roses. It's possible that Robbie felt basket-carrying was a bit demeaning. It's more likely that he was unnerved by the size of the House and angry that my father had hidden all this splendour from him. All I know is that I turned up the following day to find the library blinds drawn, the bees humming merrily outside them among the wallflowers, and my father stretched, prostrate, upon a sofa. His eyes, when he removed his dark glasses to bestow a sorrowing kiss on my cheek, were milky with tears.

'Where's your friend?' I asked. My father shook his head. He could hardly speak for sobs.

'Gone,' he said at last. 'Gone back to London. And he never wants to see me again. Oh, bloody, bloody house!'

'He didn't like it?'

'He's cockney,' my father said, as though this explained everything. 'And I love him. Is that a terrible thing to say? I love him!'

I studied my fingernails and concentrated on wondering whether they might be improved by a clear coat of varnish. By concentrating, I could block out the unwelcome sound of a renewed burst of weeping, followed by further diatribes against the House. This, clearly, was love of a new kind.

'I suppose you think I'm horribly selfish,' he said petulantly, when it became clear that I wasn't going to respond. 'But if you knew how happy Robbie and I have been—'

'I don't want to know.'

Outraged, my father glared. 'My God, but you're cold-hearted! You've never cared. It's all about you, isn't it? It never occurs to you that anyone else might deserve a few pathetic little moments of joy, when their entire life has been one long, wretched grind of duty and sacrifice . . .'

More followed: long, quaveringly familiar lamentations about the cruelty of a family who begrudged him any moment of freedom, any morsel of common happiness. I was too furious to speak. I couldn't believe that he was looking for my sympathy.

'Now, don't be so sharp,' reproves my mother. 'I'm sure he never said all that. No need to get carried away.'

'I'm not. Do you think I'd forget?'

'I think', my mother says nicely, 'you had less to complain about than me. And I put up with it.'

'Only because you had to,' I say brutally. 'Only because you weren't ever going to leave him.'

'I might have done,' she says, looking forlorn. 'You don't know everything.'

Guilty at causing pain, I squeeze her hand. 'You'd never have abandoned him. You were a good wife.'

But she still wears a sad look, and I've put it there. 'I'm not sure,' she says. 'I wasn't always kind.'

The row was quickly patched up, and Robbie was persuaded to return to the House for a second visit. After a third, he began to feel more at his ease. He was staying there in October 1982, when my father, aware that mature women dislike to be reminded of their age, adopted the charitable course of leaving my mother to celebrate her sixtieth birthday alone, while he took young Robbie off on an overnight bike trip to Scotland. Shortly after this jaunt, with my father's benevolent encouragement, Robbie decided to leave his wife. The separation and divorce were uncontested; Robbie now had even more time to place at the disposal of his mentor.

Either Robbie disliked the bachelor state or else he was an easy prey; we were never quite sure. In 1983, less than a year later, he announced that he planned once again to marry. His choice had fallen upon Della, a stolid, matronly young woman, a few years older than himself. My father, although displeased, paid for the cake and the hire of the registry office; he even offered to act, and performed as, the best man. Three weeks later, he suggested to Robbie that the Duke needed to get out for a run. They took a two-day trip on the bike to Cornwall: this expedition, as my father noted in his pocket diary, had proved '*great* fun!' Part of the fun, I'd guess, was in knowing that he'd won Robbie away from a newly-wed wife.

The homosexual friends to whom I've told the story interpret Robbie's married state as a plus for my father. He'd never shown any interest in effeminate men; they see him as the type to enjoy the challenge of a female rival. If this was the case, he must have relished the scent of victory. Robbie was either exceptionally weak or entirely under my father's spell; by the spring of 1984, less than a year after he married Della, he was travelling to Thrumpton every week, while his wife remained in London.

This marked the point at which Robbie began his new role at the House. A routine was quickly established. Each night, after a homely supper cooked by my mother, the two men would repair upstairs to my father's dressing room to change into their bikers' uniforms. My mother remained below to wash up the dishes. By nine, the House was entirely hers. She rarely saw the two of them before breakfast the following morning.

My mother said nothing and did what was asked of her; Della was not so willing to comply. She wanted her husband back with her, and earning money.

My father jotted down a terse reminder to himself, during the late summer of 1984: 'Talk with Della.' He could, when he wanted, make himself hard to resist; I'm sure Della was surprised, when he left, to find that Robbie was going to be spending just as much time at the House as before, and with her agreement. The compromise she had been offered was that the invitation now embraced them both. Robbie would continue to accompany my father on his biking expeditions. Della, meanwhile, would enjoy the pleasure of providing my mother with a companion.

Separated from my first husband and keeping myself at a distance from the House and its altered ménage, I was baffled by the insistently serene tone of my mother's letters. Having met Della once, I couldn't imagine that the two wives had anything to say to each other; on paper, my mother praised her as a helpful young woman who didn't mind helping to polish furniture and was always easy company, no trouble at all. Today, however, my mother has become less guarded. She remembers how Della enjoyed watching television game shows, with the volume turned up at full blast. The furniture-polishing was, she says, undertaken only when the television broke down, and at my mother's insistence.

'Well, she didn't do anything else!' she says. 'And all that cooking! I had to give her lunch, and him dinner. I might as well have been running a hotel.'

'Why did you pretend everything was fine in the letters?' I ask. 'You ought to have said you were having a rotten time; you know we would have backed you.'

Stubbornly, she shakes her head. 'I didn't want you causing trouble,' she says. 'It wouldn't have done any good.'

Even though I've seen her watch that film so many times, I still can't bear to hear the note of resignation in her voice. Gelsomina was a poor little waif, staying loyal to promiscuous Zampano, in part, because she had nowhere else to go; my mother is a proud woman, from a proud family. How could she allow herself to be so beaten down?

'You said you could have left him. Why didn't you?'

She looks bewildered. 'And leave all this . . .?'

Of course. It isn't only the story of Gelsomina, standing by her impossible man. Having lost that romantic family home of her own, the castle on the hill she'd always supposed was their own until her parents left it, my mother had allowed the house of her marriage to fill the void. She would have put up with anything rather than be separated from a home the contours of which had grown as reassuringly familiar as a beloved body. Here it always stands, at the heart of every family story, pulling us back, holding us fast: The House.

At about this time, bruised by the end of a marriage and a long, unhappy love affair, I turned again to the House myself, seeking comfort in its safe harbour. I hadn't been seeing much of either of my parents after that one emotional scene with my father, when he thought that Robbie had left him. I knew of Robbie's existence, and that he and Della spent time at the House. It had not occurred to me, until I began to feel the desire to spend more time there myself, that I would find myself an outsider. Robbie was now securely fixed in position. My brother and I had been displaced.

I hope that Robbie never understood how much I hated him for supplanting me. He didn't glimpse me above him, standing on the roof, looking down to where he lounged at my father's side on the bank of the lake, where he lay listening, like a perfect child, to a storybook read aloud to him by his ageing friend. He didn't read the diary in which I wrote: 'Is he *never* not here?' He didn't know how desperately I prayed for him to disappear.

Towards me, Robbie always acted cheerful and kind. He taught my son how to fish in the Thrumpton lake; when my London flat was burgled, he rode round on his new bike – my father's birthday gift to him – to offer me a brass candlestick he claimed to have picked up at a car boot sale. (Or had my father given it to him to offer me as a sop?) He was always keen to come up with a word to help me out at Scrabble, a game that our father, dispensing urgent winks and nods to signal his scheme, ensured that Robbie always won, however bizarre his spelling.

'You do like Robbie, don't you?' my father would say, hungry for appreciation of his friend.

'He's all right,' I'd say, the most that I could manage without being accused of viciousness or snobbery. (And here was another difficulty: it was impossible to express hostility to Robbie without sounding condescending. If Robbie had been rich, or well-read, or from a grand family, I would have felt no such delicacy about expressing my resentment.)

'He's very fond of *you*.' A yearning pause, while I savour the moment of power and contemplate the dangers of candour, the risk to my mother, who has begged me, almost crying, to make no more trouble than already exists in the House.

'He was saying how much he admires you for writing all those books.'

I'd like to tell him that I'd value Robbie's admiration of my works more if he had managed to do more than glance at their jackets. Instead, I thank my father for passing the tribute on; seeing Robbie himself loitering attentively in the background, awaiting his excuse to join in, I find a reason to move away, to leave the two of them alone. I hate to see them together. I hate the softness in my father's eyes when he looks at Robbie. I hate the glances that plead with me to be understanding, to be kind.

My rage, expressed as calculated reticence, was fuelled by a sense of the injustice done to our family as a whole. Why was it acceptable to my father for Robbie to boast fingernails that looked as though he'd gone grave-digging without a shovel, while my mother's honest gardening hands were criticised as unkempt? Why was my young son rebuked if he failed to post my father a weekly letter from school, while Robbie never wrote at all? Why must I drive across London – I was often working against tight deadlines – to return to Robbie a cheap plastic cigarette lighter he had left behind at the House? Why must I obtain the autograph of a singer I had once met, requesting him to write 'With Love to Robbie'? Why must Robbie always take precedence, always be without fault?

The answer, as I well knew, was love. My father was enraptured, besotted, head over heels. He treasured my mother. He was, if only behind our backs, proud of his son and daughter's achievements.

But Robbie was the passion of my father's later life. Robbie's only rival was the House.

The presiding spirit of this stage of their increasingly exclusive relationship was A. A. Milne. Teaching Robbie to read had not been an easy business, since he was quickly bored and disliked being corrected. These little foibles, as my father fondly observed, demonstrated that he had much in common with a special character in one of the few books that Robbie sincerely enjoyed: the bouncy and uncrushable 'Tigger'.

Delighted by this identification, Robbie pointed out that Tigger was referred to by Pooh as a great friend of Christopher Robin's: not just any friend, but a *great* one. If he was Tigger, then my father must surely be Christopher Robin (rapidly shortened to 'CR'). Her affection for owls made the selection of name an easy pick for my mother. Della, although her visits had become infrequent, was offered Piglet. Behind her broad back, however, my father spoke of her to Robbie as Heffalump. They both enjoyed this little joke at the expense of Della's shape, although Robbie occasionally remonstrated that it wasn't in the best of taste. (He remained quite fond of Della, and liked to point out that she had a good sense of humour. She surely needed one.)

The names were chosen in 1984. From then on, these were the characters and personalities that my parents and Robbie adopted for use in their private life.

I've managed to find my father's tattered copy of *The House at Pooh Corner*, the volume in which Tigger first appears. It's a third impression from the 1928 edition, published when George Seymour was five years old and just beginning to look upon Thrumpton as his rightful home. Ernest Shepard's delicate drawing, spread across the flyleaf, depicts a small boy, with his faithful band of followers skipping at his heels, dancing through an idealised landscape. Easily visible on the far side of the rolling fields is the outline of a tall, well-gabled house. The similarity to his own House and its pretty estate is striking enough to have caught my father's fancy when, almost sixty years later, he began reading the book aloud to Robbie.

To me, it's clear that my father was once again revisiting his childhood, burying the bad memories of abandonment, loneliness and fear in a re-enacted version over which he had gained control. In his kindness to Robbie, he was also compensating himself for the years when he had slept up on the dusty top floor, and cried, unheard, for the mother who had left him when she travelled to La Paz.

My mother argues that the connection is simpler still.

'He liked being Christopher Robin because it meant he didn't have to be responsible,' she states. 'And Tigger: well, Robbie was rather greedy, and clumsy, and always making out he knew much more than he did.'

'And were you Owl, because you were so wise?'

My mother glances again at the illustration by Shepard. 'The owl isn't following Christopher Robin,' she observes.

And she's right: the owl is off on its own, floating overhead, hovering above the frolicking troupe. Suddenly, I find myself thinking about the grand house parties with which my grandmother liked to fill her Welsh castle, and of my reclusive grandfather trotting quietly away from them, absconding up the stone stairs, fleeing to his turret and his books.

'Could you have got through it all without that ability to detach yourself?' I ask her.

My mother thinks about it, then she shakes her head.

'I doubt it,' she says. 'No. Not that last ten years . . .'

8

❧

THE HOUSE DIVIDED

Saturday, 24 April 1993
Received by George Seymour, very friendly, extremely
correct, snobbish . . . In the library we were joined for
drinks by . . . nice rugged lady resembling Violet
Powell . . . and a strange yob-like bruiser who sat mute
and gazing into space. Myles [Myles Hildyard, a
neighbour] disclosed that he is the 'friend' with whom
G.S. rides pillion all over the country on an enormous
motorbike — very strange.

JAMES LEES-MILNE, *THE MILK OF PARADISE:
DIARIES, 1993–1997*

Lacking any interest in motorbikes, I had no sense in 1985 of the
significance in my father's exchange of a Ducati for a Harley
Davidson. Today, I've become better informed.

The Ducati, affectionately known to its admirers (not just my
father) as the Duke, is the Bugatti of the bike world. A young
man's machine, it was designed for speed, for fast corners on the
Italian racetracks; later, it was adapted to suit the twists and turns
of European roads. The Ducati is swift, dangerous and elegant.
The Harley is a style of life, the icon of the seasoned biker, the
tough guy.

Image, here, is what counts. Nobody cares that Marlon Brando
actually rode a British Triumph in the film, *The Wild Ones* (or that

the author of *On the Road*, for a similar example, could not even drive). In fact, and this explains my father's change of machines, the Harley Davidson (rudely known to its critics as the Hardly Ableson) is a bike ideally suited to an ageing man. Built for long-haul riding on the straight roads of America, it is more comfortable than the Ducati, and more reliable. For a man of sixty-one who was anticipating a long future of leisurely bike tours around Britain, accompanied by Robbie, the Harley was the consummate choice.

This was not, at the time, how it seemed to us. To my brother and me, our father appeared to have taken one more step into a macho world of big machines, black leather, tough talk and loud boasts, a world into which we were unable to follow him. I myself, after my father once kidnapped my six-year-old son, sweeping him off to 'do the ton' on a busy local road, had resolved to have nothing further to do with bikes; my brother, having nearly lost his life in a biking accident, had better reason still for staying away from all such machines.

Love made my father protective of his friend: suspecting that his grander cousins and acquaintances would take a dim view of Robbie's role in the House, he took care to keep them at a distance. The Visitors' Book at the House had once been thick with names; by 1987, with rare exceptions, it displayed only one, awkwardly traced, over and over, week in, week out. On the infrequent occasions when country neighbours came to meals, Robbie stayed at the back of the House. Occasionally, for a laugh, and because he liked to have his friend close to him, my father coaxed him to come through to the dining room where, while pouring wine or gathering up the plates, Robbie took stock of the visitors. Later, he'd comment on their appearance and entertain my father with his candid views, fondly passed on in due course to my brother and myself. (No opportunity was ever missed for showing off Robbie's remarkable powers of perception.)

Robbie, while we kept our distance, was feeling increasingly at home in the House. To him, as to us all, it offered an enchanted haven. The villagers, taking their cue from my mother's smiling face, kept any doubts to themselves and offered Robbie a warm welcome when he and my parents joined in the local galas, fetes and feast days. In the gardens, on hot summer days, the two men hacked down laurels and scythed away undergrowth before settling down to a beer and sandwich lunch on the grass. Riding the bike around the county, they scoured antique markets and charity shops for bargains; irreproachably elegant in London, my father now competed with his friend for scruffiness in his country clothing, boasting of the excellent cut and comfort of a tattered and ill-fitting pair of moleskin trousers that Robbie had spotted on a secondhand stall. For supper, my mother remembers, the two of them liked nothing better than beans on toast before they went upstairs to my father's dressing room in the oldest and most remote corner of the House, to prepare for a long night ahead, on the road.

Enthusiasm for fast bikes, late night fry-ups at motorway diners, and a bit of slang had not reduced my father's acute sense of his place in the world. Visiting London, he continued to dine at his club, to visit his barber, to purchase hair lotion in Jermyn Street, and to study, at leisure, the *Daily Telegraph*, for confirmation that the civilised world was in decline. (At Thrumpton, he preferred to read, with Robbie, the jaunty and more downmarket *Sun*.) It gave him continuing joy that an earl's elderly daughter consented to chat to him twice a week on the telephone. He flinched as if pierced when a stranger failed to rhyme his surname with the capital of Peru. He cringed when I mentioned that I had forgotten, while posting off a letter, that a duchess's name should properly be preceded on the envelope by the words: 'Her Grace'.

By 1988, however, Robbie's ascendancy was almost complete, and the worlds that my father had striven to keep separate were beginning to collide. To us, his children, it seemed as though Robbie's transformation into Tigger, the stripy little tiger who thinks he can do everything better than anybody else, had encouraged a new and irritating confidence. The bike rides now often included visits to castles, cathedrals and stately homes; seeing them in the company of a man who sounded eminently authoritative, Robbie picked up fragments and then produced them, garbled, as his own opinions.

'Tigger's got very good instincts,' my father wrote to me, after proudly reporting Robbie's reaction to the gargoyles of Notre Dame. All I could think was that my mother, rather than Robbie, ought to be holidaying with her husband in Paris. Burning with self-righteousness, I urged her to stand up for her rights. When had *she* last been taken on a holiday? Did she know – I'd been shocked by this information – that there were plans afoot for a visit with Robbie to Venice? Didn't she care?

For a moment, I seemed to detect a slight chink in the armour. I didn't know, then, that my mother had been suggesting that she and my father should take a holiday in Venice, their first European jaunt, as a couple, in twenty years. Neither did she feel the need to tell me. Instead, shaking her head, she told me to stop making trouble. Everything was all right. She had no complaints, none at all. In fact, the kindest thing her children could do, she said in a voice taut with repressed emotion, was to keep their mouths shut and their opinions to themselves. All she had ever asked of us was our discretion.

'Be quiet,' she said fiercely, when I returned to the attack. 'Please. Just – be quiet.'

Silence was beyond me. I found it easier to stay away from Thrumpton, and to put all the contending forces and inhabitants of the House entirely out of my mind.

It was, as I realised later, easier for me to do this than it was for my brother. I, although I loved the House, had accustomed myself to the knowledge that it would never be mine. As my father's daughter, I had escaped the weight of future obligation. I had no need to fret about my father's determination to hold on to the House until his death (as one of an unusually long-lived family, he expected to survive into his nineties). I sympathised with my brother's fears that his inheritance, when it came, would be swallowed up by death duties; but these were not my concerns.

In 1989, I married a man whose relative youth – he was several years my junior – and friendly manner won my father's heart. Looking with hungry eyes for anybody in the family who would treat Robbie with more than frozen courtesy, he saw two potential allies, my husband and my affectionate, easygoing son, a boy of sixteen. This consoled him a little, I imagine, for the fact that my brother and I, while outwardly civil, remained hostile to Robbie, an intruder for whom our mother appeared to be meekly sacrificing her rights as a wife.

It was at about this time that, with money running low, my father, while taking no risk himself, encouraged my mother and his son into a plan to replenish the coffers at no expense. He was not alone in thinking that Lloyd's Insurance would solve the problem; or in being sucked under by the claims that almost immediately began to flood in from companies whose employees had suffered from the use of asbestos. Lloyd's, as my family were now painfully taught, had not been joking when they asked, in return for a handsome annual yield, to have the promise of unlimited security. This meant, in plain language, that they would take everything, the House included, to recoup the required amount.

My mother was wiped out; my brother became temporarily vulnerable. It was at this point that my father decided to change his will. I might not have much money, but I was not threatened by Lloyd's. I, at the stroke of a pen, became his heir; my clever, hard-working, conscientious brother, who had endured the brunt of my father's demands and expectations for half his life, was casually informed, as he was stepping on to a train, of the altered plan.

These were the facts; nevertheless, I couldn't help wondering if my father's talent for mischief-making had also influenced this transformation in his children's lives. My brother and I had always been close; our shared resentment of Robbie strengthened the bond. Was it possible, I wondered, that our father hoped by this radical action to drive us apart? If so, he was to be disappointed. My brother, conscious that I loved the House as passionately as he, told me that it was only fair that each of us should have our turn. Our affection for each other, although tested, remained undiminished.

I had not suspected, until I became my father's heir, how much this would increase my passionate aversion to Robbie. Neither had I realised how meticulously my father was planning for his friend's future. I, as a woman, was judged to be a softer touch than my brother, and, in my imagined gratitude, more susceptible to the request he now made.

My father still had no intention of yielding control of his estate; having risked nothing of his own with Lloyd's, he had no reason to do so. The full horrors imposed by inheritance and capital gains tax would be avoided, he explained, by the fact that the House would pass, for a restricted period, through my mother's hands. And what if she died before him? His answer – that this was most unlikely – didn't do much to reassure me.

This discussion took place one summer afternoon in 1992 as he left Robbie to fish in the lake while he tutored me in the daily running of the estate. We strolled along the hilltop, backs tactfully turned to the looming chimney of the station. Smiling, my father pointed down to the lake where Robbie crouched in the rushes beside his rod. Invited to comment on his evident state of contentment, I prepared to speak my mind.

'Don't you think it's time that Robbie got on with his own life?'

'Away from here? When you can see how he loves it? I've always thought', my father murmured, his hand resting like a pincer on my arm, 'that it was one of the great privileges of owning a beautiful House like this, that one can offer it to people less fortunate than ourselves. Agreed?'

'Within limits,' I said. 'Not all the time.'

Sighing, my father released his grasp. 'To be honest, I don't know what would happen to him now if he lost this.'

'He could be with Della in London,' I said. 'She is his wife, isn't she?' I glanced at him. 'I'm not going to promise to share the House with Robbie, if that's what you mean. I won't. '

'Darling, we're not talking about next year,' my father said. 'I'm not gone yet, however eagerly you might wish it.' He paused again, softened his voice. All he was asking, and surely it wasn't such a burden to add to my inheritance, was that I should never attempt to banish his friend from the House. Robbie, like some unloved heirloom, was to be a permanent fixture.

I don't know whether it says more about my father's force of personality, or my own weakness of character that I had, by the time we walked down the hillside, given up and given in. Beaming, my father gave the good news to his friend; Robbie, stretching his hand towards me and offering a cheery grin, said he expected that we'd rub along pretty well as co-habitants, so long as I learned to take my orders.

Christmas 1993 was approaching. Christmas was still one of the few occasions that had remained sacrosanct to the family. This year, however, my brother, lovingly married and with a young family of his own, sent apologies; my father promptly announced that he would be asking Robbie to come and fill the gap. Della, although still formally married, was in the process of seeking a separation; the poor chap couldn't be expected to spend the holiday season on his own.

'He's been with you all this month,' I said. 'Hasn't he got any other friends he might want to see? There must be someone.'

'You do sound desperate to be rid of him,' my father said. 'Poor Robbie. And he's always so full of inquiries about you, and how you're doing. It'd thrill him to think you actually wanted him here, you know. It's so little to ask.'

Telephones are a useful medium for communicating silence as displeasure. I waited.

'You do remember that Robbie's father killed himself at Christmas,' my father said in a voice of hushed reproach for my insensitivity. 'It's a sad, sad time for him to be alone. But if that's what you want, of course, I'll tell him. I'll say you couldn't bear to spend even two of your precious days showing a little kindness that wouldn't have cost you anything to offer . . .'

The technique was too familiar to be wholly effective, but a compromise was negotiated. I would bring my family for Christmas Eve and stay on for two days; Robbie, after spending most of December at the House, would depart, returning there on Boxing Day to remain through January. Our stays would overlap, but only for only two meals. Honour, on both sides, had been satisfied.

My father liked to map things out in advance; these plans were hatched and resolved in October. At the end of that month, he invited himself to supper at my home in London. This in itself was unusual. So was the fact that the meal was consumed without protest. No objection was made to a soufflé that had sunk, or even to the shocking absence of new potatoes to accompany the poached salmon: my father took second helpings of everything, praised my appearance and spoke kindly of the wine my husband had bought for the occasion.

'Although a Gewürztraminer might have been even more delicious,' he said, lounging elegantly back in his chair as he mentioned the wine I most detested. 'You like German wines, don't you, darling?'

I don't and was about to say so, when my father cut across me.

His smile, I noticed, had become tight-lipped, a sure sign that he was feeling uneasy.

'Speaking of that,' he said rapidly, 'I've been laying down some rather good Alsatian wines at the House.' My father examined the well-buffed tips of his nails. 'For Robbie.'

'How thoughtful,' I said. 'I thought he preferred beer.'

'I can hear that note in your voice,' he said softly. 'Do try not to be quite so unpleasant. He's so fond of you.'

I turned my back. 'I'll get the coffee.'

The subject had been delayed, but not dismissed.

'The thing is,' my father sighed as he set down his cup, 'that Robbie's a bit short of money at present. He's frightfully proud. No point in my trying to give him anything. But if you were to buy some wine from him, at a good price . . .'

Then and now, the scheme seemed baffling in its convolutions. I was to pay my father twelve pounds a bottle, for a case of wine that I didn't want. This would apparently show Robbie that I entertained friendly feelings towards him, while allowing his pride to remain intact. Wearily, I offered to write a cheque to Robbie on the spot; my father shook his head. Robbie and Della shared a bank account; better by far if I made out a cheque to George Seymour and let him complete the transaction, in cash.

Too tired to argue, I did as he asked. Rosy with satisfaction, my father pocketed the cheque, kissed my cheek, shook my husband's hand, mounted his bike and shot away down the street.

I made no effort to collect the wine. Having listened to my father's explanation, I assumed that he had immediately banked the cheque and given the cash, so badly needed, to his friend. Robbie, I supposed, had been told of my love of Gewürztraminer and my eagerness to help him by purchasing it. As always, I was astonished at the lengths to which my father was willing to go, for Robbie's sake.

On this occasion, however, he did not go far enough. He did not hand the money over to poor, desperate Robbie; instead, savouring the pleasure of his own solicitude, he put seven twenty-pound notes into an envelope, and laid it, inscribed to Tigger from Christopher Robin, to one side. I gather that he planned to bestow this handsome surprise just before I arrived for Christmas; Robbie would, so he fondly fancied, thus be persuaded of my friendly feelings and feel less mournful at being dismissed from the House on Christmas Eve. He told me this afterwards, blaming himself for his folly. But by then, it was too late.

At the beginning of December, just as my father and he had planned, Robbie arrived at the House. As usual, the two of them went out on the bike each night after dinner. Dire weather never kept them from making these expeditions; the diaries show that they rode, through heavy fog and rain, to Folkestone, to Cardiff, and to Lyme Regis. Robbie was unusually subdued; my father's references to the unstoppable cheeriness of Tiggers failed to elicit the usual grin. Apparently, he complained on several occasions of a headache, and, a further curious symptom that was giving him trouble, of a dizzying blackness behind his eyes.

It's possible that he was anxious about his state of dependence on my father. It's certain that he was worried about money. Problems with Della can't have helped; neither can the knowledge that he was approaching the age at which his father had killed himself. The mention of headaches and dizziness also suggest that Robbie may have suffered from severe mental depression, and that this condition was worsening. Later, all these possibilities were subjected to intense and painful speculation.

My mother's memory, although clear on all the preceding stages of the relationship, wavers at this point. The details that follow are based on her recollections, combined with those provided by my father to me, at three in the morning, on 12 December.

On the afternoon of the preceding day, Robbie went alone to the cupboard where the shotguns were kept, at the back of the House. He put one of the guns into the boot of the beaten-up old car that had been bought for him sometime earlier; he then went to find my father, and to let him know that he had decided to go back to London early. He offered no reason, and made no apology. My father hated his plans to be upset; he had been looking forward to a further two weeks of biking, and of Robbie's company. There was a scene.

Petulance, I imagine, prevented my father from going up to his room to fetch the cash-filled envelope, inscribed to Tigger. He may have wished to punish him; he may, in his distress, have let the envelope go out of his mind. It isn't known. No third party was present at the conversation that took place between them, before Robbie climbed into his car and drove away. My mother remembers that she heard them quarrelling; she was unaware until the end of the day that Robbie had left the House.

Towards ten o'clock that evening, when my parents sat watching the news, my father became intensely anxious. He telephoned Robbie's flat; Della answered. She confirmed that her husband had arrived safely and added that he was in a funny mood. My father asked her to bring him to the phone; Robbie, apparently, said he wasn't talking. Della, now sounding anxious, said she'd only meant to drop in to pick up a coat, but that Robbie seemed so low that she had decided to stay. She'd seen him in bad spirits before, but never like this.

At two in the morning, my father was woken by a ringing phone. It was Della once more, and she had bad news. Shortly after midnight, while she was sleeping, Robbie had gone into the kitchen, shut the door, and written a brief note to say that he couldn't see any other way out. Then he had sat down at the table, stuck the barrel of a shotgun into his mouth and blown his head off. The police had just left. The mess was terrible.

An hour later, my own phone rang. At first, I couldn't recognise my father's voice or understand the news that was delivered, between gasps, in hoarse cries, like those of a tortured animal. I heard the word: 'Dead'; after that, nothing but deep, protracted sobs. Robbie was dead? Silenced by shock, I stared at the ghost of myself that wavered in the mirror opposite the bed. This was, in a sense, all I had wished for; I had never expected my wish to be granted in such a fashion. 'I'm sorry; I'm so sorry,' I heard a voice whisper out of the receiver. I'm not sure whether it was from shock or pity that I began to tremble as I realised that, for the first time – it was not to be the last – my father was apologising to me. My poor father: he was apologising for his tears.

Ten years earlier, my father had made the arrangements for Robbie's wedding to Della. She, gone all to pieces, showed no will to fight him now, when he offered to organise and pay for the funeral. Della was not especially fond of my father – he had, after all, been her rival – but she had neither the heart nor the funds to sort things out herself. She may even have understood how much this last ceremony would mean to him.

It was a cold day, but fine. The service at the South London crematorium was scantily attended; behind us, the long brown ranks of pews stood empty. I hadn't, until now, understood how isolated Robbie had been, how entirely dependent he had been upon my father's friendship.

'All rise,' said the vicar. Heads bent, we stood, Della in a tight purple dress with a hatband that almost matched, my mother in a dark green tweed suit that didn't quite acknowledge the gravity of the occasion. I, my husband, and my son had, after consultation, gone to the opposite extreme, showing up like a trio of ravens; my father, eyes averted from the altar, stood a little apart from us, draped in a heavy black coat that weighed down his shoulders.

'All kneel,' said the vicar. Dully, I stared at the row of large Victorian windows that overlooked the chapel's car-park, willing myself to feel grief that Robbie was dead. The sense of relief was stronger, to my shame. Della was sobbing noisily; I couldn't produce a single tear.

Beyond the windows, a group of teenage boys were shouting at each other as they kicked a ball around the car park. Frowning at the interruption, the vicar rose once more to offer words of comfort to the bereaved. A small, exhausted-looking man who had evidently given little attention to my father's descriptions of the deceased, he spoke warmly of Ronnie's love of horses (my father winced at this misconstruction of his account of Robbie's bike-riding); back on familiar territory, the vicar spoke with sonorous authority of the enduring peace that Ronnie could now enjoy. And now, he went on, by the special request of Ronnie's family, we were to hear a piece of music that would remind us all of his love of laughter, his innocent sense of fun. (My father, sobbing, buried his head in his hands as the red curtains drew apart and the casket – it looked disconcertingly small – began, with a dignified hiss of moving steel, to be received.)

I should have guessed what was coming from the portable gramophone I had seen my father carrying into the chapel; unprepared for what we were about to hear, I shrank from the sudden crackle of vinyl as if it had been a gunshot. The turntable continued to spin, the record to emit a loud and tuneless crackle; nobody budged. My father was on his knees, white knuckles squeezed against his eyes as though he meant to gouge them out. My son, who loved him, slid along the pew to wrap a warm arm around his grandfather's hunched back. The coffin continued to move gradually away from us. And then, into the gloom, there burst the sound of a relentlessly jolly children's song:

The most wonderful thing about Tiggers
Is Tiggers are wonderful things! . . .
wonderful *things!* . . . wonderful *things!* . . .

The needle, clicking gently, stayed trapped in the groove. Grim-faced, the vicar leaned forward to pull the lever up. Now, all that could be heard were the stifled cries from behind my father's clenched fists.

Afterwards, gathered together in the gloom of Robbie's basement flat, we made polite conversation to Della and a woman friend of hers who had come along to help pour out cups of tea. My mother's face was stony as she sipped the cup and declined Della's offer of a room in which to freshen up. I, shaken by the bleakness of Robbie's London home, tried not to wonder which of the walls, covered by a cream woodchip paper, had been spattered, and how difficult blood might be to remove. I couldn't see any stains. I watched my father as he circled the room, holding out a plate of elegantly cut sandwiches – he had prepared them himself – that nobody wanted to eat. Now that he had taken off his winter coat, I saw his age revealed, in a body that appeared thin as paper, and in the tremor of that tentative, gracefully extended hand. Even death couldn't make me feel fond of Robbie, the usurper to whom I had been expected to offer a home for life. But no daughter could take pleasure in the sight of a parent who was so evidently suffering from a broken heart. I saw that he was willing himself to stay in control, struggling to mask the extremity of his grief. I felt, like a stab of pain, something for him at that moment that was close to love.

My father drew some comfort, I think, from designing the handsome stone tablet on which, with no sense of parody, Tigger was recorded as the beloved friend of Christopher Robin, and of Owl. He knew the memorial could not be placed where it would invite ridicule; he chose a secluded portion of the courtyard at the back of the House, making of it a kind of shrine where, so I heard later, he would sit for hours at a time, his face turned towards the wall, his hands pressed to the side of his stomach in which, as it came to seem, his grief lay stored. On other occasions, as I later gathered, he would take a chair down to the bank of the lake, placing it in the spot where Robbie had liked to fish and where, on summer days, the two of them had spent long, languid hours of perfect ease.

All roles at the House were now reversed. The paternal tyrant had become a weeping and apologetic child. We sat in silence at meals where my father, pushing his plate away, leaned forward, rocking his head in his hands, attempting to shield from sight the tears that never stopped falling. My brother and I, grim-faced, read to each other the letters in which our father thanked us for the affection we had shown to Robbie, and apologised for his own lack of control. Even the sight of a despatch rider could make him cry, he admitted; the knowledge of the money he had held back was a source of relentless self-accusation.

'I wish I could overcome this misery,' he wrote to me, but it held him as if in a vice.

My father had always been superstitious. I found for him a clairvoyant, who provided him some comfort when she told him Robbie had spoken to her. It is an indication of the depth of his love that he was willing to undertake, while suffering such tormenting pain that it hurt him by then even to stand upright, a daily round trip of a hundred miles in order to sit with this kindly woman, and to receive her message of consolation. Robbie was happy, she assured him, repeatedly; he was at peace.

My father would not go near a doctor until the physical pain, indistinguishable by now from the trauma of his grief, had grown too strong to be withstood without management. He asked for, and got, morphine, enough to keep him biking, week after haunted week, up and down the motorway. The purpose, I imagine, was to receive further comforting messages about, or from, his lost friend. Drugs helped, but couldn't sustain him. Too weak to fight the family's pleas for a diagnosis and proper investigation, he allowed himself to surrender. After two desolate nights at the local city hospital, we were advised to take him home. Cancer, five months after Robbie's death, had invaded and spread to my father's pancreas. He hadn't, the doctor said, more than a few days left.

We took him back to the House. He wouldn't let us help him up the stairs until one last call had been put through to the clairvoyant. The last words I heard him speak, to be conveyed through her, were a message to Robbie. She wouldn't take a penny in payment when I asked, later, what she was owed.

'He was such a gentleman,' she said. 'And so sad.'

'No,' my mother rebukes me gently. 'That's wrong. You've forgotten the staircase.'

She's right. I've somehow blotted out the memory of my father's last words. Stoked up on morphine, he had fought to throw us off, as we led him to his bedroom. We saw before us a silent staircase, cushioned with soft red carpet. His eyes saw flames, a blazing fire rising above us to engulf what he had given his life to save: the House. The old terror, the one put into his mind as a child by the story of Nuthall Temple, became once more real enough to cause him to shriek out, like a soul in torment.

I've never been able to uncover precisely what my mother had endured in those five months after Robbie's death. She tells me now that one of the hardest things to bear was her husband's insistence that my brother and I had truly loved his friend, as she had not. It was this last piece of wilful self-deception that eventually proved intolerable. Once again, I started from sleep to hear a telephone ringing in the darkness; once again, I heard my father's broken tones.

'She's saying terrible things,' he said. 'Tell me they're not true. She says you hated Robbie, you and your brother. It's not true, is it? Tell me it's not true.'

'And you lied,' my mother says flatly and I look away.

'What else could I do?'

'You could have supported me,' she says. 'You could have told the truth. As if he hadn't known it already.'

There was no contact between them at the end. My mother, during the last week of her husband's life, closeted herself away in the small, undistinguished bedroom that had always been used – while in their single state – by the men of the House: my father, her son, and mine. She didn't come to the room in which my father lay dying. He didn't ask for her.

My brother and I sat by his bed throughout the slow, glittering May days that bleached the walls with light. We read to him, as he had read to us when we were children, the comic scenes from *The Pickwick Papers*. He gave no sign of hearing our voices. His hands lay open upon the sheets, palms upturned, as if waiting for something to be placed within them.

We discerned at last what it was that his hands so wanted to hold: a photograph of Robbie, at nineteen, standing beside the Duke and smiling cheerily. My father's fingers closed around the frame, clasping it tight. We thought we saw him smile.

'Somebody he was fond of?' enquired the nurse who'd come out to help us. We nodded. Explanations, adequate ones, didn't seem in order, not even possible.

Death came crawling. We could hear the tick of time slow down, to the point when every movement on the bed became frustrating. And then – suddenly – he'd gone, and all around us, the air grew light and easy. Running across the wet lawn with bare feet, scything down branches until I stood knee deep in blossom, I hurled shouts at the red-brick walls and arching gables until they echoed back at me: *Free! Free!*

I didn't, at the time, understand that we'd simply passed from one phase of possession to another. My father had gone, but only from the daylight. Never from the House.

EPILOGUE:
IN MY FATHER'S HOUSE

Twelve years on, my father's spirit is present as ever, but the sense of anguish has receded. Walking through the fields, reading on the bank by the lake, playing the piano as he liked to hear me do, I'm conscious of the passion with which he cherished all this beauty and that, increasingly, I've taken on his cause as my own. I worry as he did, over the death of one of the grand old trees in the park, and the change its absence will create; I glow as he did, when friends, making their first visit, sigh with pleasure to find such an oasis. Like him, I'd sacrifice almost anything for the sake of keeping all this in place, as it was; and as, however precariously, it has remained.

They're putting up a vast marquee on the terrace above the lake this weekend; the bride is planning where to stand and greet her guests; the caterers are laying name cards on the tables; the florist has just put the final touches to a column of lilies and roses. Up in my room, above the marquee roof, I can look across the white canopy to where two swans are conducting their file of cygnets across the lake, orderly as the wedding processions to which, looking regal and faintly bored, they lend a conscious air of dignity. Beyond them, I can see the drooping branches of the old willow tree under which Robbie and my father used to sit, reading stories of Christopher Robin and watching the water for the slick of light on a carp's back, out beyond their lines. I can see myself there, sitting on Slav's shoulders as he waded out into the lake; I can see my brother, the oars of his boat sending ripples out towards where my mother stands on the bank, scattering bread for the ducks from the basket balanced between the swell of her hip and the crook of her arm.

It's an image of impossible serenity. Making it, I realise the danger of becoming too close a replica of my father, whose unappeasable wish it was to control not only the House and its setting, but the lives of those who lived there.

Following in my father's footsteps, I'll try to walk with a lighter tread – and no longer, now, to look back.